THE KOREAN WAR

Recent Titles in
Bibliographies and Indexes in Military Studies

Stress, Strain, and Vietnam: An Annotated Bibliography of Two Decades of Psychiatric and Social Sciences Literature Reflecting the Effect of the War on the American Soldier
Norman M. Camp, Robert H. Stretch, and William C. Marshall

Military and Strategic Policy: An Annotated Bibliography
Benjamin R. Beede, compiler

Investigations of the Attack on Pearl Harbor: Index to Government Hearings
Stanley H. Smith, compiler

Military Fortifications: A Selective Bibliography
Dale E. Floyd, compiler

Terrorism, 1988–1991: A Chronology of Events and A Selectively Annotated Bibliography
Edward F. Mickolus

Civil War Newspaper Maps: A Cartobibliography of the Northern Daily Press
David Bosse, compiler

War of 1812 Eyewitness Accounts: An Annotated Bibliography
John C. Fredriksen, compiler

Terrorism, 1992–1995: A Chronology of Events and A Selectively Annotated Bibliography
Edward F. Mickolus with Susan L. Simmons

THE KOREAN WAR

An Annotated Bibliography

Compiled by
PAUL M. EDWARDS

Bibliographies and Indexes in Military Studies, Number 10

GREENWOOD PRESS
Westport, Connecticut • London

Library of Congress Cataloging-in-Publication Data

Edwards, Paul M.
   The Korean War : an annotated bibliography / compiled by Paul M.
Edwards.
     p.   cm.—(Bibliographies and indexes in military studies,
ISSN 1040–7995 ; no. 10)
   Includes bibliographical references and index.
   ISBN 0–313–30317–7 (alk. paper)
   1. Korean War, 1950–1953—Bibliography.   I. Title. II. Series:
Bibliographies and indexes in military studies; no. 10.
Z3316.E36   1998
[DS918]
016.951904′2—dc21   97–40189

British Library Cataloguing in Publication Data is available.

Library of Congress Catalog Card Number: 97–40189
ISBN: 0–313–30317–7
ISSN: 1040–7995

First published in 1998

Greenwood Press, 88 Post Road West, Westport, CT 06881
An imprint of Greenwood Publishing Group, Inc.

Printed in the United States of America

The paper used in this book complies with the
Permanent Paper Standard issued by the National
Information Standards Organization (Z39.48–1984).

10 9 8 7 6 5 4 3 2 1

CONTENTS

ACKNOWLEDGMENTS

Always, in the preparation of a work like this, there are people who have made major contributions and who deserve serious recognition. Among these would have to be Joni Wilson who has provided invaluable service, sharing both her expertise about the Korean War and her editorial assistance.

Among the many librarians, as well as library staffs, I feel the need to acknowledge the Jackson County, Missouri, Mid-Continent Public Library; the Linda Hall Library in Kansas City, Missouri; the Miller-Nichols Library of the University of Missouri at Kansas City; the Kansas City, Missouri, Public Library; the Combined Arms Research Library at the Command and Staff College, Fort Leavenworth, Kansas; the Library of the Army History Center, Carlisle Barracks, Pennsylvania; the library at Maxwell Air Force Base; the Library of Congress; the Special Legislative Library, Senate of the United States; the National Archives in Washington, D. C., especially Reed Whitaker of the Kansas City, Missouri, branch; George Curtis recently of the Harry S. Truman Library in Independence, Missouri; Gregg Edwards for library research; Dr. Jeanne Allen of Temple University; Vice-President Thomas Peterman of Park College and the Park College Library Staff; and the staff at the Center for the Study of the Korean War in Independence, Missouri.

And, of course, special acknowledgment to my family and to my wife, Carolynn Jean, for accepting and being supportive of the many, many hours I had my head in a book.

COMMENT ON SOURCES

Names

Nations differ in the manner in which they record bibliographic entries. For simplicity in listing and locating entries, Korean, Chinese, and Japanese names are listed in the Western style with the family name listed as the alphabetical bibliographic entry, as: Lee, Chong-sik.

When on some occasions the Westernization of the name has been so common that the majority of bibliographic citations list the name without recognition of first and last, I have followed the custom. If at all possible, I have used the spelling on the original work, but the user needs to be aware that many Asian names are spelled differently by various officers.

Campaigns

The American military identified ten campaigns in the Korean War, to which they have awarded campaign ribbons and battle stars.

June 27 to September 15, 1950	UN Defensive
September 16 to November 2, 1950	UN Offensive
November 3, 1950 to January 24, 1951	CCF Intervention
January 25 to April 21, 1951	First UN Counteroffensive
April 22 to July 8, 1951	CCF Spring Offensive
July 9 to November 27, 1951	UN Summer/Fall Offensive
November 28, 1951 to April 30, 1952	Second Korean Winter
May 1 to November 30, 1952	Korean Summer/Fall
December 1, 1952 to April 30, 1953	Third Korean Winter
May 1 to July 31, 1953	Korean Summer/Fall

While campaign dates might well be used as a means of identifying bibliographic materials, it was quickly discovered that material is not usually restricted to a single campaign; most, in fact, stressing the crossover of time and campaigns. Therefore, the strictly military coverage is recorded en mass, identified more by subject than time period.

Primary Subject

Most of the bibliographic material covers several subjects and time periods. When looking for specific materials, always look for the primary subject first. For example, in locating "MASH units at air bases," look first at medical rather than air bases. On the other hand, all air activity is discussed under Air Force (including Army, Navy, Marine) with the exception of those units used for specifically army projects (i.e., artillery spotting).

Note

Master's theses are usually only available at the degree-granting institution or through University Microfilms. In this bibliography these theses are listed in order that the researcher might be aware of them, and are to be found in the applicable subject area. In those rare cases where they are significant contributions they have been annotated. Most, however, are simply listed. As a rule the content of master's theses closely follows the title provided.

Many units which served in Korea compiled memorial books as souvenirs for those who served. These are helpful on many occasions but hardly objective. They can be very useful but need to be supported by other works. These are annotated as "yearbook variety."

THE OFFICIAL WAR

A Brief History of the Korean War

In the early morning hours of the 25th of June, 1950, highly trained infantry of the North Korean People's Army (NKPA), led by Russian-built T-34 tanks, crossed the 38th Parallel and invaded the Republic of South Korea (ROK). The Cold War which had emerged from tension among allies in World War II suddenly heated up. The American response, made in conjunction with the newly organized United Nations, rather forcefully identified Western power determination to resist the expansion of communism. The resulting Korean War enforced President Harry Truman's policy of containment.

The Korean Conflict, as it was called for so long, continues, though the disputing nations arrived at an armistice agreement on 27 July 1953. Americans under the United Nation's flag, remain on duty along the demilitarized zone (DMZ) between North and South Korea.

This forty-seven year old Korean War, long ignored by scholars and all but forgotten by the American people, is one of the significant events in the twentieth century. Alternatively known as "a police action," the "forgotten war," the "unknown war," the "hidden war," and in one or two cases, the "unnecessary war," the Korean War remains, though it has faded from consciousness. The three-year combat phase produced some of the bloodiest fighting on record, yet it has passed into history. A history so confused and emotional that it took the American people nearly half-a-century to dedicate a monument to those who fought and died there.

Other than the 50,000 plus who perished, few American lives were touched by the war. At least not in the immediate sense that Americans had participated in World War II. There were few price controls, no food shortages, and no gas rationing. Life on the home front changed very little. America's involvement in this Asian war was as hard to explain to the person on the street as it was to the Congressional Committees which investigated it.

Over the years volumes have been written on America's decision to be involved in Korea. But however these causes are now justified or the reasons remembered, they failed in 1950 to motivate America's total commitment.

The politics of limited war were new to Americans. The political currents of the Cold War often produced a conflict between political and military victory. There were occasions when an acceptable peace settlement appeared more necessary than "unconditional surrender." But when the American warrior returned home from these limited wars, they did so without the sort of victory Americans expected.

The Korean veterans were rarely mistreated, but most returned to a people and a time with no recognition of what they had accomplished, nor was it acknowledged what the soldiers had sacrificed. Now, as then, several things make it difficult for historians to understand, and for the American people to remember the Korean War.

First, President Truman made America's commitment to Korea without a formal declaration of war by the United States Congress. Because of this, and some early comments by the president, it always appeared to be something less than a war.

Second, Americans who fought in the Korean War did so under the banner of another flag; the blue and white of the United Nations. And though ninety percent of the military force available in Korea was American, many persons felt that it was not "really an American war."

Third, while the Korean War was reported by the newly emerging television news services, it was not covered by them. That is, persons learned of events happening in the war and thus were influenced by participation in a foreign involvement. But television at the time did not cover it so that Americans participated in the daily activities of the fighting as was true of the later Vietnam War.

And finally, for many persons the mission in Korea was never understood. They understood World War II, a popular and passionate war, the outcome of which determined the freedom of millions of persons. Later, the Vietnam War produced a divided nation and considerable passion for and against involvement in it. Caught in between these two events, the Korean War seemed unnecessary and insignificant. And since the armistice little has happened in either understanding or recognition to improve public awareness.

The military period of the Korean War can best be described by five distinct phases: (1) the invasion and retreat to Pusan, (2) Inchon and the United Nations advance to the Yalu River, (3) the Chinese intervention, (4) General Ridgway's military response and, (5) the hill war, the longest and most difficult part of the Korean War to document.

Invasion and Retreat

The invasion came unexpectedly. Despite signs and warnings intelligence was poor and both the Republic of South Korea and the United States were caught off-guard. First artillery announced the break and then tanks and infantry crossed the line about 4:00 a.m. on 25 June 1950. Poorly-trained South Korean troops, caught off-guard, pulled back almost immediately and started the long retreat.

Called at his Independence, Missouri, home, President Harry S. Truman approved the evacuation of dependents and started his return to Washington. On the 26th, President Truman, advised by General MacArthur of the complete collapse of Republic of Korea (ROK) forces, ordered air support for the evacuation of Americans. The President also ordered the 7th Fleet to the Formosa Strait to discourage any clash between Communist China and Nationalist China on Formosa. Two days later the United Nations adopted an American resolution calling for the North Koreans to withdraw. But, Seoul (the capital of South Korea) fell on 28 June 1950. Within two days the president authorized General Douglas MacArthur to send ground forces into action.

What MacArthur had available were units serving occupation duty from World War II in Japan. Task Force Smith was hastily pulled together and thrown into fierce combat just a few days after notification. The 1st Battalion of the 21st Infantry Regiment (24th Division) reached Taejon and Osau by the 4th of July. On the 5th they were in battle.

The North Korean People's Army, having converged on Seoul, swung south across the Han River to the Kum River, then moved southeast to Taejon and Taegu. Despite the American presence, the North Korean People's Army moved steadily south. Poorly equipped Task Force Smith was unable to do much more than briefly slow the advancing army. The United States had nothing in Korea which could stop the T-34 Russian-built tanks. The fight was for time to organize a response by the United Nations.

Eighth United States Army, consisting of four divisions, was assigned to Korea (EUSAK) under the command of Lieutenant General Walton H. Walker. The 24th Infantry Division, under General William Dean, took much of the brunt of the early fighting. They delayed the North Koreans at the Kum River, but conditions were getting bad enough that Truman authorized the mobilization of reserve units.

By the 24th of July the Fifth Air Force relocated to Korea. Air power quickly proved effective in slowing the enemy, but it could not stop the communist advance. The ground war continued to move south. The understrength 24th Division was badly mauled by the rapidly advancing enemy, and General Dean, its commander, was taken prisoner.

As the battle continued reinforcements gathered in support of the American troops. Soon the 5th Regimental Combat Team and the 1st Provisional Marine Brigade, as well as the 2nd Infantry Division, arrived in Korea. Joining them were the first United Nations ground troops, a contingency of British and Commonwealth forces.

By the end of July the United Nations forces which began to consolidate its perimeter, included the American 2nd Division, 24th Division, 25th Division, 1st Cavalry Division, 1st Marine Brigade, and five ROK divisions. The core of their defense was the southeastern port city of Pusan. A series of battles was fought along the Naktong Bulge during which scattered American troops held the line against persistent attacks by the North Koreans.

As September 1950 emerged, General Walker's army was spread out in a perimeter around the port. A series of attacks and counterattacks had pushed the Eighth Army to exhaustion, but the units held. Supplies and reinforcements continued to arrive by ship at Pusan.

From Inchon to the Yalu River

During the first few days of the war, while surveying the growing retreat, supreme commander General Douglas MacArthur considered an amphibious landing on the west coast to cut the enemy supply lines and relieve the pressure on Walker. Called Operation Bluehearts it was originally scheduled for July, but was delayed by lack of personnel. Later, MacArthur began plans for Operation Chromite, an amphibious landing at the west coast port of Inchon.

Despite serious problems with the landing site, and opposition from the Joint Chiefs of Staff, a plan was put together. The Navy created the necessary task forces, and X Corps — consisting of the 1st Marine Division and the 7th Infantry Division — was reconstituted to lead the attack and placed, as a separate command, under General Edward (Ned) Almond.

Landing on 15 September 1950, the Marines first took the fortress island of Wolmi-do and then captured Inchon. The 7th Infantry Division landed on the 17th and pushed on to join the Marines, moving against Seoul. Eighth Army broke free of the Pusan Perimeter, pushed the North Koreans back and eventually joined X Corps. Seoul was retaken on the 29th of September and in a special ceremony General MacArthur returned the city to ROK President Syngman Rhee.

The North Korean supply lines, already stretched further than the communists could sustain, were now broken. The North Korean People's Army was in disarray, some soldiers retreating, other soldiers discarding their uniforms and blending into the population. As September ended United

Nations forces reached the 38th Parallel and halted momentarily. The initial goals of the United Nations resolution had been reached; South Korea had been freed.

General MacArthur, however, wanted to pursue the North Koreans and to occupy the land thus bringing an end to any threat they might impose. Authorized by the Joint Chiefs of Staff, and by a United Nations General Assembly resolution, American and ROK forces moved north, restricted only by orders not to cross into Manchuria or send planes north of the border.

United Nations troops crossed the 38th Parallel and began to push into enemy territory. The 1st Marines and the 7th Infantry Division, still operating as X Corps and under independent command, were pulled out of Inchon and moved by ship to the east coast, where they joined the conquest.

On the 21st of November patrols from the 17th Infantry Regiment of the 7th Division reached the Yalu River, and MacArthur announced "this should for all practical purposes end the war."

The Chinese Intervention

As the United Nations forces moved north, evidence increased that Communist Chinese troops were in Korea. The Red Chinese were concerned about American intentions, and warned of action if the advance continued. MacArthur, however, was convinced that despite a warning, Red China would not enter the war and he ordered both General Almond of X Corps, and General Walker of Eighth Army, to continue the advance. Then, on the 23rd of November, as many were eating their Thanksgiving dinner, the Chinese crossed their border en mass, and hit the United Nations troops along a wide front. The Eighth Army buckled under the weight of nearly 200,000 Communist Chinese "volunteers" who had accumulated in North Korea undetected. General Walker called for a withdrawal.

Along both sides of the Chosin Reservoir, Marine and Army units were hit hard. The primary need was to get out of the trap in which they found themselves. General Oliver Smith's "advance in another direction" was accomplished against overwhelming odds, as Marine and Army personnel pulled out. The constant pressure of Chinese troops which came at them from all directions, was aggravated by the bitter cold. At nearly forty degrees below zero, the equipment and exposed flesh froze.

The United Nations forces retreated toward both coasts where, in a series of evacuations, troops were removed. The largest of these evacuations moved through Hungnam where the Navy evacuated the 1st Marines, 7th Infantry Division, 3rd Infantry Division, and the ROK divisions, as well as 91,000 refugees between the 9th and 24th of December. The troops were disembarked at Pusan and other ports. From there they moved back into the fight.

The heavy fighting continued with the Communist Chinese moving slowly, but determinedly, south. The Communist Chinese Forces (CCF) took Pyongyang on 5 December. Seoul was abandoned once again on 3 January 1951. By 15 January lines of battle were drawn very near the 38th Parallel.

The Ridgway Response

Eighth Army Commander General Walton Walker was killed in an jeep accident in late December 1950. Command of all United Nations forces was invested in General Matthew B. Ridgway who arrived over Christmas. Ridgway, who commanded airborne units during World War II, was a hard-fighting general who took immediate command of the situation. Promised a free hand, and with X Corps reunited into Eighth Army, Ridgway planned his response.

He viewed his job not so much to take territory, which had been the primary concern of the first phase, but rather to inflict heavy casualties on the enemy. Ridgway set out to do that in a series of attacks called Operation Thunderbolt. He provided his troops with what they needed, demanded the best of them, and drove them hard. As the new year progressed the battle-wise veterans of Eighth Army were becoming better at their jobs.

The combined fighting forces of the United Nations Command started the slow road back. Supported by Navy and Air Force fire power, which cut and disrupted the Chinese supply lines, small units moved out to hit and destroy. Quickly Ridgway's Eighth Army pushed the CCF back. Seoul was recaptured, and on the 27th of March, Eighth Army reached the 38th Parallel. By the 5th of April, Operation Rugged advanced to geographical battle lines called Kansas and Wyoming which would serve as base lines for much of the rest of the war.

The "goals" of the war had changed from the restoration of a united and democratic Korea, to the acceptance of a cease-fire along the 38th Parallel. The United Nations resolution of 14 December 1950 made that clear. But General Douglas MacArthur wanted a Chinese surrender.

On 11 April 1951 President Truman relieved General MacArthur as Commander-in-Chief, Far East Command. MacArthur who had emerged from World War II as a highly respected military leader had served as military governor of Japan since the surrender. He and President Truman had disagreed on several points in fighting the Korean War. When the President determined the General's intentions might ignite World War III, he relieved MacArthur. General Matthew Ridgway was appointed to replace General MacArthur and General James Van Fleet assumed command of Eighth Army.

The Hill War

If the first phase of the Korean War represented the hit and run tactics of World War II, the second phase had much in common with the static battles of World War I. Poised along both sides of a slowly moving line, the two forces were reduced to small unit action, battles for limited locations, and the desperate fight over pieces of land which, in the overall outcome of the war, had little value.

Shortly after taking command Van Fleet faced a Communist Chinese offensive that began on 22 April and drove the United Nations forces south. The United Nations forces stopped just north of Seoul. In May a series of communist advances moved them another twenty miles south, but by the end of the month the United Nations had retaken its positions.

During all this, the peace talks, which began in July of 1951 at Kaesong, wore on. By 16 February 1952 most of the questions of territorial rights had been settled — almost exactly along those lines controlled by each nation at the outbreak of war — but the talks mired down on political issues.

On the 12th of November 1952, United Nations forces were ordered to cease any offensive action; they assumed a defensive posture. A new form of warfare — the limited war — was being imposed. The degree of action shifted to vicious small unit fights, individualized targets, and political victories.

When President Dwight D. Eisenhower took office in January of 1953, the only remaining issue preventing an armistice was disagreement over the repatriation of prisoners unwilling to return. While these negotiations dragged on, more than half of the United States casualties occurred. Success on the field of battle became a tool at the bargaining table and one hill after another — the Marines at Bloody Ridge, the 2nd Infantry at Heartbreak Ridge, I Corps on Old Baldy, the 7th Infantry at Pork Chop — became but a series of seemingly hopeless struggles.

On 5 March, Joseph Stalin died and three weeks later the Chinese broke the deadlock. The communists agreed to the screening of uncommitted prisoners by a neutral nation. On the 27th of July 1953, General Mark Clark, the final United Nations commander of the Korean War, signed the armistice. There was little joy in this fact. In the thirty-seven months and two days of combat 54,246 American soldiers, sailors, marines, and airmen had died; more than 103,000 were wounded; and 5,179 remained missing in action. In addition there were some 14,000 casualties suffered by other United Nations troops.

Repatriation was completed by 6 September 1953; the United Nations turning over 76,000 prisoners and the Communist Chinese 13,000. During their captivity many American prisoners died from mistreatment.

The success of the United Nations cause is still not clear. Many, at the time assumed the armistice reflected only a return to the status quo. There had been no victory. In the traditional military sense the war's victory was not found in land taken but rather in stopping the communist spread. Twenty-one Americans and one British prisoner refused repatriation after the war; more than a dozen were accused of collaboration, several were court-martialed.

Today the soldiers from the Second Infantry Division, a few of them grandchildren of the men who fought during the early phases of the Korean War, stand guard. Each day they prepare for an assault from North Korea, which they must expect, as they wait out the battle of boredom along the 38th Parallel.

The War

The military responded when the nation called. The soldier, sailor, marine, and airman all fought well. Many died to accomplish what the nation sought to accomplish. Americans responded as they have always done. For many veterans the war is remembered as immediate action, as friends and comrades in arms, as battles and engagements, and the great enemy of the soldier — hours and hours of boredom accentuated by moments of stark terror.

Looking back on the Korean War, however, we now see what a significant event it was in the life of the United States, and in world-wide implications. The rigid, often fearsome, ideologies of the Cold War drew heavy lines and allowed few mistakes. The "peace" in Korea, so necessarily proclaimed, did not rest well next to the American image of victory.

And while most veterans have remained silent they still question the American people: "Why do they not understand what we accomplished there?"

The outbreak of the war in Korea set in motion a program of preparedness for general war. Realizing that the Soviets might well be amassing enough weapons, including atomic, to risk a war with the United States, it became necessary that the nation's defenses be stockpiled, and an integrated National Atlantic Treaty Organization (NATO) defense truce established in Western Europe. What then is the legacy?

● The rearming of the United States was, according to Winston Churchill, the aged prime minister of Great Britain, the most essential victory in Korea.

● The containment of communism was accomplished, and the unification of Korea under a communist government was prevented. The United Nations took a stand and aggression was slowed. Lessons of preparation, response, and diplomacy, if well-learned, could have prevented much of the difficulty in the next, and most misunderstood, war in Vietnam.

● The Korean War was the remaking of Japan, economically ruined by the war, encouraging manufacturing growth and introducing the heart of trans-shipment and delivery-on-demand-production of military goods.

● South Korea, despite its problems, has finally been moving toward a pro-democracy government and is economically strong. Seoul, a city of nearly 11 million, was secure enough to host the 1988 Summer Olympics.

On 27 July 1995, forty-two years since the signing of the armistice, the National Korean War Veteran's Memorial was dedicated in Washington, D. C. Located across the reflecting pool from the Vietnam Veteran's Memorial, it is evidence that the nation is beginning to remember.

War Comparison Statistics

War	Battle Deaths	Other Deaths
World War I	53,513	63,195
World War II	292,131	115,185
Korean War	33,629	20,617
Vietnam War	47,244	10,446

United States Divisions in Korea

1st Cavalry Division
2nd Infantry Division
3rd Infantry Division
7th Infantry Division
24th Infantry Division

25th Infantry Division
40th Infantry Division
45th Infantry Division
1st Marine Division

United Nations Countries in Korea

Belgium
British Commonwealth —

Australia
Canada
India
New Zealand
United Kingdom

Colombia
Denmark - hospital ship
Ethiopia

France
Greece
Italy
Japan - logistics assistance
Netherlands
Norway
Philippines
Republic of Korea
Republic of China - offer to assist not accepted
South Africa
Sweden
Thailand
Turkey
United States

Chronology of Significant Dates

1866   <u>General Sherman</u>, an American merchant ship, was destroyed and crew killed near Pyongyang.

1871   Avenging Marines withdrew after attack led to trading treaty with Korea.

1910   Korea annexed by Japan.

1919   Syngman Rhee exiled from Korea for political activity.

1943   World War II "Big Three" promised a free Korea in the Cairo Declaration.

1945   America and Soviet Union agreed to joint occupation along 38th Parallel.

1948   Syngman Rhee returns and becomes first president of Republic of Korea (South); Russian and American occupation troops removed.

1950

25 June   North Korea invades South Korea along the 38th Parallel.

27 June   Truman authorizes air and naval operations south of the 38th Parallel; United Nations adopts United States resolution on aggression.

28 June   British forces in Japanese waters placed under United States command.

29 June   First United States ground forces arrive in Korea; General MacArthur flies to Korea to evaluate situation; Truman authorizes sea blockade and bombing of North Korea.

1 July   Task Force Smith arrives in Korea.

3 July   24th Infantry Division arrives.

7 July   United Nations authorizes military support for South Korea.

8 July   MacArthur named United Nations Commander.

13 July   General Walker arrives and is given command of Eighth United States Army; ground troops in Korea.

18 July   First Cavalry Division lands at Pohang on east coast.

23 July   MacArthur plans amphibious landing.

27 July   Truman signs Public Law 624 extending enlistments and draft.

8-18 Aug   First battle of the Naktong Bulge.

26 Aug   MacArthur creates X Corps under General Almond for the Inchon landing.

15 Sept   First Marine Division lands at Inchon.

16-22 Sept   Eighth Army breaks out of Pusan.

18 Sept   Kimpo Airfield taken.

28 Sept   Truman authorizes action north of the 38th Parallel.

29 Sept   Capital city Seoul is returned to President Rhee.

7 Oct   United Nations authorizes action north of the 38th Parallel.

15 Oct   Truman and MacArthur meet at Wake Island.

25 Oct	Chinese Communist Forces launch first phase.
8 Nov	3rd Infantry Division lands in Korea.
25 Nov	Chinese Communist Forces launch second phase.
27 Nov-9 Dec	Encircled Marine and Army forces fight from Chosin Reservoir to Hungnam perimeter.
23 Dec	General Walker killed in jeep accident.
24 Dec	Hungnam evacuation completed and harbor destroyed.
26 Dec	General Ridgway assumes command of Eighth Army.

1951

4 Jan	Seoul abandoned.
11-17 Feb	Chinese Communist Forces launch third phase.
14 Mar	Seoul recaptured.
27-31 Mar	Eighth Army reaches 38th Parallel.
5 Apr	Kansas Line established.
11 Apr	Truman relieves MacArthur.
30 Apr-21 May	Eighth United States Army contains CCF and returns to Kansas Line.
10 June	Battle of Punchbowl.
23 June	Russian delegate to the United Nations, Jacob Malik, proposes cease-fire discussions.
1 July	Chinese Communist Forces agree to begin truce talks in Kaesong.
3 Sept	Marines take Bloody Ridge.
1 Oct	Eighth Army disbands black units and integrates troops.

7 Oct	Truce talks moved to Panmunjom.
15 Oct	Army takes Heartbreak Ridge.

1952

22 Jan	40th Infantry replaces 24th Division on line.
22 Feb	North Korea charges United States with germ warfare.
7-11 May	Prisoners riot at Koje-do.
12 May	General Clark replaces Ridgway as Commander-in-Chief.
1 Sept	Largest all-navy raid, 144 planes against Aoji.
5-8 Dec	General Eisenhower, president-elect, visits Korea.

1953

20 Jan	Eisenhower becomes President and Commander-in-Chief.
10 Feb	General Taylor replaces Van Fleet as EUSAK commander.
5 Mar	Premier Stalin of the Soviet Union dies.
16-18 Apr	Battle of Pork Chop Hill.
20-26 Apr	Operation Little Switch (exchange ill prisoners).
13-20 July	Chinese Communist Forces attack with six divisions.
27 July	Armistice signed, cease-fire takes effect.
5 Aug-6 Sept	Operation Big Switch (exchange of prisoners).

◆

Archives and Documents

The official documents of the United Nations are held at Lake Success, New York. Complete sets of microfilm copies are available in several locations including the Combined Arms Research Library at the Command and Staff College, Fort Leavenworth, Kansas.

Primary sources and manuscripts on the Korean War can be found at: Harry S. Truman Library, Independence, Missouri; Dwight D. Eisenhower Library, Abilene, Kansas; Seely G. Mudd Library, Princeton University, Princeton, New Jersey; George C. Marshall Library at Virginia Military Institute, Lexington, Virginia; Hoover Institution Library on War, Revolution, and Peace, Palo Alto, California; National Archives, Diplomatic and Legislative Branch, Pennsylvania Avenue, Washington, D. C.; Douglas MacArthur Memorial Library, Norfolk, Virginia; Modern Military Branch, National Archives, Washington, D. C.; Butler Library, Columbia University, Columbia, New York; Records, United Nations Command, Far East Command, RQ407, National Archives at Suitland, Maryland; and the Archives II building in College Park, Maryland.

Additional archival and research materials on the Korean War can be located at the Library of Congress, Washington, D. C.; Center for Military History, Washington D. C.; United States Army Military History Institute, Carlisle Barracks, Pennsylvania; the Women's Army Forces Historical Division Archives, Air University Library, Maxwell Air Force Base, Alabama; the Gillman Library (National Security Archives), George Washington University, Washington, D. C.; the Combat Studies Institute at Fort Leavenworth, Kansas; Naval Historical Center, Washington, D. C.;

individual records, letters, maps, orders, and photographs are available, as well as an excellent collection of secondary works at the Center for the Study of the Korean War in Independence, Missouri.

Commonwealth records are available through the Liddell Hart Centre for Military Archives at Kings College, London; Royal Commission for Historical Manuscripts, London; National Army Museum, Chelsea; New Zealand Archives, Wellington; United Kingdom Public Records Office, Keiv; Imperial War Museum, London; Public Archives of Canada, Ottawa; Directorate of History, Department of National Defence, and Historical Section Department, Department of External Affairs, Ottawa (awaiting organization and transfer).

Captured North Korean documents can be located in National Archives Record Group 242 in United States Far East Command files. There is no single good source dealing with the North Korean People's Army, nor a prime location for this material until North Korea opens its archives. But during the Korean War those headquarters concerned with the management of the war produced a large volume of materials considering the size, organization, methods, and materials related to the North Korean People's Army and the Chinese Communist Forces in Korea. Most of this is now available in Daily Intelligence Summaries (INTSUM), Weekly Intelligence Summaries (WIS), Periodic Intelligence Reports (PIR) produced by the Offices of the Assistant Chief of Staff, G-2 at General Headquarters, United States Far East Command, Headquarters United States Armed Forces, Far East. Note should be taken that materials produced during the war (1950-1953) are far less accurate than those produced since the armistice.

Oral histories of the Korean War can be found at the Butler Library, Columbia Oral History Collection, Columbia University, Columbia, New York; the United States Army Eighth Army Historical Office which has a Korean War project; and at the Foreign Affairs Oral History Project, Lauinger Library, Georgetown University, Washington, D. C.

Collected Documents

0001 <u>American Foreign Policy: Basic Documents, 1950-1955, Part XV, Korea</u>. Washington, D. C.: Department of State Publications, 1957.

Basic documents of the outbreak, policy development, and execution of the Korean War.

0002 <u>Armistice in Korea: Selected Statements and Documents</u>. Washington, D. C.: Government Printing Office, 1953.

This collection makes available the primary documents of the negotiations, and letters of agreement, in the long struggle for a cease-fire.

0003 Chung-kuo jen. . . . <u>Documents and Materials on the Korean Armistice Negotiations</u>. Peking: Chinese People's Committee for World Peace, 1952.

Special reference to the prisoner-of-war agenda; December 11, 1951-June 17, 1952.

0004 <u>Congressional Record, 1950-1953: Proceedings and Debates</u>. Washington, D. C.: Government Printing Office, 1950-1953.

Primary source for congressional and congressional committee accounts.

0005 Democratic People's Republic of Korea. <u>Documents and Materials Exposing the Instigators of the Civil War in Korea: Documents from the Archives of the Rhee Syngman Government</u>. Pyongyang: Foreign Languages Publishing House, 1950.

Documents collected during occupation, which support the charges against South Korea as the aggressor.

0006 <u>Documents and Commentaries on the Cease-fire and Armistice Negotiations in Korea</u>. two volumes. Peking: Foreign Language Press, 1951.

     Supplement to <u>People's China</u>. Basic documents for understanding the armistice from the communist point of view.

0007 Dutt, Vidya Prakash, editor. <u>East Asia: China, Korea, Japan, 1947-50</u>. London: Oxford University Press, 1958.

     Issued under the authority of Indian Council of World Affairs. This work addresses the history, and political changes, in East Asia between these three powers.

0008 Etzold, Thomas H. and John L. Gaddis. <u>Containment: Documents on American Policy and Strategy, 1945-1950</u>. New York: Columbia University Press, 1978.

     History of the planning for American national security as well as the development of foreign relations between the United States and the Soviet Union.

0009 General Headquarters, Far East Command, Military Intelligence Section, Allied Translator and Interpreter Service. "Interrogation Reports—North Korean Forces: North Korean Logistics" <u>ATIS Research Supplement</u> 1 (19 October 1950).

     Copies of intelligence reports on the interrogation of North Korean prisoners-of-war.

0010 General Headquarters, Far East Command, Military Intelligence Section, Allied Translator and Interpreter Service. "Interrogation Reports—North Korean Forces: Typical North Korean Infantry Division" <u>ATIS Research Supplement</u> 1 (19 October 1950).

     Documents collected from prisoners, which explain the organization and operation of a North Korean Army division.

0011 General Headquarters, Far East Command, Military Intelligence Section, Allied Translator and Interpreter Service. "Enemy Documents, Korean Operations" <u>ATIS Research Supplement</u> 5 (13 December 1950).

     Translation of "Staff Department Field Manual," North Korean Democratic Republic, 1949.

0012 General Headquarters, Far East Command, Military Intelligence Section, Allied Translator and Interpreter Service. "Enemy Documents, Korean Operations" <u>ATIS Research Supplement</u> 9 (10 April 1951).

     Translation of "Combat Handbook," North Korean Democratic Republic, 1949.

0013 General Headquarters, Far East Command, Military Intelligence Section, Allied Translator and Interpreter Service. Daily Intelligence Summary. daily (1950-1953).
     Translation of materials dealing with logistics in the North Korean People's Army and the Chinese Communist Forces.

0014 General Headquarters, Far East Command, Military Intelligence Section, Allied Translator and Interpreter Service. FEC Intelligence Digest. semimonthly (17 June 1951-2 December 1952).
     Translation of daily intelligence reports (selected). These reports are continued as USAFFE Intelligence Digest.

0015 The Joint Chiefs of Staff and National Policy 1950-1952. volume 4. Wilmington, Delaware: Historical Division, Joint Secretariat, Joint Chiefs of Staff, 1979.
     Relates the history of the Joint Chiefs of Staff. Also discusses world politics, national security, and military policies relating to Korea.

0016 Korean Conflict: A Collection of Historical Manuscripts on the Korean Campaign Held by the U. S. Army Center of Military History. Washington, D. C.: Library of Congress, Photoduplication Services, 1975.
     Nine reels (unclassified microfilm). A history (both subject and date) of material available at the Army Center of Military History.

0017 MacGregor, Morris and Bernard Nalty, editors. Blacks in the United States Army Forces: Basic Documents. thirteen volumes. Wilmington, Delaware: Scholarly Resources, 1977-1981.
     A collection of documents which are essential to understanding the integration of the armed forces.

0018 "Pertinent Papers on the Korean Situation" Executive Branch: Documents and Reports. eight volumes. Washington, D. C.: United States Department of Defense: Office of Joint Chiefs of Staff, 1953.
     This is a great collection of information which consists primarily of documents concerning the decision by the United States and the United Nations to enter the Korean War. But lack of an identified compiler, and failure to provide evaluations or indexes, makes it difficult to use.

0019 Records of the Joint Chiefs of Staff, Part 2: 1946-53: Meetings of the Joint Chiefs of Staff. Frederick, Maryland: University Publications, 1980.
     Valuable reels (8) of microfilm which contain the minutes of the Joint Chief of Staff meetings.

0020 Traverso, Edmond, compiler. <u>Korea and the Limits of Limited War</u>. Menlo Park, California: Addison-Wesley Publisher, 1970.

This collection of documents on the Korean War contains a variety of important statements relating to cause, United States involvement, and the emerging concept of "limited" war. An account of the frustration created by trying to fight a military action while restricted by political limitations.

0021 U. S. Department of State. <u>Foreign Relations of the United States, 1950</u>. volume 1. "National Security Affairs" Washington, D. C.: Government Printing Office, 1977.

Basic documents dealing with data behind, and decisions concerning, national security affairs.

0022 U. S. Department of State. <u>Foreign Relations of the United States, 1950</u>. volume 6. "East Asia and the Pacific" Washington, D. C.: Government Printing Office, 1976.

Primary documents dealing with American policy concerning Asia and the Pacific.

0023 U. S. Department of State. <u>Foreign Relations of the United States, 1950</u>. volume 7. "Korea" Washington, D. C.: Government Printing Office, 1972.

Contains important documents relating to the outbreak of the Korean War and the decision for intervention. Deals with some of the more important "behind the scene" pressures and decisions.

0024 U. S. Department of State. <u>American Foreign Policy 1950-1951, Basic Documents</u>. Washington, D. C.: Government Printing Office, 1957.

Selected documents relating to American foreign policy during the first year of the Korean War.

0025 U. S. Department of State. <u>Foreign Relations of the United States, 1951</u>. volume 1. "National Security" Washington, D. C.: Government Printing Office, 1979.

Basic documents dealing with data collected and decisions concerning national security issues.

0026 U. S. Department of State. <u>Foreign Relations of the United States, 1951</u>. volume 6. "Asia and the Pacific" parts one and two. Washington, D. C.: Government Printing Office, 1977.

Documents dealing with foreign policy decisions concerning American involvement in Korea.

0027 U. S. Department of State. Foreign Relations of the United States, 1951. volume 7. "Korea and China" parts one and two. Washington, D. C.: Government Printing Office, 1983.
Copies of reports and documents dealing with American involvement in the war in Korea.

0028 U. S. Department of State. Foreign Relations of the United States, 1952-1954. volume 3. "United Nations Affairs" Washington, D. C.: Government Printing Office, 1979.
Documents dealing with the decisions concerning the United Nations policy.

0029 U. S. Department of State. Foreign Relations of the United States, 1952-1954. volume 13. "Indochina" parts one and two. Washington, D. C.: Government Printing Office, 1982.
Documents and analysis dealing with American involvement in Indochina.

0030 U. S. Department of State. Foreign Relations of the United States, 1952-1954. volume 15. "Korea" parts one and two. Washington, D. C.: Government Printing Office, 1984.
Documents dealing with the decisions concerning Korea in the later years of the war.

0031 U. S. Department of State. Guide to the U. N. in Korea. Far Eastern Series 47, Washington, D. C.: Government Printing Office, 1951.
Excellent guide to navigating the vast collection of materials on United Nations involvement.

0032 U. S. Department of State. A Historical Summary of United States-Korea Relations, 1938-1962. Far Eastern Series 11, Washington, D. C.: Government Printing Office, 1962.
Brief account of the long history of United States—Korean relations.

0033 U. S. Department of State. Policy in the Korean Crisis. Washington, D. C.: Government Printing Office, 1950.
Documents dealing with the early interpretations and interventions of the Korean War.

0034 U. S. Department of State. The Record of Korean Unification, 1953-1960: Narrative Summary with Principal Documents. Far Eastern Series 101, Washington, D. C.: Government Printing Office, 1960.
Collected documents related to the effort at unification.

0035 United States Senate, Committee on Armed Services. <u>Military Situation</u>
<u>in the Far East: Hearings before the Committee on Armed Services and the</u>
<u>Committee on Foreign Relations, United States Senate, Eighty-second</u>
<u>Congress, First Session, to Conduct an Inquiry into the Military Situation in</u>
<u>the Far East and the Facts Surrounding the Relief of General of the Army</u>
<u>MacArthur from His Assignments in That Area</u>. five volumes. Washington,
D. C.: Government Printing Office, 1951

    A major collection of documents and primary source materials
concerning the MacArthur firing.

0036 Yasamee, H. J. <u>Documents and British Policy Overseas</u>. "Korea 1950-
1951" series 11, volume 4. London: Her Majesty's Stationery Office, 1991.

    A selection of materials relevant to the first years of the war. The
selectivity leaves a lot of territory uncovered.

0037 <u>Yongsan Library Koreana Collection Seoul, Korea</u>. Seoul: Yongsan
Library, 1982.

    Multi-volume list of English language resources in Yongsan Library
in Seoul, Korea, dealing with the Korean War and the United States Army
in Korea.

Official Histories

0038 Appleman, Roy E. <u>The United States Army in the Korean War: South</u>
<u>to the Naktong, North to the Yalu</u>. Washington, D. C.: Office of the Chief
of Military History, Department of the Army, 1961.

    Covers from opening battles to mid-November. Not well received by
the military and other authors were asked to finish the series. Critical of
military blunders, and of 24th Regiment, an all black unit.

0039 Cowdrey, Albert A. <u>The Medics' War</u>. Washington, D. C.: Office of the
Chief of Military History, Department of the Army, 1987.

    Detailed analysis of the shortcomings of the Medical Department
at the end of the Korean War, as well as the great strides made in caring for
the troops in Korea. Not well covered is the physical and psychological
examination of POWs.

0040 Field, James A., Jr. <u>History of United States Naval Operations: Korea</u>.
Washington, D. C.: Government Printing Office, 1962.

    The official naval history, and still the best one volume work on the
naval war in Korea. While very active, the Navy has received little attention
in recent publications. Field's work is essential.

0041 Hermes, Walter G. The United States Army in the Korean War: Truce Tent and Fighting Front. Washington, D. C.: Office of the Chief of Military History, Department of the Army, 1966.

This is the official history for the period from mid 1951 to July 1953. He emphasizes the truce talks and primarily ignores the war in the line. No criticism of the military (as found in Appleman's work) or American policy.

0042 Meid, Pat and James M. Yingling. Operations in West Korea. volume V. Washington, D. C.: Historical Branch, G-3, Headquarters, United States Marine Corps, 1972.

Official history of Marine action in west Korea. Very detailed and prone to give too much credit to the Marines.

0043 Montross, Lynn and others. United States Marine Operations in Korea 1950-1953. five volumes. Washington, D. C.: Historical Branch, G-3, Headquarters, United States Marine Corps, 1954-1972.

Official history of Marine operations in Korea presented in five detailed volumes. The collection is a must to follow Marine operations in the Korean War.

0044 Mossman, Billy. The United States Army in the Korean War: Ebb and Flow, November 1950-July 1951. Washington, D. C.: Office of the Chief of Military History, Department of the Army, 1990.

Takes up the official army story from Appleman, going from mid-November 1950 to the 1951 early armistice talks. Institutional and poorly written; not a good follow-up on Appleman.

0045 O'Neill, Robert. Australia in the Korean War, 1950-1953. "Strategy and Diplomacy" volume I. "Combat Operations" volume II. Canberra: Australian War Memorial and the Australian Government Publishing Service, 1981, 1983.

The official history of the role the Australians played in the Korean War. Well written and full of information. The Commonwealth Division did not start out in either agreement or cooperation.

0046 Schnabel, James F. The United States Army in the Korean War: Policy and Direction: The First Year. Washington, D. C.: Office of the Chief of Military History, Department of the Army, 1972.

Deals with the Joint Chiefs of Staff, and the Army chiefs' view of policy. Weak on MacArthur and does not deal with the unpreparedness and poor performance of the army.

0047 Schnabel, James F. and Robert J. Watson. The Joint Chiefs of Staff and National Policy. "The Korean War" volume III in two parts. Wilmington, Delaware: Michael Glazier, Inc., 1979.

    The Joint Chiefs review published by the historical division of the Joint Secretariat. Long on detailed description but weak on analysis.

0048 Wood, Herbert Fairlie. Official History of the Canadian Army: Strange Battleground. The Operations in Korea and Their Effects on the Defence Policy of Canada. Ottawa: Ministry of National Defence, 1966.

    An official, statistical and narrative, study of Canada's small but highly significant role.

General Reference Works

0049 Agnew, James B. "USAMHRC—The Mother Lode for Military History" Journal of Military History 39 3 (October 1975): 146-148.

    The United States Army Military History Research Collection at Carlisle Barracks, Pennsylvania, is the mecca for scholars.

0050 Allard, Dean and Betty Bern, editors. U. S. Naval History Sources in the Washington Area and Suggested Research Subjects. Washington, D. C.: Government Printing Office, 1970.

    Identifies archives and special collections and lists the collection held in each state. Old and of limited value.

0051 American University. U. S. Army Handbook for Korea. Washington, D. C.: Government Printing Office, 1958.

    A handbook prepared for American servicemen who were being sent to Korea. It is a quick, but good, reference to the history, politics, and culture of both South and North Korea.

0052 Arkin, William M. Research Guide to Current Military and Strategic Affairs. Washington, D. C.: Institute for Policy Studies, 1981.

    While no longer current, this work is still valuable to help locate sources and identify what is available.

0053 The Army Almanac. Harrisburg: The Stackpole Company, 1959.

    Basic facts concerning the organization and management of the United States Army. The army reorganization of 1949 was tested in the early days of the Korean War.

0054 Blanchard, Carroll H., Jr. An Atlas of the War in Korea, 1950-1953. "The Pusan Perimeter" volume 2. Albany, New York: State University of New York, 1992.

Maps drawn or collected by Blanchard give a detailed and easy picture of the fighting lines, troop placement, the movement of fronts, and occupied territory at any given time.

0055 Brimmer, Brenda and others. A Guide to the Use of United Nations Documents (Including References to Specialized Agencies and Special U.N. Bodies). Dobbs Ferry, New York: Oceana Publications, 1962.
A must for anyone hoping to research in the maze of United Nations documents. Cross-checked index.

0056 Burton, Dennis A., James B. Rhoads and Raymond W. Smock, editors. A Guide to Manuscripts in the Presidential Libraries. College Park, Maryland: Research Materials Corporation, 1985.
Excellent source of research aids for the often "unused" presidential collections; Eisenhower and Truman are especially useful.

0057 A Chronicle of Principle Events Relating to the Korean Question, 1945-1954. Peking, China: World Culture, 1954.
Detailed chronology of the events leading to the war, as seen from the Chinese Communist Forces point of view.

0058 "A Chronology of Marine Corps Aviation in Korea" Leatherneck 39 11 (1956): 47-50, 81.
A limited but helpful order of events from 5 July 1950 to 27 July 1953 for Marine aviation.

0059 Controvich, James T. United States Army Unit Histories: A Reference and Bibliography. Manhattan, Kansas: Military Affairs/Aerospace Historian, 1983.
Includes some valuable information on units which participated in the Korean War. Excellent bibliography.

0060 Cooney, David M. A Chronology of the U. S. Navy, 1775-1965. New York: Watts, 1965.
Excellent chronology of naval events that covers nearly all United States Navy ships in the Korean War.

0061 Department of Defense. Semi-annual Reports of the Secretary of Defense, and Semi-annual Reports of the Secretary of the Army, Secretary of the Navy, Secretary of the Air Force, January 1 to June 30 and July 1 to December 30, 1950 through 1953. Washington, D. C.: Government Printing Office, 1950-1955.

These reports on military action are filed by field and theater commanders, including reports from both Eighth Army and Far East Command.

0062 Effenberger, David. A Dictionary of Battles. New York: Crowell, 1967.
Describes key battles from 1460 BC to 1966, including a few from the Korean conflict. Provides some descriptions of the location, major causes for the conflict, and military commanders engaged.

0063 Esposito, Vincent J., editor. The West Point Atlas of American Wars, 1689-1953. two volumes. New York: Praeger, 1959.
Volume 2, section 3, contains more than a dozen highly useful maps of major Korean War operations.

0064 Frank, Benis M. Marine Corps Oral History Collection Catalog. Washington, D. C.: United States Marine History and Museum Division, 1989.
An initial listing of oral interviews for the Marine Corps including an audiotape catalog.

0065 Gendlin, Gerry. "Archives and Research: Accessing the Archives of the Former Soviet Union" Perspectives 32 3 (March 1994).
An evaluation of what is available, and some warnings about the too rapid interpretation of what they mean.

0066 Geselbracht, Raymond H. and Anita M. Smith, compilers. Guide to Historical Materials in the Harry S. Truman Library. Independence, Missouri: Harry Truman Library, 1995.
Excellent guide to archival material at the Truman Library. Unfortunately there is less at the Library which relates to the Korean War than might have been expected.

0067 Haines, Gerald K. A Reference Guide to United States Department of State Special Files. Westport, Connecticut: Greenwood Press, 1985.
Considerably out-dated, but still a useful guide to the State Department Special Files.

0068 Hajnal, Peter I. Guide to United Nations Organization, Documentation and Publishing. Dobbs Ferry, New York: Oceana Publications, 1978.
Old, but useful for the Korean War period. Use of United Nations documents requires a knowledge of internal organization.

0069 Higham, Robin and Donald J. Mrozek, editors. Guide to the Sources of United States Military History: Supplement I, II, III. Hamden,

Connecticut: Shoe String Press, 1975; Hamden, Connecticut: Archon Books, 1981, 1986, 1993.

A good guide to military history, though there is no special section on Korea.

0070 Index to Documents of the National Security Council. Bethesda, Maryland: University Publications of America, 1994.

A cumulative index of microfilm of the United Nations National Security Council from 1945-1961. Very important.

0071 Jessup, John E., Jr. Encyclopedia of the American Military. three volumes. New York: Scribner's, 1994.

Good, short entry, look at American military history: suffers from the problems of most encyclopedias, but current on many subjects.

0072 Jessup, John E., Jr. and Robert W. Coakley, editors. A Guide to the Study and Use of Military History. Washington, D. C.: Center of Military History, 1979.

Deals with the Army's historical program, and provides essays on various aspects of the available material.

0073 Kim, Hak-Joon. "International Trends in Korean War Studies: A Review of the Documentary Literature" Korea and World Affairs 2 (1990).

Suggests Korea was the obvious result of policies which had been in place for decades.

0074 Kinnell, Susan K., editor. Military History of the United States: An Annotated Bibliography. Santa Barbara, California: ABC-Clio, 1986.

Useful collection of sources, well annotated. Outdated but still helpful.

0075 "Korean Chronology" Leatherneck 34 11 (1951): 28-29.

Marine operations 25 June 1950 until 30 June 1951. Very limited account.

0076 Kuehl, Warren, editor. Dissertations in History: An Index to Dissertations Completed in History Departments of United States and Canadian Universities. Lexington: University of Kentucky Press, 1972.

A good deal of the work being done on the Korean War is being accomplished in graduate schools. This work, and updates, is the best source.

0077 Leopold, Richard W. "A Survey of Sources Relating to the Korean War" Whistle Stop 5 2 (1977): insert.

Excellent survey of available works, especially unpublished, and narratives.

0078 Matray, James I., editor. Historical Dictionary of the Korean War. Westport, Connecticut: Greenwood Press, 1991.

A useful tool to assist in understanding the Korean War. Describes significant persons involved, controversies, military operations, and policy. Accurate and well constructed.

0079 McCune, Shannon. "Maps of Korea" Far Eastern Quarterly 5 3 (1946): 326-329.

Brief account of the maps available for use by United Nations troops at the time of the war. Significant information to those reviewing battle plans.

0080 Millett, Allan R. and B. Franklin Cooling III. Doctoral Dissertations in Military Affairs. Manhattan, Kansas: Kansas State University Library, 1972.

Listing of more than 1,500 dissertations, updated annually beginning with February 1973, in Military Affairs.

0081 Moody, Marilyn K. "The Korean War Revisited: A Selective Bibliography of United States Government Documents by Catherine M. Dwyer" Collection Building 11 4 (1991): 43-46.

A bibliography of government documents dealing with the Korean War.

0082 Moran, John B. Creating a Legend: The Complete Record of Writing about the United States Marines Corps. Chicago: Moran/Andrews, 1973.

Basic source of information on United States Marine Corps writing. Old but still useful.

0083 Moss, William. Archives in the People's Republic of China: A Brief Introduction for American Scholars and Archivists. Washington, D. C.: Smithsonian Archives, 1993.

Directory for material now available from the Chinese Archives, with entries in English and Chinese. With more material becoming available every day it is hard to stay current. But this is a very important beginning.

0084 Neutral Nations Repatriation Commission. Korea: Reports and Selected Documents. New Delhi: India Press, 1954.

Basic documents dealing with issues of the Korean War POW repatriation.

0085 Paszek, Lawrence. <u>United States Air Force History: A Guide to Documentary Sources</u>. Washington, D. C.: Office of Air Force History, 1973.
	Describes the United States Air Force Center and depositories, and cites a dozen collections dealing with the Korean War.

0086 <u>Records of the Joint Chiefs of Staff: Part II, The Far East, 1946-1953</u>. Frederick, Maryland: University Publications, 1980.
	Documents of military activities and policies during the pre-war Korean involvement, the invasion and American military reaction, as well as the first year of defense. Very helpful in trying to understand the military mind; microfilm available in 14 reels.

0087 <u>Register of World War II and Korean War Decedents</u>. three volumes. Washington, D. C.: The Commission, 1962.
	This register lists the American war dead in two major United States wars. It is not complete, but comes as close as possible.

0088 Sandler, Stanley, editor. <u>The Korean War: An Encyclopedia</u>. New York: Garland, 1994.
	Several articles written by experts which cover everything from helicopter warfare to psychological warfare. Includes 13 maps and 35 photos.

0089 Saunders, Jack. "Records in the National Archives Relating to Korea" in Bruce Cumings, editor. <u>Child of Conflict</u>. Seattle: University of Washington Press, 1983.
	This essay provides an excellent guide to materials that have become available concerning the Korean War. The declassification has come about through the use of the Freedom of Information Act.

0090 Schuon, Karl. <u>U. S. Marine Corps Biographical Dictionary</u>. New York: Watts, 1963.
	Series of brief sketches of officers and enlisted men, many of whom distinguished themselves during the early fighting in Korea. This work identifies and helps keep the players straight.

0091 Summers, Harry G., Jr. <u>Korean War Almanac</u>. New York: Facts on File, 1990.
	Compiled by a respected historian, the alphabetically listed entries are brief, but the information is accurate, insightful, and in very useful form.

0092 Thomas, Robert C. "The Campaign in Korea" <u>Brassey's Annual: The Armed Forces Yearbook</u>. Henry G. Thursfield, editor. New York: Macmillan, 1953.

This annual offering is a good, brief, source of information on the war. Encyclopedic account of the Korean War.

0093 United States National Archives and Records Service. <u>Preliminary Inventory of the Records of the Headquarters, United Nations Command: (Record Group 333)</u>. Washington, D. C.: National Archives, 1960.

Good resource for materials dealing with the United Nations command and the Korean War. Dated.

0094 Wickman, John E., editor. <u>Historical Materials in the Dwight D. Eisenhower Library</u>. Abilene, Kansas: Eisenhower Library, 1984.

Adequate guide to the valuable collection at the Eisenhower Library. Korean War material limited.

0095 Zaichikov, V. T. <u>Geography of Korea</u>. New York: Institute of Public Relations, 1951.

Russian author looks at physical and environmental factors.

Bibliographies

0096 Albion, Robert G. <u>Naval and Maritime History: An Annotated Bibliography</u>. 4th edition. Mystic Seaport, Connecticut: Marine Historical Association, 1972.

More than 5,000 works dealing with maritime history, some on the Korean War period.

0097 Anderson, Martin, editor. <u>Conscription: A Select and Annotated Bibliography</u>. Stanford, California: Hoover Institution Press, 1976.

The title is a little misleading, the focus is more on military policy than on conscription, but has some good materials on Korean War.

0098 Association of Asian Studies. <u>Cumulative Bibliography of Asian Studies 1941-1965: Subject Bibliography</u>. four volumes. Boston: Hall Publishing, 1970-1972.

Volumes three and four of this carefully collected bibliography contain numerous articles dealing with the Korean War. The lack of an index makes it difficult to use. All works listed are available in English. Updated annually by the Association.

0099 Backus, Robert L., compiler. <u>Russian Supplement to the Korean Studies Guide</u>. Berkeley: Institute of International Studies, University of California, 1958.

Important bibliography of Russian works, dealing with the Korean War which are available in English. Selective and works often unavailable.

0100 Bibliography of Social Science Periodicals and Monograph Series Republic of Korea, 1945-1961. Washington, D. C.: Government Printing Office, 1962.

A selected bibliography of articles and monographs covering the period from the American occupation through the war. All items listed are available in English.

0101 Blanchard, Carroll H., Jr. Korean War Bibliography and Maps of Korea. Albany, New York: Korean Conflict Research Foundation, 1964.

The early phase of a program to collect and identify materials dealing with the Korean War. The subject arrangements are somewhat difficult and by now the work is very dated.

0102 Brune, Lester H. The Korean War: Handbook of the Literature and Research. Westport, Connecticut: Greenwood Press, 1996.

An excellent source and discussion of the research done on the Korean War. Divided by subjects, it includes excellent bibliographic essays and good, up-to-date selections. Index contains some mistakes.

0103 Burns, Richard D. Harry S. Truman: A Bibliography of His Times and Presidency. Wilmington, Delaware: Scholarly Resources, Inc., 1984.

A good bibliography of Truman, with special emphasis on pre-war concerns, and the American occupation of Korea (1945-1950).

0104 Chung, Yong Sun, compiler. Korea: A Selected Bibliography, 1959-1963. Kalamazoo, Michigan: Korean Research and Publications, 1965.

The title is confusing, apparently meaning works published during these dates. It contains about fifty works on the war itself. These materials include some North Korean sources and are generally available in English.

0105 Coletta, Paolo E. An Annotated Bibliography of U. S. Marine Corps History. Lanham, Maryland: University Press of America, 1986.

A good basic listing, old but still of value, on Marine activities. There are better ones now available.

0106 Coletta, Paolo, compiler. A Selected and Annotated Bibliography of American Naval History. Frederick, Maryland: University Press of America, 1988.

A massive listing of works dealing with naval history includes articles, books, monographs, theses and dissertations, and includes more than a hundred works on the Korean War.

0107 Cresswell, Mary Ann and Carl Berger. <u>United States Air Force History, An Annotated Bibliography</u>. Washington, D. C.: Office of Air Force History, 1971.

Nearly 1,500 entries dealing with the Air Force, with fifty or so on the Air Force role in Korea.

0108 Davis, Lenwood O. and George Hill, compilers. <u>Blacks in the American Armed Forces, 1776-1983: A Bibliography</u>. Westport, Connecticut: Greenwood Press, 1985.

Contains references to the problem of integration in the Armed Forces during the Korean War.

0109 Dollen, Charles and the Library Staff of the University of San Diego. <u>Bibliography of the United States Marine Corps</u>. New York: The Scarecrow Press, Inc., 1963.

Well identified collection of books and articles relating to the Marine Corps. A good index makes it especially useful. Very dated but still helpful.

0110 Dornbusch, Charles E. <u>Histories, Personal Narratives, United States Army. A Checklist</u>. Cornwallville, New York: Hope Farms, 1967.

Listing of privately printed, and small run, histories and narratives. Some deal with Korean War titles.

0111 Edwards, Paul M. <u>General Matthew B. Ridgway: An Annotated Bibliography</u>. Westport, Connecticut: Greenwood Press, 1993.

A part of the Greenwood Press series, <u>Bibliographies of Battles and Leaders</u>, this work covers the life of General Ridgway who served as Assistant Chief of Staff, Joint Chiefs, as well as commander of Eighth Army.

0112 Edwards, Paul M. <u>The Pusan Perimeter, Korea 1950: An Annotated Bibliography</u>. Westport, Connecticut: Greenwood Press, 1993.

A part of the Greenwood Press series, <u>Bibliographies of Battles and Leaders</u>, this bibliography focuses on the retreat/defense at Pusan.

0113 Edwards, Paul M. <u>The Inchon Landing, Korea 1950: Annotated Bibliography</u>. Westport, Connecticut: Greenwood Press, 1994.

A part of the Greenwood Press series, <u>Bibliographies of Battles and Leaders</u>, this volume concentrates on the landing at Inchon.

0114 Ginsburgs, George. <u>Soviet Works on Korea, 1945-1970</u>. Los Angeles: University of Southern California Press, 1973.

Interesting collection of works from bacteriological warfare to international law, all presented from the Soviet point of view.

0115 Greenwood, John, compiler. <u>American Defense Policy Since 1945: A</u>
<u>Preliminary Bibliography</u>. Lawrence, Kansas: University Press of Kansas,
1973.
     More than seventy works listed on the outbreak and early political
considerations of the Korean War, including the Inchon decision and the
crossing of the 38th Parallel. A good solid collection greatly limited by the
lack of an index.

0116 Henthorn, William E., compiler. <u>A Guide to Reference and Research</u>
<u>Materials on Korean History</u>. Honolulu: East-West Center, 1968.
     This work focuses on Japanese and Korean citations, in English, of
the Korean War.

0117 Higham, Robin and Jacob W. Kipp, editors. <u>Military History</u>
<u>Bibliographies</u>. New York: Garland, 1978-1993.
     Chapters written by military authorities who provide technical data
references as well as military citations.

0118 Hillard, Jack B. and Harold A. Bivins. <u>An Annotated Reading List of</u>
<u>United States Marine Corps History</u>. Washington, D. C.: History and
Museums Division, Headquarters United States Marine Corps, 1971.
     Very dated by the mini-revival of interest in the late 1980s, but still
a good source of early publications.

0119 Horak, Stephen M., editor. <u>Russia, The USSR and Eastern Europe: A</u>
<u>Bibliographic Guide to English Language Publications, 1964-1974.</u> Littleton,
Colorado: Libraries Unlimited, 1978.
     Horak is outdated because of the 1990s availability of Soviet records,
but is still a good source of multi-language materials until 1974.

0120 Houston, Susan Hoffman. <u>McCarthy and the Anti-Communist Crusade:</u>
<u>A Selected Bibliography</u>. Los Angeles: California State University Press,
1979.
     The best, so far, on McCarthyism and its extended influences.

0121 Huls, Mary Ellen. <u>United States Government Documents on Women,</u>
<u>1800-1990: A Comprehensive Bibliography</u>. two volumes. Westport,
Connecticut: Greenwood Press, 1993.
     Excellent collection on women's issues in government, military, and
labor. Includes consideration of women in the Korean War.

0122 Hyatt, Joan, compiler. <u>Korean War, 1950-1953: Selected References</u>.
Maxwell Air Force Base: Air University Library, 1990.

A small but very valuable collection of Korean War materials collected by a bibliographic expert on the war, and available at the Air University Library.

0123 Imperial War Museum Library. The War in Korea, 1950-1953, A List of Selected References. London: War Museum Library, 1961.

This mimeographed list produced by the Imperial War Museum Library staff contains more than 350 books, articles, and monographs in English on Commonwealth forces who served in the Korean War. Dated.

0124 Kim, Han-Kyo and Hong Kyoo Park. Studies on Korea: A Scholar's Guide. Honolulu: University of Hawaii Press, 1959.

More than 3,500 entries on Korea, well arranged, and divided by sixteen subject headings. More than thirty entries are on the Korean War.

0125 Kinnell, Susan K. and Suzanne R. Ontiveros, editors. American Maritime History: A Bibliography. Santa Barbara, California: ABC-Clio, 1983.

Very selective in its entries, nevertheless a good source of naval information.

0126 Kuehl, Warren F. and Nancy M. Ferguson, editors. The United States and the United Nations: A Bibliography. Political issues series; 7 2 Los Angeles: California State University, 1981.

This brief work on foreign relations comes from the Center for the Study of Armament and Disarmament.

0127 Labaree, Benjamin W. A Supplement (1971-1986) to Robert G. Albion's Naval and Maritime History: An Annotated Bibliography. 4th edition. Mystic Seaport, Connecticut: Mystic Seaport Museum, 1988.

An update of the series started by Paolo Coletta, provides excellent source identification.

0128 Lambert, Norma K. Cumulative Indices to Military Affairs, 1932-1969. Manhattan, Kansas: Kansas State University Library, 1969.

Poor history and review of articles from the named journal. Not easy to use. The lack of Korean War coverage is support for the "forgotten war" thesis.

0129 Lee, Chong-Sik. "Korea and the Korean War" in Thomas Hammond, editor. Soviet Foreign Relations and World Communism. Princeton: Princeton University Press, 1965.

Contains nearly fifty works on the Korean War, most of them on the larger political issues. Very well annotated.

0130 Lee, Choon-kun. "Bibliographic Essay on Korean War" <u>A Study of Unification Affairs</u> 2 (Summer 1990).
          One of the few serious works on Korean bibliography, it provides some very useable insights.

0131 McFarland, Keith D. <u>The Korean War: An Annotated Bibliography</u>. New York: Garland, 1986.
          An excellent collection of materials dealing with the war, well arranged and easy to identify, cross referenced in index. The annotations are brief but crisp. Other than being dated by the appearance of new materials this the best source available.

0132 Miller, Samuel Duncan. <u>An Aerospace Bibliography</u>. Washington, D. C.: Office of Air Force History, 1986.
          Updated and expanded version of <u>United States Air Force History</u> first published in 1971. Includes history, aeronautics, and indexes.

0133 O'Quinlivan, Michael and James S. Santelli. <u>An Annotated Bibliography of the United States Marines in the Korean War</u>. Washington, D. C.: Historical Branch G-3 Division, Headquarters United States Marines, 1962. Revised edition 1970.
          A good, but dated, listing of materials dealing with the United States Marine Corps action during the Korean War. Annotations very limited.

0134 Okinshevich, Leo, compiler. <u>United States History and Historiography in Postwar Soviet Writing, 1945-1970: A Bibliography</u>. Santa Barbara, California: ABC-Clio, 1976.
          Good source on historiography, but surprisingly few of the entries relate to the Korean War.

0135 Paige, Glenn D. "A Survey of Soviet Publications on Korea, 1950-1956" <u>Journal of Asian Studies</u> (August 7, 1958): 579-594.
          For the serious student this provides a look at how the war was covered and analyzed by the Russian government and intellectual community.

0136 Park, Hong-Kyu. "America and Korea, 1945-1953: A Bibliographical Essay" <u>Asian Foreign Affairs</u> 3 1 (1971): 57-66.
          Excellent account of studies and sources on the Korean War.

0137 Park, Hong-Kyu. <u>The Korean War: An Annotated Bibliography</u>. Marshall, Texas: Demmer Co., Inc., 1971.

A brief and very selective work which concentrates on Korean entries (in English) without special annotation.

0138 Petersen, Neal H. American Intelligence, 1775-1990: A Bibliographical Guide. Claremont, California: Regina Books, 1992.
Provides a historical perspective on the use of intelligence data.

0139 Rasor, Eugene L., editor. General Douglas MacArthur, 1888-1964: Historiography and Annotated Bibliography. Westport, Connecticut: Greenwood Press, 1994.
Very specialized listing on Korean War general—less than anticipated on the Korean War period.

0140 A Revolutionary War: Korea and the Transformation of the Postwar World. Special Bibliography Series 84. Colorado Springs, Colorado: United States Air Force Academy Library, 1992.
A brief but informative bibliography which supports the idea the Korean War was more revolutionary than international.

0141 Roberts, Henry L., editor. Foreign Affairs Bibliography: A Selected and Annotated List of Books on International Relations. volume 3 (1942-1952) and volume 4 (1952-1962). New York: R. R. Bowker for the Council on Foreign Relations, 1955, 1964.
Good bibliographic reference which specializes in economic, sociological, and political entries.

0142 Rhee, Sang-woo, Paik Chong-Chun and Chang-Il Ohn, editors. "Selected Bibliography of the Korean War" Korea and World Affairs 8 2 (Summer 1984): 442-473.
Selective, but excellent bibliographic work for introduction to Korean sources.

0143 Roos, Charles, compiler. A Bibliography of Military Medicine Relating to the Korean Conflict, 1950-1956. Washington, D. C.: National Library of Medicine (United States), 1957.
Deals with most aspects of military medicine as it related to Korea. This is an update of earlier bibliography covering through 1953.

0144 Roos, Charles, compiler. Bibliography of Military Psychology, 1947-1952. Washington, D. C.: Government Printing Office, 1953.
Several hundred works which deal with military psychiatry in the United States and British Commonwealth during the Korean War.

0145 Santelli, James S. <u>An Annotated Bibliography of the United States Marine Corps' Concept of Close Air Support</u>. Washington, D. C.: Historical Branch, G-3 Division, Headquarters United States Marine Corps, 1968.

Deals with Marine Corps aviation and source materials for identifying air-to-ground close support.

0146 Schultz, Charles R., compiler. <u>Bibliography of Naval and Maritime History: Periodical Articles</u>. Mystic Seaport, Connecticut: Marine Historical Association, 1971.

An index to Navy articles (periodical) which includes a good section on the Korean War.

0147 Seeley, Charlotte Palmer, compiler. Virginia C. Purdy and Robert Gruber, revisions. <u>American Women in the U. S. Armed Forces: A Guide to the Records of Military Agencies in the National Archives Relating to American Women</u>. Washington, D. C.: National Archives, 1992.

Good up-to-date source for research on women in the armed forces. The material is cross-indexed.

0148 Sunderman, James F. "Documentary Collections Related to the U. S. Air Force" <u>Air University Quarterly Review</u> 13 1 (1961): 110-126.

Provides the reader the location of principle collections of Air Force documents. A help but not complete.

0149 Thursfield, Henry G., editor. <u>Brassey's Annual: The Armed Forces Yearbook, 1950-1954</u>. New York: Macmillan, 1950-1954.

Survey of activities by the British Forces during the Korean War period.

0150 Tillema, Herbert K. <u>International Armed Conflict Since 1945: A Bibliographic Handbook of Wars and Military Interventions</u>. Boulder, Colorado: Westview Press, 1991.

A well-done bibliography on armed conflicts which broke out during the Cold War period. Some descriptive accounts.

0151 Tsien, Tsuen-hsuin and James K. M. Cheng, compiler. <u>China: An Annotated Bibliography of Bibliographies</u>. Boston: Hall, 1978.

One of the few bibliographies of Chinese involvement. Out of date but useful as few other sources are available.

0152 United States. <u>Communist Treatment of American Prisoners of War During the Korean Conflict, 1950-1953: A Select Bibliography</u>. Washington, D. C.: The Library, 1984.

Selected bibliography of communist treatment of American prisoners-of-war.

0153 United States Defense Document Center. <u>Bibliography of Amphibious Operations</u>. four volumes. Cameron Station, Alexandria, Virginia: Defense Document Center, 1969.

Useful collection of material dealing with various amphibious landings. Their interpretation of "amphibious" is used in the widest sense, but other than being dated this is a useful source of information.

0154 United States Department of the Army. <u>Communist China; Ruthless Enemy or Paper Tiger? A Bibliographic Survey</u>. Washington, D. C.: Government Printing Office, 1962.

Works cited between 1950 and 1960 list nearly 300 books and articles on the Korean War. It does not answer the question.

0155 United States Department of the Army. <u>Communist North Korea: A Bibliographic Survey</u>. Washington, D. C.: Government Printing Office, 1962.

A very selective bibliographical source on the communist government and troops in North Korea. Not only dated but the definition of communism is not clear and listings not well conceived.

0156 <u>United Nation's Efforts Against Aggression in Korea, Bibliography</u>. Washington, D. C.: Library of Congress, no date.

A limited bibliography directed by the assumption of North Korean acts of aggression. Concerned with works which support the position of communist aggression.

0157 United States Navy Department Library. <u>United States Naval History: A Bibliography</u>. 6th edition. Washington, D. C.: Naval History Division, 1972.

Update of book first published in 1956. Includes naval history, biography, strategy, and tactics.

0158 Ward, Robert E. and Frank Shulman. <u>The Allied Occupation of Japan, 1945-1952: An Annotated Bibliography of Western Language Materials</u>. Chicago: American Library Association, 1974.

This nearly 2,500 work bibliography contains materials on General MacArthur and his dismissal, as well as some dealing with the Korean War.

0159 Werner, H. O. "Paperbacks on Modern Warfare" <u>United States Naval Institute Proceedings</u> (August 1959): 110-116.

A critical bibliography of armed forces books dealing with war, from World War II to Korea.

0160 Yang, Key Paik. <u>Korean War Bibliography</u>. Washington, D. C.: Yang Ki-baek, 1990.

  This sizable bibliography in English includes the author's personal statement in Korean characters.

CAUSES AND CONFLICTS

Korean Policy, Cold War Relations, 1865-1950

0161 American Forces in Action. fourteen pamphlets. Washington, D. C.: Government Printing Office, 1943-1947.

Popular pamphlets designed to show the locations and actions of American fighting forces. Among those considered is the occupation and first year of military government in Korea.

0162 Bell, Coral. "Korea and the Balance of Power" Political Quarterly 25 1 (1954): 17-29.

The Korean War was the result of a Russian-American international tug-of-war, and only partially related to domestic events in Korea.

0163 Borton, Hugh. "Korea Under American and Soviet Occupation, 1945-1947" in Arnold Toynbee, editor. Survey of International Affairs, 1939-1946: The World in March 1939. volume III. London: Oxford University Press, 1952.

Traces United States and Soviet involvement in the emerging Cold War conflict as Russia attempted to dominate all of Korea.

0164 Braisted, William R. The United States Navy in the Pacific, 1897-1909. Austin: University of Texas Press, 1977.

A survey coverage which tries to relate naval history as diplomatic maneuvering.

0165 Buhite, Russell D. "'Major Interests': American Policy toward China, Taiwan, and Korea, 1945-1950" Pacific Historical Review 47 3 (August 1978): 425-451.

The United States blurred the distinction between vital and major interest, then was unsure about Korea and later was too severe about Vietnam.

0166 Cho, Soon Sung. Korea in World Politics, 1940-1950: An Evaluation of American Responsibility. Berkeley: University of California Press, 1967.

Well-researched consideration of the post World War II period during which blunders by the United States and Korea led to the outbreak of war.

0167 Cohen, Warren I. "Conversations with Chinese Friends: Zhou Enlai's Associates Reflect on Chinese-American Relations in the 1940s and the Korean War" Diplomatic History 11 3 (Summer 1987): 283-289.

Excellent look at the research value to be gained from Chinese scholars when, and if, the Chinese archives are opened to complete access.

0168 Cumings, Bruce. The Roaring of the Cataract, 1947-1950. Princeton, New Jersey: Princeton University Press, 1981.

Critical of the United States, appearing to accept Russian actions at face value, and accuses all nations for the outbreak of war in Korea.

0169 Cumings, Bruce. "Korea: The Politics of Liberation, 1945-1947" Ph.D. dissertation, Columbia University, 1975.

Examines the interaction between the United States and Russia during the formation period.

0170 Dingman, Roger. "The U. S. Navy and the Cold War: The Japan Case" in Craig Symonds, editor. New Aspects of Naval History. Annapolis, Maryland: Naval Institute Press, 1981.

Selected papers about naval history, naval art, and naval science presented at the fourth Naval History Symposium at the United States Naval Academy, 25-26 October 1979.

0171 Donaldson, Gary. America at War since 1945: Politics and Diplomacy in Korea, Vietnam, and the Gulf War. Westport, Connecticut: Praeger, 1996.

Deals with the foreign policy and international relations as it existed prior to America's military involvement with these countries.

0172 The East-Asian Crisis, 1945-1951: The Problem of China, Korea, and Japan: Papers. London: International Centre for Economics and Related Disciplines, London School of Economics, 1982.

Roger Dingman paper covers the Truman-Atlee connection. Chihiro Hosoya paper covers the Dulles-Yoshida talks. Ian Hill Nish paper covers the occupation of Japan.

0173 Feaver, John H. "The China Aid Bill of 1948: Limited Assistance as a Cold War Strategy" Diplomatic History 5 2 (Spring 1981): 107-120.
    The Truman administration did not want to make a decision on the China policy, and tried to walk a line between aid and Cold War tactics with Red China.

0174 Fleming, D. Frank. The Cold War and Its Origins, 1917-1960. volume 2. Garden City, New York: Doubleday, 1961.
    This well-researched work draws some interesting conclusions and identifies the South Korean government as the primary cause of the outbreak of war.

0175 Gardner, Lloyd C. Approaching Vietnam: From World War II through Dienbienphu, 1941-1954. New York: Norton, 1988.
    Gives a broad view of United States policymaking, providing some newer interpretations, which will require answers.

0176 Gordenker, Leon. The United Nations and the Peaceful Unification of Korea: The Politics of Field Operations, 1947-1950. The Hague: Marinue Nijhoff, 1959.
    Interprets the results of United Nations collective action in the Korean question.

0177 Gordenker, Leon. "The United Nations, the United States Occupation, and the 1948 Election in Korea" Political Science Review 73 (1958): 426-450.
    Looks at earlier efforts to unite Korea and then focuses on the 1948 election and the formation of South Korea as a republic.

0178 Grey, Arthur L. Jr. "The Thirty-Eighth Parallel" Foreign Affairs 29 3 (1951): 482-487.
    Affirms that Korea was divided by military interests rather than for political or diplomatic considerations; decision was not made at Yalta as many have suggested.

0179 Harding, Harry, Yuan Ming and Pei-ching Ta Hsueh, editors. Sino-American Relations, 1945-1955: A Joint Reassessment of a Critical Decade. Wilmington, Delaware: Scholarly Resources, 1989.
    Collection of essays dealing with United States-China relations. Tends to be critical of the United States.

0180 Hausrath, Alfred. The KMAG Advisor: Role and Problems of the Military Advisor in Developing an Indigenous Army for Combat Operations in Korea. Chevy Chase, Maryland: Operations Research Office, Johns Hopkins University, 1957.

A technical memo dealing with the tactics developed for the ROK infantry groups. Includes bibliographic references.

0181 Haydock, Michael. "America's Other Korean War" Military History 13 1 (April 1, 1996): 38

On June 11, 1871, United States Marines laid seige to Kangwha in Korea. That war was not successful either.

0182 Cho, Soon Sung. Korea in World Politics, 1940-1950: An Evaluation of American Responsibility. Berkeley: University of California Press, 1967.

Moderate study of a traditional nature, which tends to support Truman's claim the Korean War was part of the Soviet Union's global plan.

0183 Iriye, Akira. The Cold War in Asia: A Historical Introduction. Englewood Cliffs, New Jersey: Prentice, 1974.

An interpretative essay on the origins of the Cold War in Asia. Focuses on the 1940s and 1950s.

0184 Joo, Seung-Ho. "Russian Policy on Korean Unification in the Post Cold-War Era" Pacific Affairs 69 1 (Spring 1996): 37-48.

An analysis of the Russian response to the political and military difficulties in Korea.

0185 Kim, Joungwoon Alexander, Divided Korea: The Politics of Development, 1945-1972. Cambridge: Harvard University Press, 1975.

Extends the earlier work done by McCune and Grey in Korea Today (1950).

0186 Kim, Young Jeung. Voice of Korea 1943-1961. Washington, D. C.: Korean Affairs Institute, 1961.

A strong appeal for a neutralized and unified Korea, made through a collection of Bulletins out of Washington, D. C.

0187 King, Lisa. The Origins of the Cold War: A Unit of Study for Grade 9-12. Los Angeles: National Center for History in the Schools, 1991.

This brief work presents world politics and foreign relations for high school students.

0188 Kwak, Tae-Hawn, editor. U. S.-Korean Relations, 1882-1982. Seoul: Kyungnam University Press, 1982.

Asserts that the United States never considered Korea as its key interest. Characterizes United States policy as indecision.

0189 Lee, Kwang-Ho. "A Study of the United Nations Commission for the Unification and the Rehabilitation of Korea: The Cold War and the United Nations Subsidiary Organ" Ph.D. dissertation. University of Pittsburgh, 1974.

Author studies the thesis that Soviets were surprised by both the Korean War and American reaction; the view of United Nations commission.

0190 Matray, James I. "An End to Indifference: America's Korean Policy During WW II" Diplomatic History 2 5 (1978): 10-14.

Traces Franklin Roosevelt's changing view on trusteeship for Korea following World War II, and the resulting Cold War confusion.

0191 Matray, James I. "Captive of the Cold War: Decisions to Divide Korea at the 38th Parallel" Pacific Historical Review 50 2 (1981): 145-158.

The decision to divide Korea at the 38th Parallel was the result of disagreements between the United States and Russia, and the American fear that Russia would dominate Korea if left alone.

0192 McCune, George M. and Arthur L. Grey, Jr. Korea Today. Cambridge: Harvard University Press, 1950.

Excellent early work which deals with Korea as a Japanese colony, and traces its movement toward occupation and war.

0193 McCune, George M. "Occupation Politics in Korea" Far Eastern Studies 15 1 (1946): 33-37.

McCune is very critical of the failures which occurred in Korea after the close of World War II.

0194 Meade, E. G. American Military Government in Korea. New York: King's Crown, 1951.

An account of American military government from October 1945 to October 1946.

0195 Min, Byong-tae. "Political Development in Korea: 1945-1965" Korean Journal 5 9 (1965): 28-33.

The United States and United Nations involvement in Korea is defended as being necessary, and was in keeping with the American desire to see a united Korea.

0196 Moris, William G. "The Korean Trusteeship, 1941-1947" Ph.D. dissertation, University of Texas, 1975.

United States entered the trusteeship for humanitarian reasons, but Japan's collapse at the end of World War II came too quickly, and unification was prevented by Soviet involvement.

0197 Nalty, Bernard C. and Truman Stonebridge. "Our First Korean War" American History Illustrated 2 5 (1967): 10-19.
    Describes the June 1871 assault by United States Marines on the Korean coast near current Inchon, and the fact that it accomplished nothing at all.

0198 Nordgaard, Vernita Helmstadter. "The Attitude of the Soviet Union Toward United Nations Actions in Korea (1950-53)" MA thesis, University of Washington, 1959.
    A less than adequate explanation of Soviet attitudes, made even less valuable by release of materials in the Russian archives.

0199 Okonogi, Masao. "The Domestic Roots of the Korean War" in Yonosuke Nagai and Akira Iriye, editors. The Origins of the Cold War in Asia. New York: Columbia University Press, 1977.
    The Korean War was the result of allowing the unrest of a domestic situation to become internationalized.

0200 Oliver, Robert T. Why War Came in Korea. New York: Fordham University, 1950.
    "Blundering good-will" created trouble in Korea despite the Russian lack of headway in making communists out of the Koreans.

0201 Park, Hong-Kyu. "American-Korean Relations, 1945-1950: A Study in United States Diplomacy" Ph.D. dissertation, University of North Texas, 1981.
    The primary goal of America was to unify Korea, but this was side-tracked by the larger goals of the Cold War.

0202 Pollack, Jonathan. "The Korean War and Sino-American Relations" in Harry Harding and Yuan Ming, editors. Sino-American Relations 1945-1955: A Joint Reassessment of a Critical Decade. Wilmington, Delaware: Scholarly Resources, 1989.
    The first major effort to use Chinese sources made available for exploring China's involvement in the war. Confirms the "China under threat" thesis.

0203 Potts, William E. "Korea: 1946 to 1950" Armor 59 5 (1950): 27-29.

Narrative of events from Cairo Conference (1943) to the outbreak of war (1950), during which the author sees the United States making an excellent contribution.

0204 Ree, Erik van. Socialism in One Zone: Stalin's Policy in Korea, 1945-1947. New York: St. Martin's Press, 1989.

Covers the background of Joseph Stalin, his politics and government. Relates the Soviet Union and Korea during these years.

0205 Rose, Lisle A. Roots of Tragedy: The United States and the Struggle for Asia, 1945-1953. Westport, Connecticut: Greenwood Press, 1976.

United States appeared to be unable to understand the Asian need for independence, and mishandled Korea.

0206 Sandusky, Michael C. America's Parallel. Alexandria, Virginia: Old Dominion Press, 1983.

Deals with the problems of American occupation of Korea during the 1945-1948 period.

0207 Sawyer, Robert K. Military Advisors in Korea: KMAG in Peace and War. Army Historical Series, Washington, D. C.: Center of Military History, 1962.

With the outbreak of the war, and the essential victory of North Korean forces, members of KMAG soon dropped their advisory role and became operational. This they did rather unsuccessfully. The Military Advisory Group was there directing, organizing, and mentoring troops. This is a revision of the original 1955 book.

0208 Sawyer, Robert K. The Military Advisory Group to the Republic of Korea. Army Historical Series, volume I (September 1, 1945, to June 30, 1949); volume II (July 1, 1949, to June 24, 1950); volume III (June 25, 1950, to July 30, 1951). Manuscript in the Office of the Chief of Military History file.

The material provided is basically the same as that in the published edition, but deals with the Advisory Group in more detail.

0209 Slusser, Robert M. "Soviet Far Eastern Policy, 1945-1950: Stalin's Goals in Korea" in Yonosuke Nagai and Akira Iriye, editors. The Origins of the Cold War in Asia. New York: Columbia University Press, 1977.

Papers on the Soviet intentions in Asia written for an international symposium in Kyoto, Japan, in 1975.

0210 Smith, Richard. "The Roots of the Korean War, 1945-1950" MA thesis, Mankato State University, 1977.

Covers the causes of the war and includes a bibliography.

0211 U. S. Department of State. The Conflict in Korea: Events Prior to the Attack on June 25, 1950. Washington, D. C.: Government Printing Office, 1951.
    Traces the political events that led from victory in World War II to the Korean War.

0212 Walsh, J. M. "British Participation in the Occupation of Japan" Army Quarterly 57 1 (October 1948): 72-81.
    The British participation in the occupation of Japan gave the British influence and responsibilities where actions in Korea were concerned.

0213 Wedemeyer, Albert C. "1947 Wedemeyer Report on Korea" Current History 20 118 (June 1951): 363-365.
    A report, suppressed until May of 1951, urged political and military support of South Korea in light of Russian and North Korean objectives.

0214 Weiss, Lawrence S. "Storm Around the Cradle: The Korean War and the Early Years of the People's Republic of China, 1949-1953" Ph.D. dissertation, Columbia University, 1981.
    Covers the politics and government of China and the international implications.

0215 Wiltz, John Edward. "Did the United States Betray Korea in 1905?" Pacific Historical Review 44 (August 1985): 243-270.
    Questions the American position taken at the Washington Conference, where the United States acted in conflict to the Korean wishes.

0216 Winder, Alice. "The Korean Failure" American Mercury 74 341 (1952): 12-14.
    Critical of the United States and its failures in Korea from 1945 to 1948. Blames Truman and the State Department.

0217 Yang, Kuisong. "The Soviet Factor and the CCP's Policy toward the United States in the 1940s" Chinese Historians 5 1 (Spring 1992): 17-34.
    The relations between Moscow and Beijing were not bad enough to drive Mao into any commitment to the United States.

Causes, Decisions, Involvement

0218 Acheson, Dean. "Crisis in Asia—An Examination of US Policy" Department of State Bulletin 22 (1950): 111-118.

Contains the 12 January 1950 speech by the Secretary of State which some historians claim so confused the issue of America's defense of Korea that it invited the North Koreans to attack.

0219 "Act of Aggression in Korea" Department of State Bulletin 23 (July 10, 1950): 43-46.
Secretary Dean Acheson, in an address to the American Newspaper Guild, reported that all actions taken so far in the Korean War was done under the authority of, and with the knowledge of, the United Nations.

0220 "Aims and Objectives in Resisting Aggression in Korea" Department of State Bulletin 23 (September 11, 1950): 407-410.
President Truman spoke to the American people from the White House on 1 September 1950, explaining to them why the United States had gone into Korea. The objectives were liberty, ours and theirs.

0221 "Authority of the President to Repel the Attack in Korea" Department of State Bulletin 23 (1950): 43-50.
Discusses the president's legal authority to take such action and to commit American troops. President Truman's decision is supported by a list of dates, places, and justification for more than eighty such previous interventions.

0222 Baldwin, Frank, editor. Without Parallel: The American-Korean Relationship since 1945. New York: Pantheon, 1974.
A series of essays which hold the theory that American intervention in Korea has proven disastrous for Korean and American foreign policy.

0223 Ballough, Harding Wilmans. "Background to United States Intervention in Korea, 1950" MA thesis, University of California: Berkeley, 1958.
Attempts to explain the long history of America's relations with Korea, right up to 1945.

0224 Bernstein, Barton J. "New Light on the Korean War" International History Review 3 2 (April 1981): 256-277.
Syngman Rhee's difficulty in supporting the United Nations effort resulted from the United Nations use of terror, bombing, and discussion of nuclear bombs.

0225 Bernstein, Barton J. "The Policy of Risk: Crossing the 38th Parallel and Marching to the Yalu" Foreign Service Journal 54 3 (March 1977): 8-11, 33-34.

The march to the Yalu River unleashed Chinese forces and brought them into the war. It was unnecessary and unwise and could easily have been avoided.

0226 Bernstein, Barton J. "The Week We Went to War: American Intervention in the Korean-Civil War" in two parts Foreign Service Journal 54 1 (January 1977): 6-9, 33-35; 54 2 (February 1977): 8-16, 33-35.

A two-part article on the United States decision to intervene. The first views Truman's and Acheson's attempts to determine Russian intentions, and the second focuses on the change which moved them from evacuation to commitment.

0227 Bo, Yibo. "The Making of the 'Lean-to-One-Side' Decision" Zhai Qiang, translator. Chinese Historians 5 (Spring 1992): 57-62.

This Chinese official during the late 1940s shows Mao's distrust of American leadership.

0228 Cavanagh, Arthur Myles. "Soviet Initiatives in the Korean War" MA thesis, George Washington University, 1975.

MA: Soviets

0229 Chaffee, William. "Two Hypothesis of Sino-Soviet Relations as Concerns the Instigation of the Korean War" Journal of Korean Affairs 6 3, 4 (1976-1977): 1-13.

One view was that Korea was a part of the Soviet expansion plan, the second was Russia's desire to control the buffer-zone while keeping Mao's friendship.

0230 "Challenge Accepted" Time 56 (July 3, 1950): 7-8.

Reports on actions by Truman, Johnson, and Acheson to meet the challenge of communist aggression when it came. When the North Korean forces moved beyond subversion to aggression they decided to act. Includes President Truman's statement.

0231 "Charging South Korea as Aggressor Reminiscent of Nazi Tactics" Department of State Bulletin 23 (July 17, 1950): 87.

Statement by Secretary Acheson indicates that free nations know the truth of who is responsible for the war, and they are not going to be misled by false versions of it.

0232 Chen, Jian. "China's Strategies to End the Korean War" Boston: Annual Meeting, Association of Asian Studies, 1994.

While author is cautious this is an excellent story of the events which led China to seek an ending to the war.

0233 Chen, Jian. "The Sino-Soviet Alliance and China's Entry into the Korean War" Working Paper 1. Cold War History Project, Washington, D. C.: Woodrow Wilson Center, 1991.

Author is challenged by the fact Soviet and Chinese archival material is so closely supportive.

0234 Chen, Chiev. "China's Road to the Korean War" Working Paper, Cold War History Project, Washington, D. C.: Woodrow Wilson Center, 1995-1996.

Challenges the view China entered because of the American push across the 38th Parallel and feels China's entry was sparked by a desire to take a lead in international communism.

0235 Cho, Li San. "Kim Started War" New York Times (July 6, 1990): A5.

Li San Cho, the former North Korean ambassador, says Kim Il Sung invented border incidents in order to provide an excuse for the outbreak of war in 1950.

0236 Cho, Soon Sung. "The Failure of American Military Government in Korea" Korean Affairs 2 3 (1963).

Maintains that both the United States and Russia dealt with Korea independently, the American failure being that it left Korea with no clear governmental control and in the midst of chaos. The expectations of these two powers were unclear and that led to irrational actions.

0237 Chung, Dae-Hwa. "How the Korean War Began" Translated by Karunakar Gupta in China Quarterly 52 (October and December 1972): 699-716.

Places the blame for the war on the South Korean government. Based on Gupta's work.

0238 "The Conflict in Korea: Events Prior to the Attack on June 25, 1950" Far Eastern Studies 45 (1951).

Discussion of the international political events which occurred prior to the North Korean invasion.

0239 The Conflict in Korea: Events Prior to the Attack on June 25, 1950. Department of State Publication Far Eastern Studies 4266 (October 1951).

Gives the diplomatic and legal background of the United States commitment to Korea. Heavily used by Appleman in his official history South to the Naktong, North to the Yalu. Very important collection of materials about American involvement and why the United States was willing to go to war at this time and under these circumstances.

0240 Connally, Thomas. My Name is Tom Connally. New York: Crowell, 1954.

   While support from members of Congress led Truman to believe he could take action without Congress, Connally maintains that Truman based his action on the United Nations treaty.

0241 Connor, W. R. "Why Were We Surprised?" American Scholar 60 (Spring 1991): 175-184.

   American leaders were surprised in Korea because of a failure of "practical intelligence," the true understanding of the adversaries.

0242 Crofts, Alfred. "The Start of the Korean War Reconsidered" Rocky Mountain Social Science Journal 1 (1970): 109-117.

   Claims the causes of the war were indigenous to Korea and the Koreans rather than some failure of national policy either by the United States or Russia.

0243 Cumings, Bruce. The Origins of the Korean War. volume I "Liberation and the Emergence of Separate Regimes" volume II "The Roaring of the Cataract" Princeton, New Jersey: Princeton University Press, 1981, 1990.

   These two volumes together provide one of the best and most responsible treatment of the causes of the war. Deals with the unbelievable complexity of events, and the interplay of persons and nations.

0244 Cumings, Bruce, editor. Child of Conflict: The Korean-American Relationships, 1943-1953. Seattle: University of Washington Press, 1983.

   In this collection of essays Cumings suggests MacArthur's attitude in Korea was designed to strengthen a political coalition.

0245 Dean, Vera M. "Justification of War" Foreign Policy Bulletin 31 (January 15, 1952): 5-6.

   Reaffirms the communist aggression as the reason for involvement, and sees the intervention of the United Nations as essential for the control of the spread of communism.

0246 Deane, Hugh. "Korea, China, and the United States: A Look Back" Monthly Review 46 9 (1995): 20.

   Claims the North Korean War was actually started by United States policy in aiding rightist forces in the south.

0247 Department of State Publication. United States Policy in the Korean Conflict, July 1950-February 1951. 4263. Washington, D. C.: Government Printing Office, 1954.

Analysis of the political and policy aspect of the American involvement in Korea and the policy considerations behind several of the military actions.

0248 Detzer, David. Thunder of the Captains: The Short Summer in 1950. New York: Crowell, 1977.

A narrative account of events in America and Korea, during the early summer of 1950, which eventually led to the United States decision to interfere. Popular account with strong personnel sketches.

0249 Dockrill, Michael L. "The Foreign Office, Anglo-American Relations and the Korean Truce Negotiations, July 1951-July 1953" in James Cotton and Ian Neary, editors. The Korean War in History. Manchester: Manchester University Press, 1989.

Suggests continuity between labor government and the conservative succession. During 1953 crisis, Churchill was willing to abandon Korea.

0250 Dockrill, Michael L. "The Foreign Office, Anglo-American Relations and the Korean War, June 1950-June 1951" International Affairs 62 3 (Summer 1986): 459-476.

The British role in Korea was augmented by a special relationship between British Ambassador Oliver Francis and American Dean Acheson.

0251 Dodson, Peter M. "The Wrong War: The Origins of the Korean War 1945-1950" MA thesis, University of Virginia, 1979.

MA: origins

0252 Doty, Mercer M. "The Decision to Cross the 38th Parallel in Korea During the United Nations Counteroffensive in the Fall of 1950" MA thesis, University of Pittsburgh, 1963.

Considers the international implications of moving the war from a local dispute to a major war effort: 1950-1953.

0253 Dresser, Robert B. How We Blundered into [the] Korean War and Tragic Future Consequences. New York: Committee for Constructive Government, 1950.

A less-than-adequate explanation for how America was used, and how this misuse will ultimately lead to disaster.

0254 "Events in Korea Deepen Interest in United Nations" Department of State Bulletin 23 (September 18, 1950): 450-451.

An address by Secretary Acheson made before the National Citizens Committee, 7 September 1950, in which he suggested that the United Nations action in Korea is symbolic of all that the United Nations stands for.

0255 Farley, Miriam S. "The Korean Crisis and the United Nations" Lawrence K. Rosinger, editor. State of Asia. New York: Alfred A. Knopf, Inc., 1951.

This essay, based on reports from the New York Times and the United Nations Bulletin, traced the development of United Nations understanding and action in Korea. One of the best statements about the why and how of the war.

0256 Fedorenko, N. "The Stalin-Mao Summit in Moscow" Far Eastern Affairs 64 2 (1989): 134-148.

These nocturnal talks between communist leaders are described by a Russian scholar who was in attendance.

0257 Feis, Herbert. From Trust to Terror: The Onset of the Cold War, 1945-1950. New York: Norton, 1970.

A classic study of the war by a man who knew the Cold War from inside the Department of State.

0258 Ferguson, Carolyn L. "The Korean Crucible: American Intervention in the Korean Conflict" MA thesis, Central Washington State College, 1974.

American involvement in the conflict in Korea was a part of the general misunderstanding of events in Asia.

0259 George, Alexander L. "American Policy-Making and the North Korean Aggression" World Politics 7 (January 1955): 209-232.

Defines a reverse in Truman's policy on Korea following the invasion, a situation which left the Soviet Union unsure as to American intentions.

0260 George, Alexander L. U. S. Reaction to North Korean Aggression. Santa Monica, California: Rand Corporation, 1954.

The Truman administration reacted to North Korean invasion by revising its Asian policy.

0261 Gillilland, William S. "Roots of Red China's Strategy in the Korean War" MA thesis, Stanford, California: Stanford University, 1960.

Examines the character of the Russian and Chinese leaders who helped shape communist China strategy in Korea.

0262 Goldman, Eric. "The President, the People, and the Power To Make War" American Heritage 21 3 (1970): 28-35.

Goldman says that Truman acted unconstitutionally, and unwisely, in his decision to commit American troops in Korea, with or without United Nations support.

0263 Gorcharov, Sergei N. "Stalin's Dialogue with Mao Zedong" interview with Ivan V. Kovalev; Craig Seibert, translator. Journal of Northeast Asia Studies 10 4 (Winter 1991-1992): 45-76.

An insightful review of Kovalev's participation in the infamous dialogue which puts the discussion in context.

0264 Gromyko, Andrei A. "World Documents—Gromyko Statement" Current History 19 (September 1950): 167-174.

On American Independence Day, 1950, Russian Foreign Minister Andrei Gromyko charged the United States with aggression in Korea. The "White Paper" is included.

0265 Gupta, Karunakar. "How Did the Korean War Begin?" China Quarterly 52 (October/December 1972): 699-716.

A well thought-out discussion of the events leading to war, the outbreak via "invasion," and an analysis of the various "invasion theories." Suggests South Korea was primarily responsible.

0266 Guttman, Allen. Korea and the Theory of Limited War. Boston: D. C. Heath, 1967.

Primarily designed for a class in decision making, this collection contains key documents for understanding the outbreak of the war. Primary in importance is the United Nations Security Council Resolution, 27 June 1950, and the text of Harry Truman's "Our Aims in Korea." Compares civilian view (Truman) and the military view (MacArthur) of the policy of limited war. The opinions of six excellent scholars are made available.

0267 Halliday, Jon. "The Korean War: Some Notes on Evidence and Solidarity" Bulletin of Concerned Asian Scholars 3 (November 1979): 2-18.

A British historian tries to make sense out of the conflicting charges as to who is responsible for the outbreak of the war. He finds the Western explanations less than convincing, and identifies the United States as primarily to blame. Makes the same argument as Riley and Schramm's The Reds Take a City.

0268 Heichal, Gabriella T. "Decision Making During Crisis: The Korean War and the Yom Kippur War" Ph.D. dissertation. George Washington University, 1984.

Holds the view that there are no "crisis" moments in international action, but rather a problem with the flow of information.

0269 Hitchcock, Wilbur W. "North Korea Jumps the Gun" Current History 20 (March 1951): 136-144.

Suggests the Soviet Union was as surprised as the United States when the North Korean People's Army crossed the 38th Parallel and invaded the South.

0270 Ho, Chong-ho, Sok-hui Kang and Tae-ho Pak. The US Imperialists Started the Korean War. Pyongyang, Korea: Foreign Languages Publishing House, 1993.
North Korean view that places the blame for the war on South Korea which, it is described, was an American puppet.

0271 Hoyt, Edwin P. The Day the Chinese Attacked: Korea 1950. New York: McGraw-Hill, 1990.
The war with China was the result of diplomatic entanglements almost as confused as the pre-World War I period. A popularized but good work.

0272 Hunt, Michael H. "Beijing and the Korean Crisis, June 1950-June 1951" Political Science Quarterly 107 3 (Fall 1992): 453-478.
Hunt's work reflects the increasing availability of Soviet and Chinese documents relating to the North Korean decision to invade and the Chinese decision to intervene.

0273 Huo, Hwei-ling. "A Study of the Chinese Decision to Intervene in the Korean War" Ph.D. dissertation, Columbia University, 1989.
This extended study looks at the Korean War as the necessary response to an international policy dating from 1945, and reflecting the nationalism, as well as practical understanding, of the Red China leaders.

0274 Judd, Walter H. "The Mistakes That Led to Korea" Reader's Digest 57 343 (November 1950): 51-57.
An opinionated and out-of-date look at the causes of the war, the main point being the withdrawal of American troops in 1948.

0275 Jung, Young Suk. "A Critical Analysis on the Cause of the Korean War" Journal of Asiatic Studies 15 1 (1972): 85-94.
War was caused by the United States failure to clarify a Far Eastern policy not, as many supposed, by Dean Acheson's talk.

0276 Kim, Chull Baum. "U. S. Policy on the Eve of the Korean War: Abandonment or Safeguard?" in Phillip Williamson, editor Security in Korea: War Stalemate and Negotiations. Boulder, Colorado: Westview Press, 1994.
Kim charged the United States did not understand its role, and confused the best interest and the international significance of South Korea.

0277 Kim, Chull Baum. "U. S. Withdrawal Decisions from South Korea, 1945-1949" Ph.D. dissertation, State University of New York at Buffalo, 1984.

United States decision to withdraw in 1948-1949 was, the author contends, the direct cause of the Korean War.

0278 Kim, Gye-Dong. Foreign Intervention in Korea, 1950-1954. Aldershot, England: Dartmouth Publishing Company, 1993.

Examines the war as the obvious results of foreign intervention in Korean affairs.

0279 Kim, Gye-Dong. "Who Initiated the Korean War?" in James Cotton and Ian Neary, editors. The Korean War in History. Atlantic Highlands, New Jersey: Humanities Press International, 1989.

North Korea had the support of China and Russia in making the decision, and they certainly were the invaders, but the United States — and to some degree the United Nations — were also to blame.

0280 Kim, Ho Joon. "Why China Goes to War: Risk-taking Factors and Patterns of Crisis Behavior: Three Comparative Case Studies" Ph.D. dissertation, George Washington University, 1990, 1996.

The risk was in China's need to consolidate its domestic control, and the balanced problem of marketing its place in international communism.

0281 Kim, John Jong-Hyun. "Shadows of History: Chinese Intervention in the Korean War" AB thesis, Harvard University, 1988.

Weak discussion of China's "historic" decision.

0282 Kwak, Tae-Hwan. "United States-Korean Relations: A Core Interest" MA thesis, Claremont Graduate School, 1969.

An analysis of relations between the two countries prior to the United States intervention.

0283 Lashmar, Paul. "Stalin's 'Hot War' — Four Decades of Speculation by Western Historians as to Stalin's Exact Role in the Korean War Can Now Be Confirmed or Rebutted, Thanks to the Opening of the Soviet Archives" New Statesman Society (February 2, 1996): 24.

The opening of Soviet archives is shedding new light on the Soviet role in support of North Korea's invasion of the South.

0284 Lawrence, David. "Why Is My Son in Korea?" US News 30 (March 16, 1951): 64.

Lists fourteen reasons why it is necessary for the United States to be fighting in Korea. Not realistic.

0285 Lee, Mary Angel. "The March to Disaster: The Decision to Cross the Thirty-eighth Parallel in Korea and Theorizing America's Foreign Policy" AB thesis, Harvard University, 1994.

The decision to march north was a decision made without any clear understanding of the implications or effects.

0286 Lee, Se Ki. "A Study on the Origins of the Korean War in Connection with Sino-Soviet Confrontation" Ph.D. dissertation, Korea University, 1980.

In this study by a Korean scholar, Stalin is accused of playing the leadership role in his decision to join the war.

0287 Lee, Victor Young. "The U. N. Decision to Intervene in the Korean War" MA thesis, Stanford University, 1957.

A very early attempt to stress the international implications of Korea over the domestic difficulties.

0288 Lewis, John W., Sergei N. Goncharov and Litai Xue. Uncertain Partners: Stalin, Mao, and the Korean War. Stanford, California: Stanford University Press, 1993.

An essential and scholarly work which provides new and important information. Based on primary source materials, most of which have recently become available, which show the support, albeit reluctantly, of Stalin and Mao for the North Korean invasion against the South. Mao's decision to intervene in the North was made weeks before the Inchon landing, thus changing many of the theories concerning North Korean reaction.

0289 Liang, Chin-tung. "The Sino-Soviet Treaty of Friendship and Alliance of 1945" in Paul K. T. Sih, editor. Nationalist China During the Sino-Japanese War, 1937-1945. Hicksville, New York: Exposition Press, 1977.

Offers some evidence of the contrast between Jieshi (national) view and Stillwell's reform movement in the State Department. Proceedings from the conference on Wartime China 1937-1945 held in 1976.

0290 Lowe, Peter. The Origins of the Korean War. London: Longman, 1986, 1997.

A good account of the tangled international background which was made worse by the continuation of civil strife and exaggerated by North Korea's dependence on the Soviet Union.

0291 Markwardt, Richard A. "A Policy of Pragmatism: United States Diplomatic Relations with Spain, 1949-1953" MA thesis, Kent State University, 1983.

MA: containment

0292 Matray, James I. "Truman's Plan for Victory: National Self-determination and the Thirty-Eighth Parallel Decision in Korea" Journal of American History 66 (September 1979): 314-333.
    Truman saw the invasion as a part of Soviet aggression and reacted to block communist expansion.

0293 McLane, Charles B. Soviet Strategies in Southeast Asia: An Exploration of Eastern Policy under Lenin and Stalin. Princeton, New Jersey: Princeton University Press, 1966.
    The distinctive foreign policy of Lenin and Stalin were such that Russia had to eventually become involved in China and then Korea.

0294 Merrill, John. Korea: The Peninsular Origins of the War. Newark, Delaware: University of Delaware Press, 1988.
    Discusses the Korean War as a civil war before 1950, and is very critical of Syngman Rhee.

0295 Morris, Richard B. "The Decision to Resist the Communist Invasion of Korea" Great Presidential Decisions. New York: J. B. Lippincott Company, 1960.
    Text of the Truman announcement giving aid to the Korean Republic, plus commentary putting the decision into political and military context.

0296 Murphy, E. Lloyd. The U. S./U. N. Decision to Cross the 38th Parallel, October 1950; A Case Study of Changing Objectives in Limited War. Maxwell Air Force Base, Alabama: Air War College, 1968.
    Brief, but interesting look at the change in Korean War policy from "stop the aggressor" to "occupy the land."

0297 "New Findings on the Korean War" Cold War International History Project Bulletin 3 (Fall 1993): 1, 14-18.
    One of the first analysis of material released from Soviet archives.

0298 Noble, Addison Grant. "The Origins of the Korean War: The Soviet Union's Involvement in and Responsibility for the Failure of Peaceful Unification of North and South Korea, 1945-1950" MA thesis, University of North Carolina at Chapel Hill, 1970.
    MA: unification

0299 "North Korean Preemptive Strike Plan in '50 Made Public in Russia" The Korean Herald (30 August 1992): 1.
    Translation of material suggesting North Korea only acted to avoid South Korean invasion.

0300 Oliver, Robert T. <u>Korean Report, 1948-1952: A Review of Governmental Procedures during the Two Years of Peace and Two of War.</u> Washington, D. C.: Korean Pacific Press, 1952.

Oliver, a close associate of Rhee, supports the view that Rhee represented the majority of the South Korean people.

0301 Oliver, Robert T. "Why War Came in Korea" <u>Current History</u> 19 (1950): 139-143.

This well-known scholar has put together a rather complicated case for the invasion based, in the largest part, on Russian desire for an expansion of influences, and on the United States failure to define a Korean policy. Published as a book with the same title. See entry 0200.

0302 Paige, Glenn D., compiler. <u>1950: Truman's Decision: The United States Enters the Korean War</u>. New York: Chelsea, 1970.

A good companion to his work <u>The Korean Decision</u>. This is a significant collection of primary documents released prior to July 1, 1950, concerning the intervention decision.

0303 Paige, Glenn D. <u>The Korean Decision: June 24-30, 1950</u>. New York: The Free Press, 1968.

Probably the best work on the Truman intervention policy. Information which was taken from the official documents is re-enforced by interviews with participants from the State Department and the military who were involved in the decision. Looks at the unbelievable optimism of the Korean Military Advisory Group, and America's serious underestimation of the enemy.

0304 Park, Mun Su. "Stalin's Foreign Policy and the Korean War: History Revisited" <u>Korean Observer</u> 25 3 (Autumn 1994): 341-381.

Essays about new findings based on papers received from President Boris Yeltsin in <u>Korean Observer</u>.

0305 Pelz, Stephen E. <u>America Goes to War, Korea, June 24-30, 1950: The Politics and Process of Decision</u>. Washington, D. C.: The Wilson Center, 1979.

An in-depth study, conducted by the Wilson Center of the six-day decision to involve the United States in the war in Korea. Excellent study.

0306 Pelz, Stephen E. "America Goes to War, Korea, July 1-October 9, 1950: Truman's Decision to Cross the 38th Parallel" Henry Luce Fellow, East Asian Institute, Columbia University, no date.

Pelz's theme is mismanagement, indecision, and failure of international understanding all laid on President Truman's shoulders.

0307 Pelz, Stephen E. "When the Kitchen Gets Hot, Pass the Buck: Truman and Korea in 1950" Reviews in American History 6 (December 1978): 548-555.

Book review of volume seven Foreign Relations of the United States, 1976. Documented account of events leading to the decision. Pelz asserts that the large degree of mismanagement, particularly during the presidencies of Roosevelt and Truman, was a, if not the, cause of the outbreak. Truman, Pelz contends, was too much influenced by others and did not think through his decision.

0308 Pritt, Denis N. New Light on Korea. London: Labour Monthly, 1951.

Pamphlet published by socialist press blames the United States and South Korea for starting the war.

0309 Quigley, John. The Ruses for War: American Interventionism Since World War II. Buffalo, New York: Prometheus Books, 1992.

Chapters 2, 3, and 4 deal with the pressures on America for entry into the Korean War. Quigley's thesis is that fear of Russian intervention served both to lead America into war, and limited them once they were involved.

0310 Raymond, Ellsworth. "Korea: Stalin's Costly Miscalculation" UN World 3 (1952): 28-31.

Soviet support in Korea was a major blunder for it derailed the Soviet relations with the Chinese.

0311 "Review of Security Council Action in Defense of Korea" Department of State Bulletin 23 (September 18, 1950): 451-454.

An address by Ambassador Warren R. Austin broadcast on CBS 31 August 1950 on the need for military action by the United Nations to prevent a communist victory in Korea.

0312 Shen, Yueliang. "The Entry of the People's Republic of China into the Korean War" MA thesis, Old Dominion University, 1995.

MA: chronological discussion

0313 Sho, Jin Chull. "Some Causes of the Korean War of 1950: A Case Study of Soviet Foreign Policy in Korea (1945-1950) With Emphasis on Sino-Soviet Collaboration" Ph.D. dissertation, Oklahoma University, 1963.

Examines Russian foreign policy and the outbreak of the Korean War, in light of Soviet long-term interest in Asia.

0314 Sho, Jin Chull. "The Role of the Soviet Union in Preparation for the Korean War" Journal of Korean Affairs 3 (January 1974): 3-14.

This article argues it was Russian training and equipment which made it possible for North Korea to launch an attack. Without this assistance there would have been no invasion.

0315 Simmons, Robert R. The Strained Alliance: Peking, P'yongyang, Moscow and the Politics of the Korean Civil War. New York: Free Press, 1975.

Maintains that Kim Il-Sung attacked because of an internal struggle and that Russia was not ready to get involved.

0316 Smith, Beverly. "The White House Story: Why We Went to War in Korea" Saturday Evening Post 224 19 (November 10, 1951): 22-23, 76-77, 80-88.

This article deals with the first ten days of the Korean War, and with decision making. It appears to have had some White House support in the writing and makes, what becomes the official case for America's involvement in the war.

0317 Snyder, Richard C. and Glenn Paige. "The United States Decision to Resist Aggression in Korea: The Application of an Analytical Scheme" Administrative Science Quarterly 3 3 (1958): 341-378.

Truman's decision to enter the Korean War is discussed as a case study in decision making.

0318 Special Report of United Nations Commanding General. "Captured Documents" Department of State Bulletin 24 (May 21, 1951): 828-830.

Includes the two captured documents, presented to the United Nations as evidence by the American government, that clearly show the North Korean forces were ordered to attack.

0319 Stevenson, Adlai E. "Korea in Perspective" Foreign Affairs 30 3 (April 1952): 349-360.

The then Democratic presidential candidate provides perspective on the decision to interfere, claiming that by supporting the United Nations the United States provided a significant move toward world security.

0320 Stueck, William W., Jr. The Road to Confrontation: American Policy Towards China and Korea, 1947-1950. Chapel Hill: University of North Carolina Press, 1981.

Supports the view that the national security policy of containment became "fixed" because of the Korean War.

0321 Stueck, William. "The Soviet Union and the Origins of the Korean War" World Politics 28 14 (July 1976): 622-635.

A review of Robert R. Simmons <u>The Strained Alliance</u> which disagrees with it and stresses the growing desire for Peking's independence of the Soviet Union.

0322 Suh, Jae-man. "The Influence of the Korean War on Turkish Foreign Policy" Ph.D. dissertation, Ankara University, 1973.
Takes a look at the role Turkey played in forming United Nations policy relating to the Korean War.

0323 Suvarnajata, Supaluck. "The Perception of Soviet-American Decision-makers in the Korean War 1950" MIS thesis, Claremont Graduate School, 1981.
Attempts to deal with the psychological aspects of international decision making.

0324 Tagor, Saumyen Dranath. <u>Stalin, Truman: Hands Off Korea</u>. Calcutta, Tarapado Gupta: Ganavani Publishing House, 1951.
Pro-socialist but anti-Stalinist warning originally issued as <u>Hands Off Korea</u>.

0325 Teiwes, Frederick C. <u>Politics at Mao's Court: Gao Gang and Party Factionalism in the Early 1950s</u>. Armonk, New York: M. E. Sharpe, 1990.
An "East Gate" book which offers a limited analysis of purges, politics, and government in contemporary China.

0326 Truman, Harry. <u>Memoirs: Years of Trial and Hope</u>. volume 2. Garden City, New York: Doubleday & Company, 1956.
President Truman was in the middle of the conflict both in and about Korea. As Commander-in-Chief his approval was necessary for any policy change and it was the president who gave final authority for the Inchon landing. He says surprisingly little about the <u>why</u> of his decision, but his early involvement is well documented, and indexed.

0327 Truman, Harry. "Preventing a New World War" <u>Department of State Bulletin</u> 24 (April 16, 1951): 603-605.
Text of President Truman's 11 April 1951, 10:30 p.m., address to the nation in which he explains that the decision to enter the Korean Conflict was a good one, and that it was the only decision to prevent World War III.

0328 <u>U. S. Policy in the Korean Crisis, 1950</u>. Department of State Publication 3922, Far East Series 34. Washington, D. C.: Government Printing Office, 1950.
Messages which established United States policy and American involvement are provided and discussed.

0329 "United States Policy in the Korean Crisis" Far Eastern Studies 34 (July 1950).
    Early collection concerning the development of American policy during the crisis in Korea.

0330 United States, Department of the Army, Office of Military History. Korea, 1950. Washington, D. C.: Government Printing Office, 1952, 1989, 1997.
    General survey of political entries and military policy relating to the outbreak of fighting and the early response.

0331 "United States Submits 'Conclusive Proof' of Captured Army Orders" United Nations Bulletin 10 (June 15, 1951): 578-579.
    Provides "documented proof" that the North Koreans planned and executed the attack on South Korea.

0332 United States Department of State. "White Paper on Korea" Current History 19 (1950): 170-174.
    On 4 July 1950, Deputy Foreign Minister Gromyko blamed the United States for the hostilities. This is the official reply which, after tracing the post-World War II history, blames North Korean aggression and stresses the fact the United States is responding to United Nations pressure.

0333 Warner, Albert L. "How the Korean Decision was Made" Harper's 202 (June 1951): 99-106.
    Traces the decision in Washington to react with military force to the North Korean invasion of South Korea. Acknowledged that even if the United Nations had not acted the United States would have entered in.

0334 Weathersby, Kathryn. "Attack or Not to Attack? Stalin, Kim Il Sung and the Prelude to War" Cold War International History Project Bulletin 5 (Spring 1995): 1, 2-9.
    Relying on newly released archives, the author suggests Russian support for a "quick" stride into Korea.

0335 Weathersby, Kathryn. "Soviet Aims in Korea and the Origins of the Korean War, 1945-1950: New Evidence from Russian Archives" working paper 8, Woodrow Wilson International Center for Scholars, Cold War International History Project Bulletin 2 4 (January 1993).
    First view of Soviet aims in Korea as reflected in newly translated and available Russian archives.

0336 Weathersby, Kathryn. "The Soviet Role in the Early Phase of the Korean War: New Documentary Evidence" Journal of American-East Asian Relations 2 4 (Winter 1993): 425-458.

Further evidence the initiative for the invasion came from Pyongyang not Moscow. Stalin was surprised by the United States response.

0337 Whiting, Allen. China Crosses the Yalu: The Decision to Enter the Korean War. New York: Macmillan, 1960.

Holds the view that, at least in 1945, there was no Moscow conspiracy to control East Asia.

0338 Who Started the War? The Truth About The Korean Conflict. Seoul: The Public Relations Association of Korea, 1973.

Provided with expected lack of objectivity this "official" work identifies the North Korean government who, with the aid of the Soviets, is blamed for a totally unwarranted attack on the South.

0339 "Why Are We Fighting in Korea?" United States Naval Institute Proceedings 9 (1950): 1016-1017.

A chronological listing of events which led to the North Korean invasion. It suggests a breakdown of understanding and places the blame on the Russians.

0340 Xiaobing, Li and Glenn Trancy, translator. "Mao's Telegrams During the Korean War, October-December 1950" Chinese Historians 5 2 (Fall 1992).

Translation and analysis of Mao's early telegrams to and from Stalin and Kim Il Sung.

0341 Xiaobing, Li and Wang Xi. Jian Chen, translator. "Mao's Dispatch of Chinese Troops to Korea: Forty-six Telegrams, July-October 1950" Chinese Historians 5 1 (Spring 1992): 63-86.

Series of telegrams and analysis of the decision to send Chinese volunteers into Korea.

0342 Yoo, Tae-ho. The Korean War, and the United Nations. Belgium: University of Louvain Press, 1965.

An excellent account of the United Nations decision to enter the Korean Conflict, based on French and English sources.

0343 Yufan, Hao and Zhai Zhihai. "China's Decision to Enter the Korean War: History Revisited" China Quarterly 121 (March 1990): 94-115.

Excellent work which maintains the American crossing of the 38th Parallel and credits MacArthur's bellicose remarks as reasons why the Chinese Communist Forces became involved.

0344 Zagoria, Donald S. "Mao's Role in the Sino-Soviet Conflict" Pacific Affairs (Summer 1974): 139-153.

Relations between American and the Chinese communist party during World War II were good enough to suggest relations with the United States were possible and explain the strange partnership between Mao and Stalin.

0345 Zhang, Shu Guang. Mao's Military Romanticism: China and the Korean War, 1950-1953. Lawrence: University of Kansas Press, 1995.

Interesting, if not well supported, study of Mao's emotive concerns which led to involvement in the Korean War.

0346 Zhang, Xi. "Peng Dehuai and China's Entry into the Korean War" Jian Chen, translator. Chinese Historians 6 1 (Spring 1993): 1-30.

Interesting account of Peng Dehuai's participation, and the case for national involvement in China and Korea.

National Involvement

General

0347 "Aid from U. N. to U. S. Forces Will Stay Small" U. S. News & World Report 29 (August 18, 1950): 24.

The military help made available by member nations of the United Nations is more reflective of their willingness to help, than it is supportive in terms of numbers.

0348 "Call to Arms Against World Aggression" Newsweek 36 (July 31, 1950): 22.

Reports, twenty-five days after the North Korean attack, that President Truman has called for ten billion dollars, the National Guard, and more military assistance to NATO.

0349 Clothier, Marcel. "Latin America and the Korean Crisis" MA thesis, Baton Rouge: Louisiana State University, 1984.

An analysis of Latin American response to the United Nations call for member nations to assist.

0350 "The Fabric of Peace" Time 56 (July 31, 1950): 10.

President Truman, glum and ill-spirited, tells the nation of the cost of Korea. He no longer calls it a police action, but has not yet accepted that it is in fact a war.

0351 Fox, William J. Inter-Allied Co-Operation During Combat Operations. two volumes. Washington, D. C.: Office of the Chief of Military History, Department of the Army, 1952.
    Korean War reports of the Eighth Army Commanders.

0352 Goodrich, Leland M. "Korea: Collective Measures Against Aggression" International Conciliation 494 (1953): 131-192.
    A condensed effort of the author's larger work [see entry 2111] on United States-United Nations relations during the Korean War.

0353 "Roll Call: The Outfits Ticketed for the Korean Job" Newsweek 36 (July 31, 1950): 13.
    The six major combat divisions to fight in Korea are described in capsule profile: 1st Cavalry, 1st Marines, 2nd Infantry, 7th Infantry, 24th Infantry, 25th Infantry.

0354 "Unflagging Use of UN Needed to Win Asian Minds" Foreign Policy Bulletin 29 (August 11, 1950): 2-3.
    Malik's return to the United Nations brings new charges of aggression against the United States. These actions will test the United Nations resolve to continue the fight in Korea.

0355 The US—ROK Alliance in Transition. Seoul: Institute for Far Eastern Studies, 1996.
    Collection of papers on the continued association of the armistice nations, delivered at Seoul, October 1995.

Commonwealth

0356 Albinski, Henry. "Australia and the China Problem during the Korean War Period" Canberra: Department of International Relations, Australian National University, 1964, 1983.
    Beginning of a broader book on Australia-China foreign relations. (Australian Policies and Attitudes toward China. Princeton, New Jersey: Princeton University Press, 1965.) Australia was not so sure it was in its best interest to take up arms against Red China.

0357 Barclay, C. N. The First Commonwealth Division: The Story of British Commonwealth Land Forces in Korea, 1950-1953. Edinburgh: Thomas Nelson, 1952.

A general history of British forces, as well as Commonwealth units formed, during the Korean War. While the British navy was on call nearly from the beginning, the British ground forces arrived just in time to take part in the defense of the Pusan Perimeter.

0358 Bartlett, Norman. With the Australians in Korea. Canberra, Australia: Australia War Memorial, 1954.
        The Australians sent an air force contingency in July of 1950, and eventually had forces on the ground (with the Commonwealth Brigade), in the air (77th Squadron), and at sea (destroyer Bataan, frigate Shoalhaven, and HMAS Warramunga, a destroyer, HMAS Sydney, HMAS Condamine, and Murchison). The New Zealand ship Pukaki was at Inchon.

0359 Battle of the Imjin River (Gloucester Hill) 22-25 April 1951. APO: Headquarters, 1990.
        A capsule look at the 8th Army, and British forces at the Imjin campaign.

0360 Bentley (pseudonym). "HMS Belfast in Korea" Naval Review (November 1950): 372-381.
        The story of her majesty's vessel which arrived early in the Korean War.

0361 "British Commonwealth Naval Operations During the Korean War" Journal Royal United Service Institution part I 96 (May 1951): 250-255; part II 96 (November 1951): 609-616; part III 97 (May 1952): 241-248.
        Considers the war effort of Commonwealth naval forces during the Korean Conflict. Commonwealth forces were involved in all phases of operations during the war.

0362 Burk, Richard J. "The Organization and Command of United Nations Military Forces" MA thesis, Yale University, New Haven, 1956.
        Traces the difficulties encountered by attempts at a United Nations command. The early days were fairly simple with only American and ROK troops involved, but during the Pusan Perimeter the landing of other troops and the involvement of other nationalities in the naval units, brought the difficulties to a head.

0363 Carew, Tim (John Carew). Korea: The Commonwealth at War. London: Cassell, 1967.
        The author lists his work as an exposé of military ineptitude. He makes an excellent case for such failure during the first few weeks, stressing American concern that the United Nations was so slow to send troops. His account of British troops, joining in the battle of August 1950, during the

fighting south west of Taegu, is very informative. Chapters one to four discuss America as the major force and supplier.

0364 Cassels, Sir A. James H. "The Commonwealth Division in Korea" Journal Royal United Service Institution 98 591 (August 1953): 362-372.
　　　The author commanded the division until 1952. His statement is very generalized about command problem in combat and the good relations with the United States forces.

0365 Cooling, B. Franklin. "Allied Interoperability in the Korean War" Military Review 63 6 (June 1983): 26-52.
　　　Korea, he contends, is a perfect example of complex lines of command and operations which were nearly unworkable.

0366 Cosgrove, Peter J. The Commonwealth Military Perspective of Commonwealth Division Operations in Korea 1950-1953. Quantico, Virginia: Marine Corps Command and Staff College, 1979.
　　　An evaluation of the performance of the Commonwealth Division which served in Korea.

0367 Cunningham-Boothe, Ashley and Peter Farrar, editors. British Forces in the Korean War. London: The British Korean Veterans Association, 1988.
　　　Report on British troops who arrived late at the Pusan Perimeter. Once they were there, the British served with distinction.

0368 Eaddy, R. R. "New Zealand in the Korean War: The First Year: A Study in Official Government Policy" MA thesis, University of Otago, 1983.
　　　The decision to join the United Nations action was quick, but by no means automatic. New Zealand had its own policy.

0369 Eaton, Hamish B. Something Extra: 28 Commonwealth Brigade, 1951-1974. Edinburgh: Pentland Press, 1993.
　　　Basically a unit history of the Commonwealth infantry.

0370 Farrar-Hockley, Anthony. The British Part in the Korean War. volume 1. "A Distant Obligation" volume 2. "An Honourable Discharge" London: Her Majesty's Stationary Office, 1990, 1995.
　　　An excellent work by this British participant-historian. Volume one deals with the British involvement in the Inchon landing, most of which was naval and all related to diversionary tactics. Appendix L in volume one is the best listing to locate specific commanders, ships, and duties. British forces were involved in several deception attempts during the Inchon landing, and naval forces provided deception duties near Kunsan.

0371 Farrar-Hockley, Anthony. The Edge of the Sword. London: Buchan & Enright, Publishers, 1954.

Primarily an account of the 1st Battalion Gloucestershire Regiment, at the battle of Imjin River in April 1951.

0372 Gallaway, Jack. The Last Call of the Bugle: The Long Road to Kapyong. St. Lucia: University of Queensland Press, 1994.

A brief account of the 3rd Battalion Royal Australian Regiment during the campaign at Kapyong.

0373 Gaston, Peter. Thirty-Eighth Parallel: The British in Korea. Glasgow: A. D. Hamilton and Company, Ltd., 1976.

Gaston's account of the British forces in Korea is good but lacks objectivity.

0374 Geer, Andrew. "Eight Perilous Hours Inside Red Lines" Saturday Evening Post 224 (1951): 26-27, 92-96.

An account of the 41st British Independent Commandoes who entered the war shortly after hostilities and took part in a raid 150 miles behind the lines. Great Britain was an aggressive partner during the early days of the war.

0375 Grey, Jeffrey. "British Commonwealth Forces in the Korean War: A Study of A Military Alliance Relationship" Ph.D. dissertation, University of New South Wales, 1985.

Looking for "combat effectiveness" Grey considers the combined operation of the Commonwealth Division which, despite problems of command, supply, finance, fought well.

0376 Grey, Jeffrey. The Commonwealth Armies and the Korean War: An Alliance Study. New York: Manchester University Press, 1988.

Grey, a well-respected British historian, deals throughout with individual Commonwealth nations, and Commonwealth units. The most impressive aspects of this work, however, lie in the appendix, a careful listing of units involved, and in the wide bibliographical and archival sources listed for both Commonwealth and American materials.

0377 Grey, Jeffrey. "The Formation of the Commonwealth Division, 1950-1951" Journal of Military History 51 1 (January 1987): 12-16.

The shared heritage and common materials made the Commonwealth Division possible, but the differences with American equipment made attachment difficult.

0378 Halliday, Jon. "The United Nations and Korea" in Frank Baldwin, editor. Without Parallel: The American-Korean Relationship Since 1945. New York: Pantheon Books, 1974.

One of the better articles in a good book. An effort to show how American and Korean interests were generated by United Nations efforts at unification, and finally of defense.

0379 Holles, Robert O. Now Thrive the Armourers. London: British Book Centre, 1953.

Outlines the role of British forces in service in Korea by looking at the 1st Battalion, Gloucestershire Regiment.

0380 Horan, H. E. "British Aircraft Carriers in Korean Waters" Royal Air Force Quarterly 5 (April 1953): 133-138.

The British carriers provided the "depth" for United Nations actions. Describes planes used for deception and interdiction during the early phase.

0381 Kyle, Ronald K. "Killer of Communists, Saver of Soldiers: U. S. Army Field Artillery in the Korean War, 1950-1953" MA thesis, Ohio State University, 1995.

MA: field artillery

0382 Landsdown, John R. P. With the Carriers in Korea: The Fleet Air Arm Story, 1950-1953. Worcester: Square One Publications, 1992.

A brief history of air operations, via carrier, with the Royal Navy in Korea. Complete and helpful.

0383 Lee, David. "The National Security Planning and Defence Preparations of the Menzies Government, 1950-1953" War and Society 10 2 (October 1992): 119-138.

Lee argues that the Korean War extracted a heavy cost for participation and started a long increase in Australian defense spending.

0384 Linklater, Eric. Our Men in Korea. London: Her Majesty's Stationery Office, 1952.

Accounts of the British 27th Brigade, which consisted of the 1st Battalion of the Middlesex Regiment and the 1st Battalion of the Argyll and Sutherland Highlanders Regiment, and the 45th Field Artillery Regiment, Royal Artillery. A battalion of Australian volunteers was added during the summer of 1950. These troops saw action along Congchon.

0385 Lowe, Peter. "An Ally and a Recalcitrant General: Great Britain, Douglas MacArthur and the Korean War, 1950-1" The English Historical Review 105 416 (July 1990).

The British had their own problem with MacArthur and were pressuring for his removal when Truman issued the recall.

0386 Lowe, Peter. "The Frustration of Alliance, the United States and the Korean War, 1950-1951" in James Cotton and Ian Neary, editors. The Korean War in History. Manchester: University of Manchester Press, 1989.
     Lowe's contribution deals with the British problems in working with the United States because of the American tendency to act unilaterally.

0387 MacDonald, Callum. Britain and the Korean War. Oxford: Basil Blackwell, Ltd., 1990.
     Charts the political and military investment of the British people, with comment on the impact of the war on the nation.

0388 MacDonald, J. F. M. The Borders in Korea. no publisher, 1952.
     Basically a unit history of the King's Own Scottish Borderers, British.

0389 Malcolm, George I. The Argylls in Korea. London, Nelson, 1952.
     A brief account of the Argyll and Sutherland Highlanders, holders of a great military tradition, thrown into the fighting in 1950 more as a token than a military unit. The Argylls went on to make a significant contribution.

0390 McCormack, Gavan. Cold War Hot War: An Australian Perspective on the Korean War. Sydney: Hale and Iremonger, 1983.
     Australia's relations with both China and Korea were different than the United States, and their decision to be involved in the United Nations activity was difficult.

0391 McGibbon, Ian. New Zealand and the Korean War. volume 1. New York: Oxford University Press, 1992.
     A survey of New Zealand's political and diplomatic efforts to maintain early relations with North Korea, China, and the United Nations.

0392 McLeod, Alan L. " Australia and the War in Korea" Korean Survey 2 7 (1953): 6-7.
     Primarily an assessment of the view of the average Australian looking at their country's involvement in the war.

0393 New Zealand, Department of External Affairs. New Zealand and the Korean Crisis. Wellington: Owen, 1950.
     A tract which describes why New Zealand felt obligated to join the United Nations effort to stop aggression.

0394 Odgers, George. Across the Parallel: The Australian 77th Squadron with the United States Air Force in the Korean War. London: Heinemann, 1953.
    Organization and deployment of the Australian Fighter Air Squadron, attached to the Far East Air Force.

0395 Prince, Stephen. "The Contribution of the Royal Navy to the United Nations Forces During the Korean War" Journal of Strategic Studies 17 2 (June 1994): 94-120.
    The Royal Navy's contribution was to subsidiary operations, and was second only to the United States in overall effort.

0396 Ra, Jong-yil. "British-American Relations During the Korean War" Ph.D. dissertation. Cambridge University, 1971.
    Great Britain's involvement in Korea was dependent, to a significant degree, on her need to remain an equal partner with the United States.

0397 Ra, Jong-yil. "Political Settlement in Korea: British Views and Policies, Autumn 1950" in James Cotton and Ian Neary, editors. The Korean War in History. Manchester: University of Manchester Press, 1989.
    Author looks at British influence in Korea, and the English stand on the emerging war.

0398 Ra, Jong-yil. "Special Relationship at War: The Anglo-American Relationship During the Korean War" Journal of Strategic Studies 7 3 (September 1984): 301-317.
    The Korean War was essential and timely in terms of cementing British-American relations.

0399 The Royal Ulster Rifles in Korea. Belfast: William Mullan, 1953.
    A regimental history.

0400 16th Field Regiment: Royal New Zealand Artillery, 1950-1954. no publisher, 1954.
    A regimental history also captioned as "Kiwi Tracks in Korea."

0401 Smurthwaite, David and Linda Washington. Project Korea: the British Soldier in Korea 1950-1953. London: National Army Museum, 1988.
    A brief account of the standing army and nationals service used as the narrative for an exhibition held at the National Army Museum, Great Britain.

0402 Soward, F. H. "The Korean Crisis and the Commonwealth" Pacific Affairs 24 (June 1951): 115-130.

Good look at the attitude of the Commonwealth nations toward China at the outbreak of the war, many of which had good relations with the communists.

0403 Stairs, Denis. The Diplomacy of Constraint: Canada, the Korean War and the United States. Toronto: University of Toronto Press, 1974.
This is the war from the Canadian point of view and is directed more toward United States-Canadian relations than the war itself. The significant aspect of this work is the contention that the Canadian government, like the Russian government, did not expect the United States to make a military response in Korea. Canada had the job of "containing America" during this period when she seemed to be interested in swinging the big stick.

0404 Stairs, Denis. "The United Nations and the Politics of the Korean War" International Journal 25 2 (Spring 1970): 302-320.
President Truman took the Korean question to the Untied Nations, at least according to Stairs, to cement the legitimacy of the body (United Nations), not to support America's war in Korea.

0405 Steinberg, Blema S. "The Korean War: A Case Study in Indian Neutralism" Orbis 8 (Winter 1965): 937-954.
Discusses the value of India's neutrality during the Korean War, as well as some of the failures of their efforts.

0406 Stueck, William. "The Limits of Influence: British Policy and American Expansion of the War in Korea" Pacific Historical Review 55 1 (February 1986): 65-95.
Though terribly worried about Korea expanding into World War III, Great Britain had little influence and often held to a separate policy.

0407 Thomas, Lieutenant Colonel Peter. 41 Independent Commando Royal Marines, Korea: 1950-1952. Portsmouth: Royal Marines Historical Society, 1990.
Unit history of a special and independent command.

0408 Thomas, R. C. W. "First Commonwealth Division in Korea" Army Quarterly 64 1 (April 1952): 33-47.
At the conclusion of the first six months, the commander of the Royal Wise Kent Regiment reports on how well the unit fought together.

0409 Thomas, Robert C. W. "Some Impressions of Life in the Commonwealth Division in Korea" Army Quarterly 67 1 (October 1953): 33-41.

The division's whole life was spent in Korea where it served well, fought bravely, and made a significant contribution.

0410 Thorgrimsson, Thor and Edward C. Russell. Canadian Naval Operations in Korean Waters, 1950-1955. Ottawa: Department of National Defence, Canadian Forces, Headquarters Naval Historical Section, 1965.

Canada provided a good initial response to the Korean War. This is an account of Canadian forces which fought with the United Nations during the war. An excellent account of the eight destroyers and 3,600 men contributed by Canada to the United Nations cause.

0411 War History Editing Committee. The Account of Defensive Operations Along the Nak Dong River. Seoul: South Korean Defense Ministry, 1970.

Less biased than many of the "official" publications of South Korea, this work provides fairly detailed material about unit involvements.

0412 War History Editing Committee. History of the United Nations Forces in Korea. five volumes. Seoul: South Korean Defense Ministry, 1967-1970.

This official version is very useful in terms of accounting United Nations involvement, especially the formation of units.

0413 War History Editing Committee. The Invasion by Chinese Forces. Seoul: South Korean Defense Ministry, 1972.

Biased account of the why and how of the communist involvement in the Korean War.

0414 War History Editing Committee. The Invasion of the North Korean Puppet Forces. Seoul: South Korean Defense Ministry, 1967.

Very biased report of the invasion of South Korea. Interesting but of limited value to the scholar.

0415 War History Editing Committee. The Participation of UN Forces. Seoul: South Korean Defense Ministry, 1980.

Good information on the military involvement of the various nations fighting under the United Nations flag.

0416 "The War in Korea—A Chronology of Events, 25 June 1950-25 June 1951" World Today 7 8 (1951): 317-328.

A day-by-day account of the political and military events of the first year. It is very helpful to the student who is working out the order of the fast moving events leading to, and during, the first phase of the war.

0417 "The War in Korea: Diaries for June 25-July 30, 1950; August 1-October 31, 1950" Journal Royal United Service Institution 95 (1950): 486-491, 601-611; 96 (1951): 148-155, 298-305.

British orientation describes the day-by-day activities of the first four months of the war. Includes involvement of the British army and navy in the alternative bombardment prior to the action at Inchon.

0418 Wilson, David. Lion Over Korea: 77 Fighter Squadron RAAF, 1950-1953. Canberra: Banner Books, 1994.

Wilson discussed the fact that the Royal Australian Air Force was driven by poor equipment rather than wise doctrines and policy, yet made a significant contribution.

0419 Worden, William L. "Britain's Gallantry is Not Dead" Saturday Evening Post 223 (1951): 28-29, 94-96.

The 27th British Brigade fought effectively against North Korean troops advancing against the Pusan Perimeter.

Japan

0420 Dingman, Roger. "The Dagger and the Gift: the Impact of the Korean War on Japan" in William J. Williams, editor. A Revolutionary War: Korea and the Transformation of the Postwar World. Chicago: Imprint Publications, 1993.

The Korean War helped to reconstruct Japan, giving it a "fraudulent independence" with the United States still calling the shots.

0421 Drifte, Reinhard. "Japan's Involvement in the Korean War" in James Cotton and Ian Neary, editors. The Korean War in History. Atlantic Highlands, New Jersey: Humanities Press International. 1989.

Japan was not only the logistical base for United States and United Nations activities, but an active participant in the war.

0422 Nimmo, William, editor. The Occupation of Japan: the Impact of the Korean War. Norfolk, Virginia: General Douglas MacArthur Foundation, 1990.

A volume of essays which deals with political, cultural, as well as military characteristics of Japan's involvement in the Korean War.

Canada

0423 Ahern, Neal J. "Killer Offensive" Combat Forces Journal 3 4 (November 1952): 35-36.

In support of General Ridgway's "Operation Killer," thirty-five infantry units successfully attacked and captured their assigned objectives.

0424 Canada, Army Headquarters. General Staff Historical Section. Canada's Army in Korea: A Short Official History. Ottawa: Queen's Printers, 1956.
Discusses the political pressures and implications of Canada's military involvement in the Korean War.

0425 Canada, Army Headquarters. General Staff Historical Section. Canada's Army in Korea: The United Nations Operations, 1950-1953, and Their Aftermath. Ottawa: Queen's Printer, 1956.
The Canadian official account of the Canadian army contribution to the United Nations effort.

0426 "Canada's Army in Korea" Canadian Army Journal 9 (1955) part 1: 5-29, part 2: 20-42, part 3: 20-42, part 4: 16-34, part 5: 21-34.
A five-part history of the Canadian involvement during the war. Three destroyers joined the United Nations forces on 30 June 1950. Contains a brief bibliography of Canadian and communist forces.

0427 Coad, B. A. "The Land Campaign in Korea" Journal Royal United Service Institution 97 585 (February 1952): 1-14.
A quick, but excellent overview of the first months of the Commonwealth forces and the land campaign.

0428 Evans, Paul and B. Michael Frolic, editors. Reluctant Adversaries: Canada and the People's Republic of China, 1949-1970. Toronto: University of Toronto Press, 1991.
Examines Canada's policy toward communist China, a major alteration because of the Korean War.

0429 Geisler, Patricia. Valour Remembered: Canadians in Korea. Ottawa: Department of Veterans Affairs, 1982.
Discussion of heroic deeds and national service performed by Canadian forces in Korea.

0430 McDougall, C. C. "Canadian Volunteers Prepare for Combat" Soldiers 6 6 (June 1951): 54-57.
Canada responded to the United Nations request for support by putting together an all volunteer brigade, which was trained at Fort Lewis, Washington, in the United States.

0431 McGuire, F. R. Canada's Army in Korea. Ottawa: Historical Section, Army General Staff, 1956.
    Semi-official work which chronicles the Canadian participation.

0432 McNair, Charles T. "The Royal Canadian Navy in Korea" Army Information Digest 6 11 (November 1951): 50-53.
    Brief account of Canada's naval response which was operationally at sea by August 1, 1950.

0433 Melady, John. Korea: Canada's Forgotten War. Toronto: Macmillan, 1983.
    General discussion of Canada's contribution, especially ground troops.

0434 Meyers, Edward. Thunder in the Morning Calm: The Royal Canadian Navy in Korea, 1950-1955. St. Catharines, Ontario: Vanwell Publishing, 1991.
    This basic account of the Canadian Navy in Korea includes excellent coverage of the role of the Marine Royale.

0435 Newman, Peter C. "The Royal Canadian Navy" United States Naval Institute Proceedings 80 3 (March 1954): 295-299.
    A very brief general overview of the Canadian contribution to the Korean War.

0436 Prince, Robert S. "The Limits of Constraint: Canadian-American Relations and the Korean War, 1950-1951" Journal of Canadian Studies/Revue d'etudes Canadiennes (Winter 1992-1993): 129-152.
    The author reviews the work of Denis Stairs and finds that there were limits on Canada's ability to influence events.

0437 Roy, Reginald H. "The Seaforth Highlanders of Canada, 1919-1965" Vancouver, British Columbia: Seaforth Highlander, 1969.
    Regimental history of a Canadian outfit which fought in World War II and Korea.

0438 Stairs, Denis. "Canada and the Korean War: The Boundaries of Diplomacy" International Perspective 6 (1972): 25-32.
    Canada used its influence on the United States to press its case through the United Nations.

0439 Stairs, Denis. "The Role of Canada in the Korean War" Ph.D. dissertation, Toronto: University of Toronto, 1969.
    Analysis of Canadian policy in relation to its influence in Korea.

Republic of Korea (South)

0440 Berbert, Henry. "Engineer Field Notes—Korea: Delaying the Advance in the First Few Days" Military Engineer 42 (1950): 433-434.

The role of the ROK engineers, guided by American advisors, during the retreat 30 June-5 July 1950 when destruction of key bridges and cratering of roads was about all that could be done to slow the enemy. The other side of the argument is that the premature blowing of key bridges cut off or destroyed hundreds of ROK troops.

0441 Braitsch, Fred, Jr. "The Korean Marine Corps" Leatherneck 36 1 (1953): 30 - 33.

The Republic of Korea's Marines were participants in the Inchon landing, acting both as diversionary forces and in the attack on Kimpo.

0442 Edwards, Spencer P., Jr. "KATUSA—An Experiment in Korea" United States Naval Institute Proceedings 84 1 (January 1958): 31-37.

A good look at the KATUSA effort and the role of the 7th Infantry Division which served as trainer and host division. The KATUSA did better than expected, but were not without difficulty as a military unit.

0443 Hall, Thomas A. "KMAG and the 7th ROK Division" Infantry 79 16 (November-December 1989): 18-23.

This previously unavailable and unpublished material provides a daily journal of KMAG activities at Uijongbu during the difficult and intense days of 25-26 June 1950.

0444 Holly, David C. "The ROK Navy: Reorganization After World War II with US Aid; Its Record During the Korean Conflict" United States Naval Institute Proceedings 78 11 (November 1952): 1218-1225.

Two United States destroyers were recommissioned in the ROK navy. The United States developed a naval force for South Korea, its first in 375 years. While small and primarily American trained and equipped, the ROK navy did play an important role at the Inchon landing.

0445 Hong, Kyudok. "Unequal Partners: ROK-US Relations During the Vietnam War" Ph.D. dissertation, University of Southern California, 1991.

Discusses South Korea's participation in the Vietnam War, stressing it was not "repayment" for Korean War involvement, but a shared Asian policy between allies.

0446 Jeung, U. H. "ROK Marines: Battle Hardened Heroes" Korean Survey 6 8 (1957): 6.

The ROK Marine Corp was activated in 1949 and, after initial training, was active in the Inchon invasion, and the attack on Seoul. Though small they played an important role in the landing.

0447 Kubloin, H. "The ROK Navy" United States Naval Institute Proceedings (October 1953): 1134-1135.
A short note on the rendering of Korean nautical terms in English.

0448 Lee, Young-Woo. "Birth of the Korean Army, 1945-1950: Evaluation of the Role of US Occupation Forces" Korea World Affairs 4 (1980): 639-656.
Compares United States influence on the development of the military army of the Republic of Korea with North Korean growth under Soviet influence.

0449 Lucas, Jim Griffing. Our Fighting Heart . . . The Story of the Republic of Korea. Washington, D. C.: Korean Pacific Press, 1951.
A collection of articles on the Korean War appearing in Scripp-Howard newspapers during November-December of 1951.

0450 The Ministry of National Defense, The Republic of Korea. The History of the United Nations Forces in the Korean War. five volumes. Seoul, South Korea: Ministry of National Defense, 1972-1974.
Provides the South Korean point of view on the United Nations forces, and on the military leadership of the United Nations troops. It is an excellent source of Korean and United Nations units, action dates, and casualties. These books are a totally subjective history of the "three years' fratricidal tragedy" designed to excuse the excesses of the war. Acknowledging the contribution of the twenty-one nations involved in the conflict, it draws attention to the continuing menace of the communist view.

0451 United States Operations Research Office. Integration of ROK Soldiers into U. S. Army Units (KATUSA). Washington, D. C.: Government Printing Office, 1990.
The KATUSA project brought on many critics, but it made possible the 7th Infantry Division (Army) landing at Inchon and their contribution to the battle of Seoul.

Other Nations

0452 Brecher, Michael. Israel, The Korean War and China: Images, Decisions, and Consequences. Jerusalem: Jerusalem Academic Press, Hebrew University, 1974.

Israel aided the United Nations but felt the United States policies failed to maintain much needed relations with Communist China.

0453 Crocker, Isabel. Burma's Foreign Policy and the Korean War. Santa Monica, California: Rand Corporation, 1958.
Brief but useful look at the relations between Burma and Korea.

0454 Danisman, Basri. Situation Negative! The Hague: International Documentation and Information Centre, 1973.
Turkish regimental history.

0455 Daskalopoulos, Ioannis. The Greeks in Korea. Washington, D. C.: Department of the Army, Office of the Assistant Chief of Staff for Intelligence, 1988.
An evaluation of Greek forces serving in Korea, as translated from the Greek.

0456 Davison, Daniel P. "The Columbian Army in Korea: A Study of Integration" MA thesis, University of South Dakota, 1958.
A study of the integration of a Columbian Battalion into the 31st Infantry Regiment. Based on the experiences of Major General Lloyd R. Moses.

0457 Dayal, Shiv. India's Role in the Korean Question. New Delhi, India: Chand, 1959.
A study of India's role in the settlement of international disputes under the flag of the United Nations. India spent considerable effort trying to get the United Nations to steer a moderate course.

0458 DeVaney, Carl N. "Know Your Allies" Military Review (March 1953): 11-19.
Language, national politics, customs, military policy, and plans all negatively affect coordination and cooperation among allies. Operation orders in Korea are an excellent example of the difficulties.

0459 Ensslen, R. F., Jr. "Numbah One Shot" Army (August 1957): 30-35.
Ethiopian troops served in combat with forces of the United Nations.

0460 Fanning, Anne K. "Turkish Military in the Korean War" MA thesis, Texas Tech University, 1993.
A modest account of the services of the Turks in Korea. Their unit was known for its harsh and violent methods.

0461 Galbraith, C. "Colombian Participation in the Korean War" MA thesis, University of Florida, 1973.
        MA: Colombian participation

0462 Gallego, Manuel. The Philippine Expeditionary Force to Korea: Before the Eyes of the Law. Manila: no publisher, 1950.
        Discusses Philippines forces in Korea from a legal perspective.

0463 Gogate, Rajaram V. "How India Looks at Korea" Korean Study 2 2 (1953): 7-8.
        India felt it was a political pawn in the battle between Russia and the United States.

0464 Heimsath, Charles. "India's Role in the Korean War" Ph.D. dissertation. Yale University, 1957.
        Assisting the United Nations to achieve peace was India's primary concern, and they were successful in arranging the POW exchange.

0465 Jensen, Peter K. "The Turkish Military Contribution to the United Nations Command in the Korean War, 1950-1953" MA thesis, Princeton University, 1978.
        MA: Turkey

0466 Jimenez, Ernesto T., editor. These Are Your Boys—The Avengers. Tokyo: International Printing, 1954.
        Rare history of the Philippine 14th Battalion Combat Team (14th BCT) in the Korean War.

0467 Loesch, Robert J. "Korean Milestones: 1950-53" Soldiers 8 9 (September 1953): 57.
        Brief listing of United Nations allies and the date and location of their arrival in the Korean War.

0468 Martin, Harold H. "The Greeks Know How to Die" Saturday Evening Post 224 1 (1951): 26-27, 83-84.
        Greeks attached to the United States 7th Cavalry brought combat experience with them when they joined the United Nations command.

0469 Martin, Harold H. "Who Said the French Won't Fight?" Saturday Evening Post 223 45 (1951): 19-21, 107-108.
        Surveys the French all volunteer unit which served with the United Nations command; an effective force.

0470 McGregor, P. M. J. "History of No. 2 Squadron, SAAF in the Korean War" Military History Journal 42 6 (June 1978): 82-89.
South Africans joined Canadians and Australians to play an important, if minor, role in Korea.

0471 Moore, Dermot M. "SAAF in Korea" Militia 4 (1980): 24-34.
Contribution of a South Africa Air Force fighter squadron in the United States Far East Air Force.

0472 Murti, Bhaskarla. India's Stand on Korea. New Delhi, India: Congress Party in Parliament, 1953.
Brief discussion of India's role as a peacemaker, and its position as communication link for diplomatic considerations for Red China.

0473 Ozselcuk, Musret. "The Turkish Brigade in the Korean War" International Review of Military History 46 (1980): 253-272.
The 5,000 man Turkish force suffered very high losses, but was a highly effective military unit.

0474 Pacholik, Robert M. "India as Advocate: The Role of a Nonaligned State in the Settlement of the Korean War" MA thesis, California State University at Sacramento, 1976.
MA: India

0475 Ramsey, Russell W. "The Colombian Battalion in Korea and Suez" Journal of InterAmerican Studies and World Affairs 9 4 (October 1967): 541-560.
A description of Colombia's dispatch of a naval frigate and an infantry battalion.

0476 Royal Netherlands Navy, Historical Section, Naval Staff. "On the Way from Tread" United States Naval Institute Proceedings (September 1952): 966-971.
Royal Netherlands Navy in cooperations with the United States Navy during the Korean War.

0477 Skordiles, Komon. Kagnew, The Story of the Ethiopian Fighters in Korea. Tokyo: Radio Press, 1954.
Analysis of the contribution of Ethiopian forces attached to the United Nations.

0478 Villasanta, Juan F. Dateline Korea: Stories of the Philippine Battalion. Bacolod City, Philippines: Naleo, 1964.
Accounts of the Philippines 10th Infantry Battalion.

North Korea

0479 Cumings, Bruce. "Kim's Korean Communism" Problems of Communism
23 2 (1974): 27-41.
        Discusses Kim's rather unique brand of communism in the post
World War II years.

0480 Koon, Woo Nam. The North Korean Communist Leadership, 1945-
1965. Birmingham: University of Alabama Press, 1974.
        The role of the North Korean high command in the nationalization
of North Korea.

0481 Paige, Glenn D. The Korean People's Democratic Republic. Stanford,
California: Hoover Institution, 1966.
        Discusses the nationalistic implication of the Korean War and Kim's
communism developing in the post-1948 period.

0482 United States. North Korea. Washington, D. C.: Office of Intelligence
Research, 1951.
        Case study dealing with North Korea as a Soviet satellite.

0483 United States Army Field Forces. Impressions of North Korean
Division. Washington, D. C.: Army Field Forces, 1950.
        Organization data gained from hasty analysis of 252 interrogated
POWs.

0484 United States Army Forces Far East, General Staff. Materiel [sic] in
the Hands of or Possibly Available to the Communist Forces in the Far East.
APO: Army Forces, Far East, 1953.
        Considers the availability of supplies and equipment the communists
could put in the fight against United Nations forces.

0485 Yang, Key P. "The North Korean Regime, 1945-1955" MA thesis,
American University, 1958.
        Relying heavily on North Korean sources it explores communist
backed North Korea's growth

Soviet Union

0486 Glasgow, William M., Jr. "Korean Ku Klux Klan" Combat Forces
Journal 2 7 (February 1952): 18-24.
        More than 2,000 torch-carrying North Koreans attacked the 2nd
Platoon, Company B, 23rd Infantry, 2nd Division and cut them off. Many of
the men moved back through enemy lines to their own areas.

0487 Lineer, Thomas A. "Evolution of Cold War Rules of Engagement: the Soviet Combat Role in the Korean War" MA thesis, Fort Leavenworth, Kansas, Command and General Staff College, 1993.
    MA: rules of engagement

0488 Park, Gap-dong. The Korean War and Kim Il-sung. Seoul: Baram gwa Mulgyol Publishing, 1990.
    Memories of a South Korean Workers Party official who depicts Pyongyang's responsibility for the war.

China

0489 Bueschel, R. M. Communist Chinese Air Power. New York: Praeger, 1968.
    A surprisingly useful history of the development of Red China's air power and its reliance on, as well as independence from, Russia.

0490 Chang, Tao-Li. Why China Helps Korea. Bombay: People's Publishing House, 1951.
    The relation between China and Korea, focusing on an effort to explain China's interest in Korean politics.

0491 Chen, Jian. China's Road to the Korean War: The Making of the Sino-American Confrontation. New York: Columbia University Press, 1994, 1996.
    Studies in social, economics, and political interaction based on China's gradual decision to be involved in the Korean War.

0492 Chilimuniya, Aurosimov and Shih-ku-li-tieh-tzu. Chinese Communist General Principles of Army Group Tactics. two volumes. Manila: General Headquarters, Far East Command, Military Intelligence Section, General Staff, 1951.
    The translation of captured documents outlining Soviet military doctrines adapted by the People's Liberation Army.

0493 Chinese Tactics and Lessons Learned. APO: Headquarters, 2nd Infantry Division, United States Army, 1952.
    An outline of what was learned, by 1952, of Chinese tactics, drill, and logistics.

0494 Chung, Se Yung. "Communist China's Intervention in Korea: 1950-1953" MA thesis, Miami University, 1957.
    MA: China

0495 Clegg, Arthur. No War With China. London: Communist Party, 1951.

This socialist author states Great Britain's case against getting into a war with the Chinese.

0496 Corr, Gerard H. The Chinese Red Army: Campaigns and Politics Since 1949. New York: Shocken Books, 1974.
     Popularized version of Corr's book on the formation of the Red Chinese Army. A little on Korea.

0497 Creighton, John J. "Chinese Intervention in Korea" MS thesis, Defense Intelligence College, 1985.
     MS: Chinese intervention

0498 Farrar-Hockley, Anthony. "A Reminiscence of the Chinese People's Volunteers in the Korean War" China Quarterly 98 (June 1984): 287-304.
     Though fighting well, the Korean War raised some serious questions about party leadership among the volunteer troops.

0499 George, Alexander L. The Chinese Communist Army in Action: The Korean War and Its Aftermath. New York: Columbia University Press, 1967.
     Using POW interviews the author discusses the political base of the military units, finding they fought well, but quickly lost initial morale.

0500 Gittings, John. The Role of the Chinese Army. New York: Oxford University Press, 1967.
     Excellent writing on the Chinese Army viewpoint.

0501 Griffith, Samuel B. II. The Chinese People's Liberation Army. New York: McGraw-Hill Book Company for the Council on Foreign Relations, 1967.
     An excellent account of the Chinese Army from the "Long March" to Korea. While written for popular audiences, it is a fair work.

0502 Headquarters, United States Army Forces, Far East (advanced), Office of the Assistant Chief of Staff, G-2, "Chinese Communist Army and North Korean Army Logistics and Class Supply" USAFFE Intelligence Digest. 6 4 (April 1956): 49-68.
     Outline and brief description of logistics as maintained by China and North Korea.

0503 Headquarters, United States Army Forces, Far East (advanced), Office of the Assistant Chief of Staff, G-2. "Chinese Communist Army Supply System" USAFFE Intelligence Digest 4 4 (June 1954): 31-46.

Fairly complete accounting of the supply system set-up by the Chinese communists; more information is now available but still a good source.

0504 Jan, Ji Bao. "China's Policies toward the Soviet Union and the United States before and in the Korean War" MA thesis, Portland State University, 1995.

Discusses the political relations between United States and the Soviet Union as it affected China.

0505 O'Ballance, Edgar. The Red Army of China: A Short History. New York: Frederick A. Praeger, 1963.

Excellent account of the formation and battle awareness of the people's army of China.

0506 Park, Doo bok. "A Study of Chinese Participation in the Korean War" Ph.D. dissertation, Mun Hwa University, 1975.

Puts forth the position that China sent troops to Korea to assure Stalin of Mao's support for international communism and secure China's future.

0507 Riggs, Robert B. Red China's Fighting Hordes. revised edition. Harrisburg, Pennsylvania: The Military Service Publishing Co., 1952.

Accounts by United States officer with firsthand knowledge of the People's Liberation Army.

0508 Segal, Julius. A Study of North Korean and Chinese Soldiers' Attitudes Toward Communism, Democracy, and the United Nations. Chevy Chase, Maryland: Operations Research Office, The Johns Hopkins University, 1954.

Using POW interviews Segal examines the pro-communist anti-democratic attitudes of the communist soldiers.

0509 Spurr, Russell. Enter the Dragon: China's Undeclared War Against the United States in Korea, 1950-1951. New York: Newmarket Press, 1988.

Interesting but weakened by the author's lack of objectivity in his interviews, and a lack of focus to his analysis.

0510 Weller, Donald. Chinese Communist Strategic and Tactical Doctrine. no publisher, 1964.

Communist doctrine as it relates to communication with anti-communist forces.

0511 Xu, Yan. "The Chinese Forces and their Casualties in the Korean War: Facts and Statistics" Li Xiaobing, translator. Chinese Historians 6 2 (Fall 1993): 45-58.

Good source of statistical information about the Chinese forces in Korea including Navy, Air Force, and People's Liberation Army.

0512 Zelman, Walter A. Chinese Intervention in the Korean War. Berkeley: University of California, 1967.

The United States totally misunderstood the Chinese interests in Korea and misjudged their willingness to enter the war.

Leadership, Command, United Nations Political Command

0513 Acheson, Dean. Present at the Creation: My Years at the State Department. New York: Norton, 1968.

Deals with the State Department from 1941 to 1953, but is especially powerful in the coverage of the Korean War period. An excellent account and source.

0514 Albert, John G. "Attlee, The Chiefs of Staff and the Resurrection of the 'Commonwealth Defense'" Ph.D. dissertation, Oxford: Merton College, 1986.

The renewal of British reliance on the Commonwealth nations for common defense.

0515 Alexander, Jack. "Stormy New Boss of the Pentagon" Saturday Evening Post 222 5 (1949): 26-27, 67-70.

Commentary on the controversial Louis A. Johnson, Secretary of Defense during the early war. He made many enemies in the service.

0516 Allen, Richard C. (pseudonym). Korea's Syngman Rhee: An Unauthorized Portrait. Rutland, Vermont: Charles E. Tuttle Co., 1950.

A fairly simple, but very useful, history of the South Korean president during the Korean War until his 1960 overthrow.

0517 Amos, Zachary D. "Harry S. Truman's Leadership in the Korean War" MSE thesis, Arkansas State College, 1960.

MS: Truman

0518 Army Times, editor. The Banners and the Glory: The Story of General Douglas MacArthur. New York: G. P. Putnam's and Sons, 1965.

A hazy, publicity directed, account of General Douglas MacArthur, from the time when he was identified as Commander-in-Chief of United

Nations forces through the victory at Inchon. This account displays a strong case for the singular role the General played in the "successes" of Korea.

0519 Baik, Bong. Kim Il Sung: Biography. 3 volumes Tokyo: Miraisha, 1969-1970.
Translated version of North Korean publication about the patriot of communism.

0520 Belmonte, Laura. "Anglo-Americans Reactions and the Dismissal of MacArthur" MA thesis, University of Virginia, 1991.
Compares British and American responses to the firing of MacArthur. The British were not as concerned about the dismissal as were Americans.

0521 Blair, Clay. MacArthur. London: Futura Publications, 1977 and Garden City, New York: Doubleday, 1977.
A well-written and sound biography of MacArthur, but not a complimentary one.

0522 Bradley, Omar N. Substance of Statements Made at Wake Island on October 15, 1950. Washington, D. C.: United States Senate, 1951.
The second-hand transcript of the MacArthur-Truman meeting, which supports Truman's view he was misled about China's ability.

0523 Bradley, Omar N. and Clay Blair. A General's Life. New York: Simon and Schuster, 1983.
Open and interesting account of the life of General Bradley, chairman of the Joint Chiefs during the Korean War.

0524 Campbell, David R. "East of the Chosin: A Study of Leadership" United States Army Center of Military History: Archives, 1987.
Looks at the role of command which moved down to junior officers as communications failed. Deals with the 1st Battalion of the United States Army, 32nd Infantry Regiment, and Task Force Faith under the leadership of Lieutenant Colonel Don C. Faith Jr.

0525 Carlton, David. Anthony Eden: A Biography. London: Allen & Unwin, 1986.
Affirms that British support of the Korean War, and rearmament, was bipartisan.

0526 Carpenter, Ronald H. "General Douglas MacArthur's Oratory on Behalf of Inchon" Southern Communication Journal 58 1 (Fall 1992): 1-12.

This collection is obviously more concerned with the oratory than the contents but it provides a good source of General MacArthur's obvious ability to use words to achieve his purposes.

0527 Cerami, Joseph. Wrestling the Initiative: Ridgway as Operational Commander in the Korean War: December 1950 to April 1951. Fort Leavenworth: School for Advanced Studies, United States Army Command and General Staff College, 1988.
        After his assignment to 8th Army, Ridgway revitalized his forces, and turned the communists back. Cerami's analysis is very impressive.

0528 Chen, Chien-Ping. "The Role of Dean Acheson in the Korean War" MA thesis, Ball State University, 1988.
        MA: Acheson

0529 Chesterton, A. K. "General MacArthur and the Far East" Journal Royal United Service Institution 96 (May 1951): 306-307.
        The sacking of MacArthur, the author contends, did not result in a conflict between military and civilian control, but MacArthur's desire to bomb targets in China.

0530 Chesterton, A. K. "The War in Korea" Journal Royal United Service Institution 95 580 (November 1950): 612-615.
        The author feels it is too much to believe the communists are defeated, but they were certainly set back. Especially impressed with America's "petrol-bomb."

0531 Choe, Sunki. "The Korean Question Before the U. N." MA thesis, University of Massachusetts, 1964.
        MA: United Nations

0532 Chou, Ching-wen. The Years of Storm. New York: Holt, Rinehart and Winston, 1960.
        The memoirs of a Chinese Communist Forces general.

0533 Chou, En-lai. Selected Works of Zhou Enlai. two volumes. Beijing: Foreign Language Press, 1981.
        Translation of the major works of Zhou Enlai with biographical and bibliographical aids.

0534 Clark, Mark W. From the Danube to the Yalu. New York: Harper, 1954.
        Clark's memoirs of his military career; strong on the period of the Korean War, and how the armistice agreement was reached.

0535 Clark, Mark W. "The Truth about Korea" Collier's 113 3 (1954): 34-38; 113 4 (1954): 88-93.

Tries to explain the frustrations of trying to fight a limited war, especially the problems created by President Rhee's failure to work with the United Nations.

0536 Collins, Joseph Lawton. War in Peacetime: The History and Lessons of Korea. Boston: Houghton Mifflin, 1969.

United States Army Chief of Staff gives an excellent account of decision making and war in Korea.

0537 Coombs, Robert M. "Changjin (Chosin) Reservoir, Korea, 1950: A Case Study of United States Army Tactics and Doctrine for Encircled Forces" MMAS thesis, Fort Leavenworth: United States Army Command and General Staff College, 1975.

MA: Chosin

0538 Davis, Burke. Marine: The Life of Lt. General Lewis B. (Chesty) Puller, USMC (Ret.). Boston: Brown, 1962.

More than any other man, Lieutenant General Lewis B. "Chesty" Puller, USMC, was the symbol of the fighting marine. From the command of horse Marines in Peking to the landing at Inchon, Puller was at the center of America's military efforts.

0539 Davis, William J. The Story of Ray Davis, General of Marines. Faquay Varina, North Carolina: Research Triangle Publishing, 1995.

Biographical analysis of lessons learned by and about General Davis in war and in peace.

0540 Dean, William F. and William L. Worden. General Dean's Story. New York: Viking Press, 1954.

General Dean was captured during the early months of the Korean War and held captive until the end of the war. His accounts of the early confusion during the first communist drive are lively, entertaining, frustrating, and a frightening reminder of just how under-prepared America was for a war of any kind.

0541 Dingman, Roger. "Truman, Attlee and the Korean War Crisis" in The East Asian Crisis, 1945-1951, The Problem of China, Korea, and Japan: Papers London: International Centre for Economics and Related Disciplines, London School of Economics, 1982.

Part of the difficulty arising at the opening of the Korean War, was the differing views held by Great Britain and America.

0542 Dofflemyer, Leonard H. "An Appraisal of the Military Leadership of Douglas MacArthur" MA thesis, University of the Pacific, 1966.

A somewhat limited effort to evaluate MacArthur's leadership styles and effectiveness in World War II and Korea.

0543 Domes, Juergen. Peng Te-huai: the Man and the Image. Stanford, California: Stanford University Press, 1985.

A limited biography of a significant Communist Chinese Forces commander.

0544 Donovan, Robert J. Nemesis: Truman and Johnson in the Coils of War in Asia. New York: St. Martin's Press, 1984.

An interesting comparison of presidential crises between the Korean and Vietnam Wars. Both had the unique characteristics of being totally misunderstood. Has excellent discussion of the effect of the United Nations response, as well as certain key failures to respond, and on the retreat and final defense of Pusan.

0545 Falk, Stanley L. "Comments on Reynolds: 'MacArthur as Maritime Strategist'" Naval War College Review 33 (March/April 1980): 92-99.

The author attacks Clark G. Reynolds who called MacArthur a great maritime strategist. According to Falk's well presented argument MacArthur's planning was limited and outdated. The General failed to appreciate the logistical aspects of naval operations. Highly critical of the Inchon landing.

0546 Flint, Roy K. "The Tragic Flaw: MacArthur, The Joint Chiefs, and the Korean War" Ph.D. dissertation. Duke University, 1976.

Author claims that a basic weakness in the command structure and MacArthur's shortsightedness led to failure at war.

0547 Fuller, Francis F. "Mao Tse-tung: Military Thinker" Journal of Military History 22 3 (Fall 1958): 139-145.

Admits Mao was a military genius who utilized every aspect of his nation to achieve military victory. Fuller says his weapon was "psychological disintegration."

0548 Gaver, Pierce H. Characteristics of Command and Control During the Korean War. Menlo Park, California: Stanford Research Institute, 1960.

This it the text of SRI research memo WSL 50, dealing with the facts of, and limitations of, communication and how it alters command.

0549 Gordon, Rosalie M. The MacArthur-Korea Story. New Rochelle, New York: American's Future, Inc., 1961.

Interesting, but not very significant, account of MacArthur's role in Korea.

0550 Gunther, John. The Riddle of MacArthur: Japan, Korea and the Far East. New York: Harper, 1951.

Written far too early to be very informative about the Korean War, and a number of the conclusions he draws are proven wrong by the end of the war. But he does try to explain MacArthur in sort of a folksy account in which he identifies General MacArthur's farsighted understanding of the Inchon situation, his victory at Inchon, and the unkindness of criticism leveled against MacArthur.

0551 Hearings on the Military Situation in the Far East. Congressional Record, Senate, 82nd Congress, 1st session, 1951.

Voluminous collection of testimony concerning the military situation, United States and United Nation objectives and General MacArthur's release from command.

0552 Hetzel, Frederick A. and Harold L. Hitchens. "An Interview with General Matthew B. Ridgway" Western Pennsylvania Historical Magazine 65 4 (October 1982).

Ridgway focuses on the frustration of commanding the United States Eighth Army in Korea from 1950-1951.

0553 Higgins, Trumbull. Korea and the Fall of MacArthur: A Précis in Limited War. New York: Oxford University Press, 1960.

An interesting study of the relationship between civilian and military command during wartime. The author concludes MacArthur was basically a military genius but he did not understand the political implications of either his victory at Inchon, or his push to cross the 38th Parallel.

0554 Hillman, R. L. "End of a Leader" Army 13 8 (March 1963): 25-29.

The death of Lieutenant Collins (presumably a fictional characterization of a platoon gunnery officer) designed to show the initiative of command at all phases of leadership. Set during the early months of the war.

0555 Holloway, James Y. "The Role of General MacArthur in the Korean War" MA thesis, Vanderbilt University, 1954.

Outdated and of questionable value. The author tries to define MacArthur's real contribution.

0556 Horner, D. M. "High Command—The Australian Experience" Defence Forces Journal 48 (September/October 1984).

The Australians had little experience with "high command," and Horner recommends the staff work needed for such a role, be accomplished.

0557 Horrell, Mason E. "MacArthur, Correspondents and Controversy: Censorship in the Korean War" MA thesis, University of Kentucky at Lexington, 1991.
MacArthur tried to recapture the easy relations which he and the press enjoyed during World War II, but found it was impossible in Korea.

0558 Hunt, Frazier. The Untold Story of Douglas MacArthur. New York: The Devin-Adair Company, 1954.
Hunt was a friend of General MacArthur, and covered his headquarters for the press. The author focuses on "the war he [MacArthur] was not permitted to win." This reporter's objectivity is completely lost, but he has interesting "insider" comments about MacArthur, as well as commentary on the general's success prior to the time Truman pulled his "crime of the century."

0559 Ickes, Harold L. "MacArthur Is Always Right" New Republic 124 11 (March 12, 1951): 16.
Ickes reminds the reader that MacArthur's ability to turn defeat into victory lies is in his use of words, not troops. Questions MacArthur's association with Nationalist China.

0560 James, D. Clayton. "Command Crisis: MacArthur and the Korean War" The Harmon Memorial Lectures in Military History 24 Colorado Springs, Colorado: United States Air Force Academy, 1982.
Early look at the author's longer and more complete work published in 1993.

0561 James, D. Clayton and Anne S. Wells. Refighting the Last War: Command and Crisis in Korea, 1950-1953. New York: Free Press, 1993.
The authors claim that the Korean War was not only fought with equipment and materials left over from World War II, but that the strategic and tactical doctrines used were also left over from the previous war.

0562 James, D. Clayton. The Years of MacArthur. three volumes. Boston: Houghton Mifflin, 1967-1985.
Good treatment of MacArthur, strong on the Korean period. The author found MacArthur grossly insubordinate and felt this was the reason he was fired. Truman preferred to use the issue of civilian control.

0563 Katzedbach, Edward L., Jr. and Gene Z. Hanrahan. "The Revolutionary Strategy of Mao Tse-tung." in Franklin Mark Osanka, editor.

Modern Guerrilla Warfare: Fighting Communist Guerrilla Movements, 1941-1961. New York: Free Press, 1962.

A good analysis of Mao in light of twentieth-century military history, and the emergence of communist military strategy

0564 Keefer, Edward C. "President Dwight D. Eisenhower and the End of the Korean War" Diplomatic History 10 3 (Summer 1986): 267-289.

Eisenhower considered his support of an atomic threat as the prime instrument in the peace. It forced China to choose between peace and nuclear expansion.

0565 Kein, Warren. "The Truman-MacArthur Controversy During the Korean War" MS thesis, Queens College, New York, 1963.

MS: Truman — MacArthur

0566 Kennan, George. Memoirs, 1925-1963. two volumes. Boston: Little, Brown, 1967, 1972.

Discusses the key decisions in Korea, including the decision to cross the 38th Parallel. Kennan was top United States advisor on Soviet affairs and played an important role during this period.

0567 Kenney, George C. The MacArthur I Know. New York: Duell, Sloan and Pearce, 1951.

A "political biography" written by a close MacArthur associate who uses the occasion to engage in more than a little hero worship. He discusses the Korean connection in broad terms and identifies the Inchon landing as a stroke of genius and as if it were the only military action open to them at the time.

0568 Khrushchev, Nikita. Khrushchev Remembers: The Last Testament. Strobe Talbott, translator. two volumes. Boston: Little, Brown, 1970, 1974.

In these memoirs the Soviet premier denies any Russian involvement and claims Kim Il Sung was the initiator. Should be read with considerable caution as the authenticity has been questioned by some scholars.

0569 Khrushchev, Nikita. "The Korean War" Ogonek 1 (January 1991).

Thy only Russian leader to write about Korea, Khrushchev is fairly open about Stalin's war interest.

0570 "Kim Il Sung" Army Digest 24 10 (1969): 32.

A brief account (1912 to 1965) of the life of the North Korean leader Kim Il Sung. It identifies Kim as the primary power in his roles as premier, general secretary of both the Central Committee and the Korean Labor Party, and as the Supreme Commander of the Armed Forces.

0571 Korb, Lawrence J. "The Truman-MacArthur Controversy Over the Korean War" MA thesis, St. Johns University, 1962.
     MA: Truman — MacArthur

0572 "The Korean War and Related Matters" Report of the Subcommittee on Internal Security to the Senate Judiciary Committee. 84th Congress, 1st session. Washington: Government Printing Office, 1951.
     Primarily concerned with the MacArthur dismissal, but considers earlier aspects of his command, and the X Corps versus Eighth Army command structure.

0573 Lee, Clark and Richard Henschel. Douglas MacArthur. New York: Holt, 1952.
     Amazingly objective account of MacArthur as told by Associated Press correspondents who knew him well.

0574 Lim, Young-Chahng. "The Korean War and General Douglas MacArthur (July 1950-April 1951)" MA thesis, New Mexico Highland University, 1968.
     MA: MacArthur

0575 Lim, Um (pseudonym). The Founding of a Dynasty in North Korea—An Authentic Biography of Kim Il Sung. Tokyo: Jiyusha, 1962.
     The author, a North Korean exile, relates early evidence of Kim's preparation for war, and the organization and training of his army along Soviet lines, and with Soviet weapons.

0576 Lofgren, Charles. "Congress and the Korean Conflict" Ph.D. dissertation, Stanford University, 1966.
     Despite the extremes represented, Congress held a fairly supportive, middle-of-the-road view during the war.

0577 Lowitt, Richard, editor. The Truman—MacArthur Controversy. Chicago: Rand McNally, 1967.
     A study of these two very different men by using Congressional materials, public statements, and personal memoirs.

0578 "The MacArthur Story" U. S. News & World Report 30 (May 11, 1951): 52-64; 30 (May 18, 1951): 52-66+.

Report of MacArthur hearings conducted before the Senate Armed Services Committee. It is directed toward his career, but focuses on the decision to release him.

0579 MacArthur, Douglas A. MacArthur's Address to Congress April 19, 1951, with Highlights of His Career. New York: Rand McNally, 1951.

A chronological report on the general's life ending with MacArthur's report to Congress.

0580 MacArthur, Douglas. Reminiscences. New York: Da Capo, 1964.

This is a great disappointment, considering it is really the only major effort on the part of a world figure to explain his actions. Part nine of this memoir deals with the war in Korea.

0581 Marshall, S. L. A. with Cate Marshall, editor. Bringing Up the Rear: A Memoir. San Francisco: Presidio Press, 1979.

Marshall, one of America's most respected military historians, saw military service for over thirty years and wrote his history of his role in military affairs. Includes opinion and analysis of the defense at Pusan.

0582 Maihafer, Harry J. From the Hudson to the Yalu: West Point '49 in the Korean War. College Station: Texas A & M University Press, 1993.

A well-written personal account which follows the lives of the West Point class of 1949. Many of these young officers served in Korea. Good account of life in the field at the second lieutenant level.

0583 Manchester, William. American Caesar: Douglas MacArthur, 1880-1964. New York: Dell, 1978.

Manchester is not afraid to expose MacArthur's warts, nor to express appreciation for his efforts and abilities. MacArthur was no more or less than his times and environment demanded. The Korean War was a final call for an old hero and he took full advantage of it.

0584 Mao, Tse-tung. On the People's Democratic Dictatorship. Peking: Foreign Language Press, 1961, 1963, 1965, 1967 and New Haven: Yale University Press, 1965, 1968.

Translation of Chairman Mao's thoughts on his dictatorship.

0585 Martin, Harold H. "Toughest Marine in the Corps" Saturday Evening Post 224 38 (March 22, 1952): 40-41, 105-110.

Another account of the infamous Lewis B. "Chesty" Puller, commander of a Marine unit in Korea. In recounting his "beer versus ice cream" story it tells us more about Puller's unorthodox behavior and views than it does the events in Korea.

0586 Mazuzan, George T. Warren R. Austin at the UN, 1946-1953. Kent, Ohio: Kent State University Press, 1977.

Excellent account of the United States delegate to the United Nations who was very influential in getting the United States wishes implemented into United Nations policy and action.

0587 McCullough, David. Truman. New York: Simon and Schuster, 1992.

By far the most readable, if not the most complete biography of Truman. President Harry Truman was a full participant in military and political decisions concerning Korea. This author provides a clear understanding of Truman's policies and attitudes and is essential to fully comprehend and analyze this period of confusion.

0588 McLellan, David S. "Dean Acheson and the Korean War" Political Science Quarterly 83 (1968): 16-39.

Determines that Acheson miscalculated China's intentions in Korea, thus Truman acted with less than a realistic assessment in 1950.

0589 McNeal, Robert H. Stalin: Man and Ruler. New York: New York University Press, 1988, 1990.

A better than average biography of Stalin (1879-1953) including the Korean War period.

0590 Millett, Allan R. In Many a Strife: General Gerald C. Thomas and the U S. Marine Corps, 1917-1956. Annapolis: Naval Institute Press, 1993.

A short history of the Marines as told through the life of General Thomas. Very informative and easy to read.

0591 Nam, Koon Woo. The North Korean Communist Leadership: 1945-1965. Birmingham: University of Alabama Press, 1974.

Describes how Kim Il Sung united North Korea under his power by removing rival leadership.

0592 Oliver, Robert T. Syngman Rhee: The Man Behind the Myth. New York: Dodd Mead and Company, 1954.

This biography, written by a man who knew and worked with Rhee, is a very sensitive account of the turbulent years of his life, and deals in considerable depth with the years identified as the war for Korean independence.

0593 Park, Young. "Mao Tse-tung's Military Strategy and Tactics in Theory and Application: China, the Korean War, and Vietnam, 1927-1954" MA thesis, Flagstaff: Northern Arizona University, 1981.

MA: Mao

0594 Parrott, L. "And Now MacArthur of Korea" <u>New York Times Magazine</u> (August 20, 1950): 50-51.

A high profile "public relations" type effort which identifies MacArthur, then 70, as a powerful and hardworking leader who may well be the salvation of the United States in Asia.

0595 Parry, Francis F. <u>Three-War Marine: The Pacific * Korea * Vietnam</u>. Pacifica, California: Pacifica Press, 1987.

Colonel Parry commanded an artillery battalion in Korea; at Inchon, Seoul, and later at the Chosin Reservoir. His account is of taking a "makeshift unit into combat at the outset of a war for which his nation was unprepared." (cover). Good on the daily activities of an artillery unit, and one of the few dealing with Marine artillery.

0596 Peng, Te-huai. <u>Memoirs of a Chinese Marshal—The Autobiographical Notes of Peng Dehuai (1898-1974)</u>. Beijing: Foreign Language Press, 1984.

One of the few, and best, of material about Chinese military leaders in English. Very important to the war.

0597 Potter, Allen R. "The Truman—MacArthur Controversy, A Study in Political-Military Relations" MMAS thesis, Ft. Leonard wood: United States Army Command and General Staff College, 1972.

MA: Truman — MacArthur

0598 <u>Records of the Joint Chiefs of Staff: Part I, Meetings of the Joint Chiefs of Staff, 1946-1953</u>. Frederick, Maryland: University Publication, 1980.

Minutes of the meetings of the Joint Chiefs during the Korean War, especially useful in considering both the military view of why the United States was involved, and how it fought the first period. Microfilm available in eight reels. Declassified in 1970.

0599 <u>Records of the Joint Chiefs of Staff: Part II, The Far East, 1946-1953</u>. Frederick, Maryland: University Publication, 1980.

Documents of military activities and policies during the pre-war Korean involvement, the invasion and American military reaction, as well as the first year of defense. Very helpful in trying to understand the military mind, the policy of involvement, and how the war was to be fought. Microfilm available in fourteen reels.

0600 Reynolds, Clark G. "MacArthur as Maritime Strategist" <u>Naval War College Review</u> 33 2 (March-April 1980): 79-91.

The author develops great praise for the maritime strategies (the combined use of Navy, Army, Air Force in a seaborne operation) of General

MacArthur who developed a strong policy in Korea. MacArthur had more faith in the Navy, than the Navy did in themselves.

0601 Rhee, Syngman. Korea Flaming High, Excerpts from Statements by President Syngman Rhee in Crucial 1953. Seoul: Office of Public Information, 1954.
        Portions of speeches primarily dealing with expanded war aims and the release of prisoners.

0602 Ridgway, Matthew B. "My Battles in War and Peace: The Korean War" Saturday Evening Post 228 35 (1956): 36, 127-130.
        The general tells how he stabilized the Eighth Army when he assumed command in December of 1950.

0603 Riggs, James R. "Congress and the Conduct of the Korean War" Ph.D. dissertation. Purdue University, 1972.
        Congress took surprisingly little action related to the Korean War. Riggs looks at why.

0604 Rovere, Richard H. and Arthur M. Schlesinger. The General and the President, and the Future of American Foreign Policy. New York: Farrar, Straus and Young, 1952.
        An excellent account of what many call the apologist point of view.

0605 Schaller, Michael. Douglas MacArthur: The Far Eastern General. New York: Oxford University Press, 1989.
        A far from flattering account of Douglas MacArthur as the supreme military commander in the Far East. Schaller includes a look at MacArthur's view of his commanders. Of particular interest is his comment on General Walker who he felt had lost the fighting edge.

0606 Schaller, Michael. "MacArthur's Japan: The View from Washington" Diplomatic History 10 1 (Winter 1986): 1-23.
        MacArthur's attitudes about Japan, his determination to include Nationalist China in his plans, and his clash with civilian authorities means revisionists are giving him a small role in United States—Asian history.

0607 Schram, Stuart R. Mao Tse-tung. New York: Simon and Schuster, 1966.
        A well-written biography of Mao (1893-1976) and the making of modern China.

0608 Sebald, William J. and Russell Brines. With MacArthur in Japan: A Personal History of the Occupation. New York: W. W. Norton & Company, Inc., 1965.

This is primarily an account of the highly successful occupation of Japan, and MacArthur's role as the Allied representative. The Korean War is a minor part of this work, but the discussion of the relationship between the Inchon landing and General MacArthur's foreign policy is explained in detail and well done.

0609 Seltzer, Robert U. "The Truman-Johnson Analog: A Study of Presidential Rhetoric in Limited War" Ph.D. dissertation, Wayne State University, 1976.
    Uses analogies to justify United States entrance into, and sustained effort, in the Korean Conflict.

0610 Shi, Zhe. "With Mao and Stalin: The Reminiscences of a Chinese Interpreter" Jian Chen, translator. Chinese Historians 5 (Spring 1992): 35-46.
    These memoirs of Mao's bodyguard have some interesting stories, but give very little new information.

0611 Smith, Robert. MacArthur in Korea: The Naked Emperor. New York: Simon and Schuster, 1982.
    Designed as a tribute to Douglas MacArthur it nevertheless deals openly with the leader's limitations, primarily his arrogance and recklessness. Inchon is an example of both of these characteristics.

0612 Soffer, Jonathan Milton. "General Matthew B. Ridgway: Postwar Warrior, 1946-1986" Ph.D. dissertation, Columbia University, 1992.
    An intellectual biography of Ridgway with emphasis on his diplomatic missions.

0613 Spaatz, Carl. "General MacArthur Read General Wolfe" Newsweek 36 15 (October 9, 1950): 26-27.
    Spaatz relates that General MacArthur had drawn deeply in his historical background and knowledge, and that MacArthur had conceived his idea about Inchon following "in the footsteps as Wolfe at Quebec . . . It was the answer to the problem." This is an illusion which some have attributed to MacArthur himself.

0614 Spanier, John W. The Truman-MacArthur Controversy and The Korean War. New York: W. W. Norton & Company, Inc. 1965.
    The success at Inchon reaffirmed MacArthur's conviction that it was wise to follow the bold course whenever the military situation appeared bleak. Inchon, based on the concept of the Wolfe campaign against Quebec (at least according to the press), was the clear-cut difference between the "will to win" and "vacillation." Despite General Omar N. Bradley's feelings

to the contrary, MacArthur proved that amphibious warfare and its success was not a thing of the past.

0615 Steinberg, Alfred. Douglas MacArthur. New York: G. P. Putnam's Sons, 1961.
    A typical short account of the life of the highly controversial general, Douglas MacArthur. What is surprising is the seemingly insignificant role of Korea in this account, and the lack of any real understanding of the Korean War.

0616 Suh, Dae-Sook. Kim Il Sung: The North Korean Leader. New York: Columbia University Press, 1988.
    This North Korean leader held power longer than most heads of government, and was a central power in international affairs. This work shows his strength and weakness, deals with accomplishments during the war.

0617 Tarr, James K. "The Truman-MacArthur Controversy" MA thesis, East Stroudsburg University, 1989.
    MA: civil supremacy

0618 Taylor, Maxwell. Swords and Plowshares. New York: Norton, 1972.
    A United States Army commander of Eighth Army in Korea said that the atomic bombs were not used because of the limited number available.

0619 Timmons, Bascom M. "MacArthur's Greatest Battle" Collier's 125 25 (December 16, 1950): 13-15, 65-66.
    This is a better than average account of MacArthur's background and the suggestion that the General's classic inception of amphibious warfare was the turning point of the war. "One of the most decisive strategic operations of all times." Timmons writes a convincing article in support of the "only action possible" thesis.

0620 Titus, Donald. "The Recall of General Douglas MacArthur from Korea: A Study and Appraisal of a Presidential Decision" MS thesis, Central Connecticut State College, 1969.
    MA: MacArthur

0621 "Tokyo-Washington Messages Behind Dismissal of MacArthur" U. S. News & World Report 30 (April 20, 1951): 46-49.
    A brief account, including excerpts, of messages between Washington and Tokyo which show that General MacArthur had indeed violated assumed polities.

0622 Truman, Harry. <u>Memoirs: Years of Trial and Hope</u>. volume 2. Garden City, New York: Doubleday & Company, 1956.

President Truman was in the middle of the conflict both in and about Korea. As Commander-in-Chief his approval was necessary for almost any policy change. His early involvement is well documented, and indexed.

0623 Twedt, Michael. "The War Rhetoric of Harry S. Truman During the Korean Conflict" Ph.D. dissertation, University of Kansas, 1969.

A discussion of President Truman's efforts to unite the American people behind the war, using his speeches.

0624 United States Congress House Committee on Appropriations. "Statement of General Hudelson on Korea" Washington, D. C.: Government Printing Office, 1952.

Transcript of testimony by General Daniel H. Hudelson.

0625 Walker, Ronald Lee. "The Truman-MacArthur Controversy: A Reappraisal" MA thesis, Eastern Illinois University, 1967.

Walker considers the conflict between the president and General MacArthur as an issue of civilian rather than military control of national policy.

0626 <u>Webster's American Military Biographies</u>. Springfield, Massachusetts: Merriam, 1978.

Contains numerous brief sketches of military leaders who served in the early years of the Korean Conflict.

0627 "What's the Use of Korea?" <u>Life</u> 31 (August 6, 1951): 28.

One of the key elements in General MacArthur's eventual replacement was a series of "unwise," and generally unnecessary, speeches given. This is the report of one such speech given by MacArthur, in which he suggests the "utter uselessness of the Korean War."

0628 Whitney, Courtney. <u>MacArthur: His Rendezvous with History</u>. New York: Alfred A. Knopf, 1956.

A strong biography of MacArthur as military commander. The author supports MacArthur in the "great debate" over the Inchon landing, though he provides little defense other than MacArthur's wisdom, military knowledge, and a general ability.

0629 Whitson, William W. <u>The Chinese High Command</u>. New York: Praeger, 1973.

A history of the military politics of China from 1927 to 1971. Excellent and informative.

0630 Wildman, Richard. "The Impotence of Office: Mr. Truman's War" MA thesis, University of San Diego, 1973.

Discusses President Truman and his inability to deal with the Korean War as he wanted to.

0631 Willoughby, Charles A. and John Chamberlain. MacArthur 1941-1951. New York: McGraw-Hill Book Company, Inc., 1954.

An excuse for MacArthur's behavior. It provides little of the analysis that would be possible twenty years later.

0632 Wiltz, John Edward. "The MacArthur Hearings of 1951: The Secret Testimony" Military Affairs 39 4 (December 1975): 167-173.

Secret testimony from the MacArthur hearings paint a far darker picture of Korea in 1951 than was given to the American public.

0633 Wiltz, John Edward "The MacArthur Inquiry, 1951" in Arthur Schlesinger and Roger Burns, editors. Congress Investigates: A Documental History 81792-1974. volume 5. New York: Chelsea House, 1975.

An account of the political reasons behind MacArthur's dismissal, all very well supported by a collection of pertinent documents and a bibliographic essay.

0634 Wiltz, John Edward. "Truman and MacArthur: The Wake Island Meeting" Military Affairs 42 4 (December 1978): 169-176.

Wiltz holds that serious political problems for Truman, not military concerns, caused their meeting in Korea.

0635 Wodock, Ruth C. "The Recall of General Douglas MacArthur From His Command in Korea" MS thesis, Western Connecticut State University, 1967.

A not-very-useful recount of events leading up to the recall of MacArthur, a view altered by recent understandings.

HISTORIES

General

0636 Acheson, Dean. <u>The Korean War</u>. New York: Norton, 1971.
   Former Secretary of State defends American military involvement in the Korean War, and the dismissal of General MacArthur. Based primarily on materials in <u>Present at the Creation</u>.

0637 Alexander, Bevin. <u>Korea: The First War We Lost</u>. New York: Hippocrene Books, 1986.
   This excellent history is one of the first to make good use of the unpublished narratives of combat historians, X Corps, and Eighth Army command reports. More than half the work is on the first year of the war. Alexander, who served as an Army combat historian, suggests the United States (United Nations) fought two very different wars. One, with the North Koreans, was won as a result of the Inchon landing and the liberation of Seoul. The second, the war with the Chinese, was lost.

0638 Andariese, Walter S. <u>World War II through Korea</u>. no publisher, 1973.
   A "history" of the war provided by personal narrative, caricatures, and cartoons.

0639 Appleman, Roy E. <u>Disaster in Korea: The Chinese Confront MacArthur</u>. College Station: Texas A & M University Press, 1989.
   Explains the Eighth Army defeat in great detail, and is critical of both MacArthur and General David Barr (7th Division commander) during withdrawal.

0640 Appleman, Roy E. East of Chosin: Entrapment and Breakout in Korea, 1950. College Station: Texas A & M University Press, 1987.
Excellent account of the Chinese trap sprung east of the Chosin Reservoir. One of the few accounts which provides any indepth view of the Army's role in the ensuing breakout.

0641 Appleman, Roy E. Escaping the Trap: The U. S. Army X Corps in Northeast Korea, 1950. College Station: Texas A & M University Press, 1990.
This work is primarily about the Marines, but deals with the command division of X Corps and Eighth Army.

0642 Appleman, Roy E. Ridgway Duels for Korea. College Station: Texas A & M University Press, 1990.
Describes Ridgway's role in putting the army back together and holding the line in 1951.

0643 Bachrach, Deborah. The Korean War. San Diego, California: Lucent Books, 1991.
Explains just why America was involved in Korean War and discusses the legacy of the war for youth.

0644 Berger, Carl. The Korean Knot: A Military-Political History. Philadelphia: University of Pennsylvania Press, 1957, 1965, 1968.
A rare history which covers the political events of both the causes and the war itself. Excellent overview, but limited to the political intrigue with little new information.

0645 Blair, Clay. The Forgotten War: America in Korea, 1950-1953. New York: Times Books, 1987.
Blair is not all that certain the cost of containing communism was worth the war in Korea. Critical of Truman's failure to keep the nation armed, and critical of military leaders still fighting World War II, he condemns MacArthur.

0646 Bong-yon, Choy. Korea: A History. Rutland, Vermont: Charles E. Tuttle Company, 1971.
This biased history of the Korean War is written by a professor at the Seoul National University. His thesis is that the Korean War was a revolution, and discusses both the United Nations and the American involvement in creating and supporting the revolution.

0647 Burchett, Wilfred G. Again Korea. New York: International Publishers, 1968.

Socialist Australian who claims Korean War was started by the South Koreans.

0648 Burchett, Wilfred G. This Monstrous War. Melbourne, Australia: Waters, 1953.
Very biased view of the Korean War from this socialist newspaperman. Blames the United Nations for germ warfare.

0649 Cheshire, George. "Korea and the Korean Conflict" Black Hills Teachers College, 1951.
Thesis: Korean War

0650 Cho, Soon Sung. Korea in World Politics, 1940-1950: An Evaluation of American Responsibility. Berkeley: University of California Press, 1967.
Social history of Korea with special interest in World War II, discusses numerous blunders which were committed despite the good intentions of the United States.

0651 Choy, Bong Youn. Korea: A History. Rutland, Vermont: Charles E. Tuttle, Company, 1971.
This terribly biased history of the Korean War is written by a professor at the Seoul National University. His thesis is that the Korean War was a revolution, and discusses both the United Nations and the American involvement in creating and supporting the revolution.

0652 Confrontation in Asia: The Korean War. West Point: Department of History, United States Military Academy, 1981.
General history text used at the Naval Academy, excellent map of the Inchon landing.

0653 Doughty, Robert A. Limited Warfare in the Nuclear Age. Lexington, Massachusetts: D. C. Heath and Company, 1996.
Chapter two of the work offers an excellent brief and up-to-date account of the origins, fighting, and armistice of the Korean War.

0654 Edwards, Richard. The Korean War. Hove, England: Wayland, 1987. Vero Beach, Florida: Rourke Enterprises, 1988.
History written for juveniles, but fairly good coverage of the origins of the war, the events, conclusions, and aftermath.

0655 Fehrenbach, T. R. The Fight for Korea; From the War of 1950 to the Pueblo Incident. New York: Grosset & Dunlap, 1969.
Survey for high school readers giving an overview of the Cold War strain during and following the Korean War.

0656 Fehrenbach, T. R. This Kind of War: A Study in Unpreparedness. New York: Macmillan, 1963.

One of the first general survey histories to appear. An excellent account of the early war by a man with some firsthand experience. He stresses American unpreparedness for limited war and governmental inability to "get started." A good study of the tension created by this political reality.

0657 Fincher, Ernest. The War in Korea. New York: Franklin Watts, 1981.

A book for youth designed to show how the United States involvement in Korea contained the spread of communism.

0658 Fleming, Dan B. and Burton I. Kaufman. "The Forgotten War: Korea" The Education Digest (December 1990).

An interesting and significant analysis of Korean War history as found in educational texts and classrooms. What they found is a near void of information.

0659 Flint, Roy K. "Task Force Smith and the 24th Division: Delay and Withdrawal, 5-19 July, 1950" in Charles E. Heller and William A. Stofft, editors. America's First Battles, 1776 - 1965. Lawrence: University of Kansas Press, 1986.

A detailed account of the first battle, but more than that, a seasoned account of military unpreparedness and uncoordinated action. An important and brave sacrifice, but for what?

0660 Forty, George. At War in Korea. London: Allen, 1982. New York: Bonanza Books, 1985.

Well-written book which focuses on United Nations soldiers and how well they fought the war. Good illustrations.

0661 Fraser, Haynes. "The Korean Conflict with Special Reference to the Theory and Dynamics of Collective Security" Ph.D. dissertation, University of Southern California, 1956.

Evaluates the Korean War as a case study in collective security and the limitation of international aggressors.

0662 Gardner, Lloyd, editor. The Korean War. Chicago: Quadrangle Books, 1972.

Series of excellent articles by authors like James Reston and John Foster Dulles, which appeared originally in New York Times Magazine.

0663 Gay, Martin and Kathlyn Gay. The Korean War. New York: Twenty-First Century Books, 1996.

Discusses events leading to the Korean War, and some coverage of the military events. Geared for youth.

0664 Goulden, Joseph C. Korea: The Untold Story of the War. New York: McGraw, 1982.

A good journalist's history told from the view of the leaders. The author used the Freedom of Information Act to locate previously unexplored material. Goulden is strongly supportive of MacArthur as the Allied commander. The author is one of the few who deals with "Operation Bluehearts," an early plan to put the 1st Cavalry Division at Inchon on 22 July 1950.

0665 Halliday, Jon and Bruce Cumings. Korea: The Unknown War. New York: Pantheon Books, 1988.

Uses interview materials from China, Russia, North and South Korea as well as United States sources. The authors depict a war which was essentially a civil war, and one which the nations involved allowed to grow into an international conflict with threats of a third World War.

0666 Hankuk, Jon Jang Sa. History of the Korean War. five volumes. Seoul: Hangrim Publishing, 1990-1992.

A massive account of the war which tries to cover every angle. A reasonably good, if less than objective, account from the view of South Korean scholars.

0667 Hastings, Max. The Korean War. New York: Simon and Schuster, 1987.

Hastings, a respected English military historian, recounts the personal experience of the individual soldiers, as well as the strategies and politics of the leadership. He blames most of the failure in Korea on the poor quality of American infantrymen. He also identifies the intelligence failure which led to the Chinese intervention. He says the American "can do" improvisation and risk-taking grew to a magnificent scale.

0668 Hooker, John. Korea, The Forgotten War. Sydney, New South Wales: Time-Life Books, 1989.

A short but good account of Australians at war in Korea.

0669 Hoyt, Edwin P. America's Wars & Military Excursions. New York: McGraw-Hill Publishing Company, 1987.

A brief, and very general account, of the early days of the Korean War, including some discussion of the defense of the Pusan Perimeter.

0670 Hoyt, Edwin P. The Bloody Road to Panmunjom. New York: Stein & Day, 1985.

A brief overview of the Korean War by a popular author. He concentrates on the Ridgway policy of "punishing the Chinese" rather than the quest for land to occupy.

0671 Isserman, Maurice. The Korean War: America at War. New York: Facts on File, 1992.
    This volume recalls a "momentous but now largely forgotten conflict" the Korean War. This is primarily a text, written for students, but is well done and accompanied by some outstanding maps.

0672 Kaufman, Burton I. The Korean War: Challenges in Crisis, Credibility, and Command. Philadelphia: Temple University Press. New York: Knopf. New York: McGraw-Hill, 1986, 1997.
    Primarily about the politics of international conflict. Concerned with what the author considers a series of command failures early in the war.

0673 Kim, Chum-kon. The Korean War: The First Comprehensive Account of the Historical Background and Development of the Korean War (1950-1953). Seoul, Korea: Kwongmyang Publishing, Ltd. 1973.
    The author, a division commander during the Korean War, provides the South Korean point of view, including comments on the "counterattack" on Inchon. Good source on both North Korean attitudes and actions, and insightful concerning the military utility and movement of the North Korean People's Army.

0674 Kim, Soo Nam. "The Conduct of the Korean War, 1950-1953" Ph.D. dissertation, University of Aberdeen, 1987.
    The author explores civilian control over the military in the United States and tries to explain it in terms of the Korean War.

0675 Knox, Donald and Alfred Coppel. The Korean War: Uncertain Victory: The Concluding Volume of an Oral History. volume 2. San Diego: Harcourt Brace Jovanovich, 1988.
    The second volume of Knox's oral history, finished after Knox's death by Alfred Coppel. Takes firsthand look at the war from January 1950 to the "uncertain victory." Excellent firsthand accounts.

0676 Korea (Republic). The History of the United Nations Forces in the Korean War. six volumes. Seoul: Ministry of the National Defense, Republic of Korea, 1972-1977.
    A vast record of the United Nations involvement in Korea. Less than objective.

0677 "The Korean War, 1950-1953" in R. Ernest Dupuy and Trevor N. Dupuy. The Encyclopedia of Military History: From 3500 B. C. to the Present. New York: Harper and Row, 1970.

A typical encyclopedia entry, but a good source of statistics.

0678 Kurland, Gerald. The Korean War. Charlotteville, New York: Samhar Press, 1973.

Brief overview of the political and military events of the war. The material is not new, but the author makes a strong case for the military.

0679 LaFeber, Walter. "Crossing the 38th: The Cold War in Microcosm" in Lynn H. Miller and Ronald W. Pruessen, editors. Reflections on the Cold War: A Quarter Century of American Foreign Policy. Philadelphia, Pennsylvania: Temple University Press, 1974.

The decision to move north of the 38th Parallel was a costly military mistake which greatly heated up the Cold War.

0680 Lawson, Don. The United States in the Korean War. New York: Abelard, 1964.

High school history, not widely used, provides a reasonable account which focuses on political and military heroes.

0681 Leckie, Robert. Conflict: The History of the Korean War, 1950-53. New York: Putnam's, 1962.

A controlled and competent history by a World War II Marine who specialized in military history. Leckie concludes the stalemate was, in fact, a victory because the "Korean invasion" was repelled, and communism suffered a major defeat.

0682 Leckie, Robert. The March to Glory. Cleveland, Ohio: World Publishing Company, 1960.

A well-written, if often-told, account of the 1st Marines at the Chosin Reservoir.

0683 Leckie, Robert. The War in Korea: 1950-1953. New York: Random House, 1963.

An overly simple high school history which sees the war as a clash between good and evil.

0684 Lee, Seoksoo. "The Anatomy of the Korean Conflict: Its Genesis, Process, and Management" Ph.D. dissertation, University of Kentucky, 1993.

Tries to place the war within the context of the unification of the two Koreas, and views it from a wholistic and a comprehensive manner, seeing the cause as a confluence of international and domestic perception.

0685 Liem, Channing. <u>The Korean War: An Unanswered Question</u>. Pyongyang, Korea: Foreign Languages Publishing House, 1993.

Discusses who is to blame for the Korean War, diplomatic history, and causes.

0686 MacDonald, Callum A. <u>Korea: The War Before Vietnam</u>. New York: The Free Press, 1986.

Obviously an attempt to relate the two Asian wars, it is a useful source. While MacArthur turned the victory at Inchon into an excuse for overriding the limitations of his military directive from the United Nations, he did so either with Washington's backing, or in their ignorance.

0687 Manawis, Mariano D. <u>The Fighting Tenth: War Account of the First and Most Embattled Filipino Units Ever to Fight on Foreign Soil</u>. no publisher, 1955.

Limited narrative of the 10th Battalion Combat Team which fought in Korea.

0688 Marshall, S. L. A. <u>The Military History of the Korean War</u>. New York: Franklin Watts, Inc., 1963.

Written for young people, but it is done with Marshall's usual style. The coverage of Inchon and the "illusion of victory" is simply and clearly stated and accompanied by good maps.

0689 McGowen, Tom. <u>The Korean War</u>. New York: Franklin Watts, 1992.

A brief (sixty-three pages) account written for juveniles, which stresses a war of three years duration which caused over two million lives to be lost and resolved nothing.

0690 McMahan, Steven. "Limited War: Korea to Vietnam" MA thesis, Salt Lake City: University of Utah, 1969.

Deals with the political concepts of limited war.

0691 Middleton, Harry J. <u>The Compact History of the Korean War</u>. New York: Hawthorn Books, Inc. 1965.

One of the better short histories of the Korean War. This journalist and professional documentarian has written a readable, short, and negative history of the Korean War. Provides insights on General MacArthur's ability to provide forceful presentations while avoiding answers to serious questions.

0692 Miller, Francis. <u>War in Korea, and the Complete History of World War II</u>. Ann Woodward Miller, 1955.

General account of the political causes for the war, and then covers the first few months of the war. A "quick" addition to an established book.

0693 The Ministry of National Defense, The Republic of Korea. The History of the United Nations Forces in the Korean War. five volumes. Seoul: Ministry of National Defense, 1972-1974.

A totally subjective history of the "three years' fratricidal tragedy" designed to excuse the excesses of the war. It acknowledges the contribution of the twenty-one nations involved in the conflict, and draws attention to the continuing menace of the communist's view. Provides the South Korean point of view on the United Nations forces, and on the military leadership of the United Nations troops. Is an excellent source of units, action dates, and casualties.

0694 O'Ballance, Edgar. Korea 1950-53. London: Faber, 1969.

A general history which claims that President Truman waited to make his decision until he had some indication from Russia that they would not become involved on the North Korean side. Also considers the retreat and defense of Pusan from the view that MacArthur did not understand the Pusan situation.

0695 Okonogi, Masao. The Korean War: The Process of U. S. Intervention. Seoul: Chung Gye Yon Ku So, 1986.

Translation of a Ph.D. thesis "The Korean War Seen from the Context of Diplomatic History" which called for a new interpretation of Japan's role.

0696 Oliver, Robert T. Verdict in Korea. State College, Pennsylvania: Bald Eagle, 1952.

Undisguised bias which supports the Republic of Korea (South) and praises the great job they were doing.

0697 Osgood, Robert. Limited War: The Challenge to American Strategy. Chicago: University of Chicago, 1957.

Published early, this author challenged the ability of the United States to meet the needs in Korea without unleashing World War III.

0698 Paik, Son-Yup. From Pusan to Panmunjom. Washington, D. C.: Brassey's, 1992.

Reflections on the desperate battles the author led with ill-equipped troops, untrained, and unmotivated men. Discusses some of the key battles of the war.

0699 Park, Pong-Shik. "The Korean War 1950-1953" Korean Journal (July 1, 1967): 15-20.

Sees the conflict between the United States and Soviet Russia as the major cause behind the war itself, and later for the efforts at an armistice.

0700 Pran Nath, Dr. A Condensed Study of the War in Korea; in Question Answer Form. Dehradun, India: E. B. D. Publishing and Distribution Company, 1968.

A very interesting history of United Nations at war in Korea, done in an unique question and answer style.

0701 Rees, David. Korea: The Limited War. New York: St. Martin's Press, 1953, 1964, 1970.

Still one of the best histories of the Korean War, the British author combines political and military history in a unique manner.

0702 Rees, David, editor. The Korean War: History and Tactics. New York: Crescent Books, 1967, 1984.

Good single volume of the military aspects of the war. One of the best treatments of policy in relation to military operations. Highly supportive and considers "American involvement in Korea, the greatest act in recent American history."

0703 Ridgway, Matthew B. The Korean War: History and Tactics. Garden City, New York: Doubleday and Company, 1967.

While General Matthew B. Ridgway came late to Korea he had a greater understanding of it than many military leaders. In this work he covers the war from the beginning. During this early phase Ridgway was involved in the planning and was, in a real sense, Chief of Staff for Korea.

0704 Ridgway, Matthew B. "The Korean War, Issues and Policies" Manuscript, Center of Military History, Washington, D. C., no date.

A book-length document developed by General Ridgway concerning the political, as well as military, aspects of fighting the Korean War. This manuscript has been used extensively by Billy C. Mossman in Ebb and Flow, but is available for further research.

0705 Ridgway, Matthew B. The War in Korea: How We Met the Challenge. How All-Out Asian War was Averted. Why MacArthur was Dismissed. Why Today's War Objectives Must be Limited. London: Cresset Press and Barrie and Rockliff, 1968.

The London edition of Ridgway's work, The Korean War, published in the United States.

0706 Sin, Hwa-Bong. The Forgotten War Remembered, Korea 1950-1953: A War Correspondents' Notebook and Today's Danger in Korea. Elizabeth, New Jersey: Hollym International, 1996.

A war correspondent's diary with a contemporary warning.

0707 Smith, C. Carter. The Korean War. Englewood Cliffs, New Jersey: Silver Burdett Press, 1990.

Short (sixty-four page) history written for juveniles which stresses events and persons, with very little analysis.

0708 Stein, R. Conrad. The Korean War: "The Forgotten War." Hillside, New Jersey: Enslow Publishers, 1994.

History written for young persons with a stress on heroic personal events.

0709 Stokesbury, James L. A Short History of the Korean War. New York: Quill, William Morrow, 1988.

This volume, one in a series of "Short Histories," is well done, but has all the problems of a brief history. The tone of this work is the inevitability of the United States involvement in Korea once military action began.

0710 Stone, Isidor F. The Hidden History of the Korean War. London: Turnstile, 1952. Boston: Little, Brown, 1952, 1988. New York: Monthly Review Press, 1952, 1969, 1970, 1971.

This is still one of the more controversial works on the war, even though published before the war was over. Stone, a well known liberal journalist introduces the United States—Republic of Korea (South) conspiracy, placing much of the blame for the war on the United States.

0711 Stueck, William. The Korean War: As International History. Princeton, New Jersey: Princeton University Press, 1995.

Discussion of Korea as an international war which substituted for, and thus prevented, World War III. Excellent book.

0712 Summers, Harry G., Jr. "The Korean War: A Fresh Perspective" Military History 13 1 (April 1, 1996).

While the United States was busy in Europe, Kim Il Sung convinced Joseph Stalin that an invasion of South Korea involved little risk.

0713 Summers, Harry G. "An Unofficial History" Infantry 53 6 (November-December 1963): 28-29.

Interesting tongue-in-cheek account of the "real" infantry in Korea.

0714 Taylor, Maxwell D. The Uncertain Trumpet. New York: Harper, 1959.

Taylor, who was the United States Army Chief of Staff and Commander of the Eighth Army during the final period, is critical of the United States running of the Korean War, and of command decisions in the early phase.

0715 Thomas, Robert C. W. The War in Korea, 1950-1953. Aldershot, England: Gale, 1954.

While this book was written very early and without benefit of the numerous recent studies and analysis, this British officer/historian provides a good general survey and strong support for both the United Nations involvement, and for General MacArthur's handling of the war.

0716 Toland, John. In Mortal Combat: 1950-1953. New York: William Morrow and Company, 1991.

This popular historian has produced a sound history, weakened by his re-creation of situations and dialogue where there is little historical support. He has been one of the few writers to locate and use detailed North Korean and Chinese sources.

0717 Tow, William T. "The Military Dimensions of the Korean Conflict" Monterey, California: Institute of International Relations, 1991.

A forty-five page paper presented at the DARSP-M115 Conference on Military/Political Conflicts.

0718 United States Department of State. The Conflict in Korea: Events Prior to the Attack on June 25, 1950. Washington, D. C.: Government Printing Office, 1951.

Far Eastern series on Japanese and Korean history from 1945-1950.

0719 United States Department of the Army, Office of Military History. Korea—1950. Washington, D. C.: Government Printing Office, 1952, 1981, 1982.

Excellent collection with maps and illustrations which covers political, government, and economics of Korea in 1950.

0720 United States Military Academy, Department of Military Art and Engineering. Operations in Korea. West Point, New York: United States, Department of Military Art and Engineering, Government Printing Office, 1956.

Brief operations history and point of view as presented by the United States Army.

0721 Whelan, Richard. Drawing the Line: The Korean War, 1950-1953. Boston: Little, Brown, and Company, 1990.

Fairly good general history which addresses "why World War III was risked to save an undemocratic republic." His answers are more descriptive than analytical.

0722 Yoo, Tae-ho. The Korean War and the United Nations: A Legal and Diplomatic Historical Study. Louvain, Belgium: Institute for Political and Social Sciences, 1965.

Both the United States and Russia were working on their own agendas, with little or no regard to the needs of Korea.

Army

0723 Armstrong, Frank, editor. The 1st Cavalry Division and Their 8th Engineers in Korea: America's Silent Generation at War. South Burlington, Vermont: Bull Run, 1997.

More than 130 first person narratives, limericks, songs, poems, of these units at war.

0724 Ayers, Charles. The U. S. Army and the Development of the ROK Army, 1945-1950. MA thesis, Old Dominion University, 1989.

Discusses the role played by the United States Army in formatting the ROK Army.

0725 Barth, George B. Tropic Lightning 1 Oct 1941 to 1 Oct 1966. Doralville, Georgia: Albert Love, 1967.

This unit arrived in Korea at the beginning of the war and fought throughout. They won a Presidential Unit Citation for action 1-11 August 1950.

0726 Baya, G. Emery. "Army Organization Act of 1950" Army Information Digest 5 8 (1950): 28-37.

This reflects the organization of the Army as it operated throughout the war. Signed into law by President Truman just three days after the North Korean invasion, it consolidated several previous organizational laws, and was the military configuration from which the war was fought.

0727 Boatner, Mark M. III. Army Lore and the Customs of the Service. Japan: Kyoyua, 1954.

Provides a brief history of the regular army unit which served in Korea.

0728 Boelsche, Fred, compiler. Unofficial History of the 11th Engineer Combat Battalion, June 1916-August 1989. privately printed, 1995.

A "narrative' version of a unit history from World War I to Korea.

0729 Brown, Howard F. 43rd Infantry Division. Paducah, Kentucky: Turner Publishing Company, 1994.

"Winged Victory" regimental history.

0729A Busch, George B. Duty: The Story of the 21st Infantry Regiment. Sendai, Japan: Hyappan, 1953.

History of the 21st Infantry from its entry into the Korean War in July of 1950, through the long retreat and the establishment of the perimeter and defense of Pusan. Continues, in less detail, on through the armistice.

0730 Chandler, Melbourne C. Of Garry Owen in Glory: The History of the 7th U. S. Cavalry. Annandale, Virginia: The Turnpike Press, 1960.

Chronological account of the 7th Cavalry in Korea. Includes action in the Naktong River defense.

0731 The Cold Steel Third: 3rd Airborne Ranger Company, Korean War (1950-1951). Franklin, North Carolina: Genealogy Publishing Services, 1993.

More than eight hundred pages on commando operations as part of a regimental history, assembled from records, letters, and journals of the unit members.

0732 The Complete History of the 62d Engineer Battalion from October 1939 through December 1989. United States Army Engineer Battalion, 62nd, Fort Hood, Texas: The Battalion, 1990.

Narrative of the battalion in World War II, the Korean War, and the Vietnam War. Korean coverage is brief but helpful.

0733 Connor, Arthur W. "A Study of Armored Combat During the Korean War, June 1950-February 1951" MA thesis, Temple University, 1991.

MA: Armored combat

0734 Daily, Edward L. Skirmish: Red, White and Blue, the History of the 7th U.S. Cavalry 1945-1953. Paducah, Kentucky: Turner Publishing Company, 1992.

A Korean War unit history of the famed 7th Cavalry Division.

0735 Dalton, John J. and Bernard F. Brown The Thunderbird. A 45th Division History. Tokyo: Toppan, 1954.

A unit history of limited value.

0736 David, Alan A., editor. Battleground Korea: The Story of the 25th Infantry Division. Tokyo: Kyoya, 1952.

This administrative history traces the division activities from the first conflict in July 1950, through the long retreat, at the Pusan Perimeter, and during the following two years.

0737 David, Alan A., editor. Seventh Infantry Division, Public Information Office. Bayonet: A History of the 7th Infantry Division in Korea. Tokyo: Dai Nippon, 1953.

A somewhat exaggerated administrative history of the 7th (Hourglass) Infantry Division from its involvement in the summer of 1950 to the end of 1952.

0738 Diminyatz, Kerry L. "The 40th Infantry Division in the Korean Conflict: The Employment of the California National Guard in an Undeclared War" MA thesis, Sonoma State University, 1990.

The regimental history of a National Guard unit which served in Korea.

0739 Dolcater, Max W., editor. 3rd Infantry Division in Korea. Tokyo: Toppan, 1953.

An extensive look at the 3rd Infantry Division through the Korean war. Lists activities, battles, awards, and those killed in action.

0740 Dornbusch, Charles E. Histories of American Army Units, World Wars I and II and Korean Conflict, With Some Earlier Histories. Washington, D. C.: Department of the Army, Office of the Adjunct General, 1956, 1962.

A general collection of brief histories of units, which fought in these three wars of the twentieth century.

0741 Dupuy, R. Ernest. The Combat History of the United States Army. New York: Hawthorne Books, Inc., 1973.

A good one volume history of the organization and development of the United States Army. Chapter on the army in Korea discusses the impact of the reorganization of 1947 on the ability to field troops. Includes an analysis of efforts to bring about the disintegration of the army.

0742 Eighth United States Army, Military History Section. The First Ten Years: A Short History of the Eighth United States Army 1944-1954. Tokyo: Army AG Administrative Center, 1954.

This fairly light account of the Eighth Army, focuses on administrative rather than combat coverage, but is informative, particularly about TO&E.

0743 Farner, F., editor. The First Team. Atlanta: Love, 1952.

Primarily a yearbook of the United States 1st Cavalry Division in Korea, with descriptive unit histories from 18 July 1950 to January 1952.

0744 Farquhar, William J., Henry A. Jeffers and Charles Hendricks. <u>Bridging the Imjin: Construction at Libby and Teal Bridges During the Korean War (October 52-July 53)</u>. Fort Belvoir, Virginia: United States Army Corps of Engineers, 1989.

Story of the 84th Engineer Battalion which built two bridges over the Imjin River during combat in Korea.

0745 Fautua, David T. "The 'Long Pull' Army: NSC 68, The Korean War and the Creation of the Cold War U. S. Army" MA thesis, North Carolina State University, 1994.

MA: Cold War army

0746 <u>1st Battalion 37th Artillery: History, 1918-1966</u>. United States Army: Artillery Regiment, 37th, 1967.

A unit history of the yearbook variety.

0747 Gardner, Bruce. <u>Seventh Infantry Division, World War I, World War II, Korean and Panamanian Invasion, 1917-1992</u>. Paducah, Kentucky: Turner Publishing Company, 1991.

This limited edition (1000 copies) was prepared by the 7th Infantry Division Association. Not very useful.

0748 Gray, David R. "The First Rangers in Korea: The Eighth Army Ranger Company in Combat August 1950-March 1951" MA thesis, Ohio State University, 1990.

MA: Rangers

0749 Gugeler, Russell A. <u>Combat Actions in Korea: Infantry, Artillery, and Armor</u>. Washington, D. C.: Combat Forces Press Institute, 1954, 1970.

Contains numerous battle narratives of the early days which were compiled by official army historians from action reports. Original manuscripts, longer and more detailed, are available for study at the Army's Center of Military History, Washington, D. C.

0750 Hanley, James M. <u>A Matter of Honor: A Memoir</u>. New York: Vantage Press, 1995.

442nd Regimental Combat Team, Army biography, World War II, Korea.

0751 Harris, W. W. <u>Puerto Rico's Fighting 65th U. S. Infantry: From San Juan to Chorwon</u>. Novato: California, Presidio Press, 1982.

Follows the history of this famous unit from the Spanish-American War to the Korean War by the author who commanded the unit in Korea.

0752 Harrity, Ralph D. "A Forward Observer Reports from Korea" Combat Forces Journal 1 9 (April 1951): 28-29.

The role of the forward observer, never very safe, increased in importance during the fluid nature of the first weeks of fighting. In most cases any observation for direct fire came from the observer, who was also the only eyes available to many small unit commanders.

0753 Hermes, G. "The United States Army in the Korean War: The Last Two Years, July 1951-July 1953" Ph.D. dissertation, Georgetown University, 1966.

Focuses on the problems of trying to conduct a war while also involved in serious negotiating.

0754 Historical Division, 7th Infantry. Bayonet: A History of the 7th Infantry Division. Tokyo: Toppan Printing Company, Ltd., 1952.

An early publication designed for new troops assigned to the division. Has a history of each organizational unit, including those who landed at Inchon. Contains a TO&E for the division at the time it landed.

0755 A History of the 38th U. S. Infantry: The Rock of the Marne. no publisher, 1959.

A regimental history of a famous unit. Yearbook format.

0756 Jacobs, Bruce. Soldiers: The Fighting Divisions of the Regular Army. New York: Norton, 1958.

Brief history of the twenty-one divisions of the regular army, with considerations of 2nd, 7th, 24th, 25th, 43rd infantry and the 1st cavalry which were involved in Korea, several in the retreat and defense at Pusan.

0757 Johnson, Courtland ("Corky") R. Unit History, Able Company, 1st Battalion 1st Marine Regiment, 1949-1951, Also, a Brief History of 1st Marine Regiment with Lineage and Honors, 1899-1967. no publisher, 1967.

A company history seen in the frame of the larger Marine Corps history. Good but very limited focus.

0758 The Legacy of Custer's 7th U. S. Cavalry in Korea. Paducah, Kentucky: Turner Publishing Company, 1990.

The 7th Cavalry arrived in Korea in July of 1950 and were immediately put into combat. This unit history does a good job covering the division activities during the retreat and defense of Pusan.

0759 Liell, William. "United States Airborne" Journal Royal United Service Institution 92 (1962): 139-148.

Describes the use of airborne troops in World War II and their disposition in the Korean War.

0760 Lightning Lancer: A Review of the 68th Fighter-Interceptor Squadron. no publisher, 1953.

A unit history of the yearbook variety.

0761 Marshall, S. L. A. "Our Army in Korea: The Best Yet" Harper's 203 (1951): 21-27.

A most favorable account of the first year of the Eighth Army in Korea. Marshall, a first class military historian, gives an eye-witness account of the best of the Eighth Army. Repeated in Combat Forces Journal and Detroit News.

0762 McGrath, Paul C. U. S. Army in the Korean Conflict. no publisher, 1950.

Limited work on the role of the Army, as well as the origins of the war and United States, Russian, and Japanese relationships with Korea at the end of 1940s and into the 1950s.

0763 McKee, Norris, editor. The Victory Division: 1941-1961: Organization Day, October 1, 1961. no publisher, 1960.

Unit history of the yearbook variety.

0764 Meloy, G. S., Jr. "The Eighth Army Story" Army Information Digest 18 6 (June 1963): 2-13.

Brief history of Eighth Army 1949-1962 with good section on the United States Eighth in Korea.

0765 Military History Section. The First Ten Years: A Short History of the Eighth United States Army, 1944-1954. Eighth United States Army, no date.

Brief history with simple, but excellent, maps that trace the role of the Eighth Army.

0766 Munroe, Clark. Second to None: History of the Second United States Infantry Division in Korea. volume I (1950-1951). volume II (1953-1954). Tokyo.

Privately printed yearbook narratives with photos of the units in combat.

0767 Munroe, Clark C. The Second United States Infantry Division in Korea. Nashville, Tennessee: Battery Press, 1951, 1992.

Yearbook history of the division.

0768 Moore, Clark C. U. S. 1st Cavalry Division: The Second United States Infantry Division in Korea 1951. Tokyo: Toppan Printing Company, 1951, 1992.

A yearbook presentation of the military, social, and personnel activities of the 1st Cavalry Division in the first year of the war. Has all the problems of a service book, but does provide a good bit of information about the division.

0769 IX Corps, Historical Section, The IX Corps in Korea: A Brief Informal History of IX Corps in Korea, 23 September 1950 to 1 September 1954. Tokyo: Army A G Administration Center, 1954.

Brief overview, primarily a yearbook which contains narratives and individual division experience.

0770 Novak, William J. "The 301st Signal Photographic Company: A Unit History" Huntington Station, New York: Bill Novak, 1992.

Regimental history of the yearbook variety. Helpful but limited.

0771 O'Connell, William R. The Thunderbird: A 45th Division History: The Story of the 45th Division's Action in the Korean Conflict. Tokyo, Toppan, 1953.

Record of Oklahoma National Guard unit which fought in Korea.

0772 196th Regimental Combat Team. no publisher, 1951

Yearbook history of the 196th infantry, 147th artillery, 200th engineers, South Dakota, militia.

0773 "Operational Use of the Scout Dog Platoon: Reconnaissance Operations" APO: EUSAK, 1953.

A brief seven-page book, but one of the few discussions of the use of dogs during the Korean War.

0774 Patrick, Stephen B. 1st Battalion 68 Armor: A History, 1918-1968. United States Army Institute of Military History archive/manuscript control, 1968.

A typescript history of the Battalion available at the Army Institute.

0775 Strong, E. D. Armor Report (8 July-8 August 1951). Operation Research Office, General Headquarters, Far East Command, 1951.

Analysis of the limited success of armor units in Korea, as determined by research and intelligence reports.

0776 Unit History 213th Armored Field Artillery Battalion. Military History Institutes archives/manuscript control, 1954, 1990.

A typescript history, available at the archives of the 213th armored unit.

0777 United States. History of the 92d Armored Field Artillery Battalion "Red Devils". no publisher, 1971.
A yearbook type history which covers the three wars fought by this battalion.

0778 United States. The 7th Infantry Division in Korea: September 1950-July 1954. Atlanta: Love, 1954.
Yearbook history of the 7th Division.

0779 United States. 13th, The Devil's Own Grim Reapers. no publisher, 1952.
Yearbook history of the aerial operations of the 13th Bombardment Squadron.

0780 United States Army 1st Cavalry Division. The First Team: The First Cavalry Division in Korea 18 July 1950-18 January 1952. Atlanta: Love, 1952.
A social history of the 1st Cavalry Division from its commitment in the first weeks of the war, to its return to Japan in 1951.

0781 United States Army Signal Corps, 51st Signal Battalion. History of Fifty-First Signal Battalion . . . Signal Corps, United States Army. no publisher, 1959.
Yearbook history of limited value.

0782 United States Army 3rd Division. 3rd Infantry Division in Korea. Tokyo: no publisher, 1955.
Yearbook history which concentrates on early contribution.

0783 United States Army 25th Infantry Division. Tropic Lightning in Korea. Atlanta: Love, 1954.
Yearbook history of limited value.

0784 United States Army 25th Infantry Division. Twenty-fifth Infantry Division: Tropic Lightning. Paducah, Kentucky: Turner Publishing Company, 1988.
Yearbook history which is more informative than most.

0785 United States Army 24th Infantry Division. 24th Infantry Division, 16th Anniversary. no publisher, 1957.
A basic history of the 24th during World War II and Korea; one of the better unit histories.

0786 United States Engineer Agency for Resources Inventories. <u>Landmine</u> <u>and Countermine Warfare: Significant Landmines and Booby Traps</u> <u>Employed by U. S. and Allied Forces 1940-1970</u>. Washington, D. C.: Engineer Agency for Resources Inventories, 1972.

  Rather involved explanation of countermine measures used in the World War, Korea, and Vietnam.

0787 Ward, Orlando. <u>Small Unit Actions in Korea</u>. Washington, D. C.: Government Printing Office, 1953.

  Good quick reference to small units operating in the Korean War.

0788 Warren, Shelby P. <u>24th Infantry Division. A Brief History: The Story</u> <u>of the 24th Division's Actions in the Korean Conflict</u>. Tokyo: 24th Division, 1954.

  Brief yearbook presentation.

0789 Whitesides, Joe E. <u>204th Field Artillery Battalion in Korea</u>. Utah: no publisher, 1990.

  This yearbook history of the Utah National Guard in Korea has little to recommend it.

0790 Wood, Lt. Col. "Artillery Support For The Brigade In Korea" <u>Marine</u> <u>Corps Gazette</u> (June 1951): 16-23.

  Very interesting account of an artillery commander who set up the first marine artillery support for the brigade when it landed during August of 1950 in defense of the Pusan Perimeter.

Navy

0791 "Air War in Korea" <u>Naval Aviation News</u> (October 1950): 20-21.

  A mini-look at the role of jet panthers, F4Vs and helicopters in naval air action in Korea.

0792 Alexander, Joseph H. and Merrill L. Bartlett. <u>Sea Soldiers in the Cold</u> <u>War: Amphibious Warfare 1945-1991</u>. Annapolis, Maryland: Naval Institute Press, 1995.

  An operational history of amphibious warfare as employed by major powers through the Cold War.

0793 Amador, Richard. <u>The United States Ship Cruise Book, 1950-1951</u>. Tokyo: Toppan, 1951.

  Account of a World War II carrier, USS <u>Essex</u>, which was converted for duty in Korea.

0794 Amphibious Construction Battalion One. Tokyo: Toppan, 1952.
	Discusses the early years at Korea primarily building air fields for the ground forces in Korea.

0795 Beach, Edward L. The United States Navy: 200 Years. New York: Henry Holt and Co., 1986.
	An excellent one volume history of the Navy by a fine historian. Provides good general coverage of naval action in Korea.

0796 Berry, James. "Operation Fishnet" United States Naval Institute Proceedings 116 12 (December 1990): 107-108.
	One of the few accounts of the attempt to weaken North Korea by interfering with their fishing operations. Very interesting account.

0797 Blanton, Sankey L. "Damnreservists" United States Naval Institute Proceedings 116 10 (October 1990): 83-86.
	Discusses the value of the reserves who served in Korea. Blanton questions if reserves will be available in future conflicts.

0798 Blanton, Stephen Dwight. "A Study of the United States Navy's Minesweeping Efforts in the Korean War" MA thesis, Texas Tech University, 1993.
	MA: minesweeping

0799 Blassingame, Wyatt. The U. S. Frogmen of World War II. New York: Random House, Landmark Books, 1964.
	This is a book for youth, and very generalized, but it is one of the few which deal with the Underwater Demolition Teams in Korea. Includes a list of personnel who were involved in the early mine-clearing activities.

0800 Blood, Christopher G., Richard T. Jolly and Michael S. Odowick. An Analysis of Shipboard Casualty Incidence During Naval Combat Operations. San Diego, California: Naval Health Research Center, 1995.
	Data and analysis of on-board casualties during several combat situations, including the Korean War.

0801 Burns, Harry A. "The Case of the Blind Pilot" Saturday Evening Post 225 22 (1952): 41, 66-67, 69.
	A pilot for Yellow Devil Squadron was talked down by a fellow pilot after he was hit and blinded.

0802 Cagle, Malcolm W. and Frank A. Manson. The Sea War in Korea. Annapolis, Maryland: United States Naval Institute, 1957.

The naval war in Korea is excellently covered. Inchon was a major event for the navy and an account of the amphibious effort is considered in detail. Includes MacArthur's overwhelming "preoccupation with defense of his coastline."

0803 "Carrier Strike" Military Review 32 10 (January 1953): 57-62.
     Narration of the 7th Fleet activities in providing close air support for ground troops.

0804 Clark, Joseph J. "Jocko" with Clark G. Reynolds. Carrier Admiral. New York: David McKay Company, 1967.
     A biography of Admiral Joseph Clark, who served in carrier command.

0805 Cole, Charles. Korea Remembered: Enough of a War. Las Cruces, New Mexico: Yucca Tree Press, 1995.
     Story of Charles Cole and the first tour of the USS Ozbourn 1950-1951. A lot of material on Underwater Demolition Teams.

0806 Coletta, Paolo E. "The Defense Unification Battle, 1947-1950: The Navy" Prologue 7 1 (1975): 6-17.
     Discusses why navy and marines were understrength at the beginning of the Korean War, blaming an ill-conceived effort to unify the services under the Secretary of Defense.

0807 Cruise Book of U. S. S. Bairoko (CVE-115) from September 1950 to August 1951. no publisher, 1951.
     Cruise book of the USS Bairoko tour in Korea.

0808 Cruise Book of the USS Essex (CVA-9) and Carrier Air Task Group Two: Second Korean Cruise. Nashville, Tennessee: Benson, 1953.
     Narrative of a carrier support cruise in 1952.

0809 The Cruise of the U. S. S. Los Angeles, 1952-1953. Long Beach, California: Press-Telegram, 1953.
     Cruise book of the heavy cruiser USS Los Angeles in Korea.

0810 Davis, Vincent. The Admirals Lobby. Chapel Hill: University of North Carolina Press, 1967.
     Author attempts to untangle the naval effort to keep the Navy strong during the unification crisis.

0811 Denson, John. "Captain Thach's Phantom Carrier" Collier's 126 (October 14, 1950): 18-19, 52-56.

Describes the operations of the escort carrier (CVE) USS <u>Sicily</u> and its destroyer escort, USS <u>James E. Kyes</u> and USS <u>Doyle</u> which formed a task group designed to harass the enemy's east coast, striking with phantom-like characteristics.

0812 Doyle, James H. and Arthur J. Mayer. "December 1950 at Hungnam" <u>United States Naval Institute Proceedings</u> 105 4 (April 1979): 44-65.

Discusses the mass evacuation of the Army X Corps, and acknowledges the vital role played by the Navy.

0813 Edwards, Harry W. "A Naval Lesson of the Korean Conflict" <u>United States Naval Institute Proceedings</u> 80 (December 1954): 1337-1340.

A short but good article on the use of mines, mine warfare, and defense. Calls for a new approach to clearing naval minefields.

0814 Fane, Francis D. and Don Moore. <u>The Naked Warriors</u>. New York: Appleton-Century-Crofts, Inc., 1956.

A brief personalized history of the Underwater Demolition Teams operating during World War II and Korea. A chapter deals with the Korean period of these unusual underwater warriors.

0815 <u>Fighting Saints' Third Korean Cruise: USS St. Paul CA 73</u>. San Angelo, Texas: Newsfoto Publishing Company, 1953.

Cruise account of the <u>St. Paul</u> which includes Korean War involvement.

0816 "Frogmen in Korea" <u>Collier's</u> 131 8 (1953): 50-51.

Popularized account of Navy frogmen (SEALS) in Korea. Includes an account of Operation Fishnet.

0817 Griffin, Harry K. "The Navy in Korean Waters" <u>Army Information Digest</u> 6 12 (December 1951): 12-22.

A brief but inclusive account of the navy during the first year of the war. Griffin points out that the navy was heavily involved in the war from the very beginning, offering support both in terms of firepower on selected targets and logistical support to the ground troops. This work includes material on amphibious supply, off-shore bombardment, and minesweeping.

0818 Hayler, W. B. "Hail, Hail, the Gang's All There" <u>United States Naval Institute Proceedings</u> 79 (July 1953): 749-751.

Considers the significant role played by the United States naval forces during the Korean War.

0819 Howarth, Stephen. To Shining Sea: A History of the United States Navy, 1775-1991. New York: Random House, 1991.

Excellent history of the United States Navy, showing the growth of naval resources and tactics. Chapter 18 gives a good overview of the Korean War.

0820 Hoyt, Edwin P. Carrier Wars. New York: McGraw-Hill Publishing, 1989.

The Navy had three fast carriers and two escort carriers as a part of the Inchon landing and air cover. Hoyt discusses the Korean War in chapter 19 giving a good overview of the place of carrier action.

0821 Hoyt, Edwin P. Pacific Destiny: The Story of America in the Western Sea from the Early 1800s to the 1980s. New York: W. W. Norton and Company, 1981.

The story of the American presence in the Western sea. Chapter 30 deals with involvement in the Korean War. Generally such a wide view that it offers little which is not covered well elsewhere.

0822 "Iowa—Class Battleships Off Korea" United States Naval Institute Proceedings 78 (July 1952): 785-789.

Discusses the role of USS Missouri, New Jersey, Wisconsin, and primarily the Iowa in support of ground forces.

0823 Isenberg, Michael T. Shield of the Republic: The United States Navy in an Era of Cold War and Violent Peace. volume 1, 1945-1962. New York: St. Martin's Press, 1993.

Very interesting, if strongly opinionated, general history of the United States Navy with good coverage of the Korean War.

0824 Jenkins, R. A. V. "The Navy in Korea" Canadian Shipping (March 1952).

Short account of the Canadian Navy's small but useful force in Korea.

0825 Karig, Walter, Malcolm W. Cagle and Frank Manson. Battle Report volume 6 — The War in Korea. New York: Rinehart, 1952.

Eyewitness account of the Navy during the first six months of the Korean War.

0826 Karneke, Joseph S. as told to Victor Bosen. Navy Diver. New York: G. P. Putnam's, 1959.

The account of individuals working in anti-mine operations in Korea, primarily in Wonsan Harbor. One of the few such accounts available.

0827 Kelly, Orr. Brave Men, Dark Waters: The Untold Story of the Navy SEALS. Novato, California: Presidio Press, 1992.

Chapter five deals with Underwater Demolition Teams (the pre-SEAL designation) in Korea and with their efforts at and for the Inchon landing. A heavily personalized account of a small and unique force which, other than Inchon, served primarily as reconnaissance and interdiction forces. Three UDT groups were available during the war.

0828 Kim, Sang Mo. "The Implications of the Sea War in Korea" Naval War College Review 20 (Summer 1967): 105-139.

A South Korean naval officer discusses the lessons learned during the war, including the significance of amphibious operations.

0829 King, D. L. Korean Encore: The Story of the USS Philippine Sea Berkeley, California: Lederer, 1952.

Describes a second tour of this carrier, 31 December 1951-9 August 1952.

0830 Kinney, Sheldon. "All Quiet at Wonsan" United States Naval Institute Proceedings 80 (August 1954): 859-867.

Concerns the 861-day siege of Wonsan harbor and the ships which manned this strategic blockade.

0831 Knight, Charlotte. "Men of the Mine Sweepers" Collier's 128 19 (November 10, 1951): 13-15, 66-68.

Account of the mine sweepers which were responsible for clearing the harbors off the coast of Korea. Basically a high-risk "one-on-one" exercise. Seems to be an acknowledgement of the high percentage of naval casualties.

0832 The Korean Cruise of the USS Tingey DD 539. San Diego, California: Davidson, 1951.

Brief discussion of destroyer action during the Korean War.

0833 Korean Cruise USS St. Paul CA 73. Berkeley, California: Lederer, 1951.

The account of the USS St. Paul, one of the first heavy cruisers to arrive in Korean waters, 12 August 1950, in support of ground troops. It continued on station until 21 May 1951.

0834 Lansdown, John. With the Carriers in Korea: The Fleet Air Arm Story—1950-1953. Worcester: Square One Publications, 1992.

A long-awaited and much heralded study of the use of carriers in Korea, and their role in the air war. British in approach and concern but of value for any serious look at the naval air war.

0835 List, William F. History of the First USS Dextrous: With Collateral Notes on Minesweepers, Minesweeping, and Collateral Events. Linthicum, Maryland: W. F. List, 1994.

Very informative account of Dextrous (AM341) and the minesweeping operation during World War II and Korea.

0836 Lott, Arnold S. Most Dangerous Sea. Annapolis, Maryland: United States Naval Institute, 1959.

A personal, and interesting, history of the United States Navy anti-mine warfare. In chapter 16, "A Few Minesweepers," Lott tells the story of the Korean campaign and the effort of the understrength minesweepers to clear and keep clear, the harbors of Korea.

0837 Lovell, Kenneth C. "Navy Engineer Support in Korea" Military Engineer 44 (November-December 1952): 413-417.

A rare account of the significant actions of the 104th Naval Construction Battalion (Seabees) who were in direct support during the Inchon landing.

0838 Marcus, J. W. USS Rochester CA-124 Operation Korea. New York: Yearbooks, 1951.

Fairly good account of the heavy cruiser in Korea 1950-1951, but is limited by its "yearbook" characteristics.

0839 McGraw, Harry. "The Seabees—1952" Military Engineer 44 298 (1952): 81-84.

Account of construction battalions in Korea, focuses on the fact that sixty percent of the Seabees were reservists.

0840 McMaster, Donald W. "The Evolution of Tactical Airpower—With Particular Emphasis Upon Its Application By the U. S. Navy and U. S. Marine Corps in the Korean War, June 1950-July 1953" MA thesis, University of Maryland, 1959.

Looks at air tactics during the Korean War and how they were modified to meet the changing nature of the war.

0841 McMullen, Robert A. and Nicholas A. Canzona. "Wolmi-do: Turning the Key" United States Naval Institute Proceedings 82 3 (March 1956): 290-297.

Up until 10 September 1950, the North Koreans were having a good war. Then the bombardment of Wolmi-do began. Indepth account of the planning for, and execution of, the taking of the island Wolmi-do was the necessary first step in the Inchon landing.

0842 Meacham, James. "Four Mining Campaigns: An Historical Analysis of the Decisions of the Commanders" Naval War College Review 19 (June 1967): 75-129.

A comparison of the effects of four mining campaigns, with an analysis of the wisdom of the commanders involved in handling the situation. In the process the author provides a good look at the Inchon versus Wonsan mine situation and the lack of preparation on the side of the United States.

0843 Melia, Tamara Moser. "Damn the Torpedoes": A Short History of U. S. Naval Mine Countermeasures, 1777-1991. Washington, D. C.: Naval Historical Center, 1991.

A brief, but informative look at the role of mines, and how the United States developed successful counter-measures. Contains good coverage on Korea.

0844 Miller, Max. I'm Sure We've Met Before: The Navy in Korea. New York: E. P. Dutton & Company, 1951.

An interesting and firsthand account of the Navy's role in the early days of the Korean War. In command of men who thought they were heading home for a long peace, Lieutenant Commander Miller recounts the difficulties while the Navy provided firepower, and supplies, during the dark days, and the eventual breakout.

0845 "Naval Air War" Naval Aviation News (December 1952): 1-7.

Claims that one-third of all combat strikes in Korea were naval. Good for statistics and names of air group commanders.

0846 One Year of Naval Operations in Korea. Annapolis, Maryland: Nimitz Library, 1951.

The USS Juneau fired the opening salvo of the war which, for the Navy, eventually expended more than seventy million pounds of high explosives in support of troops. The first year of the war, including Inchon, is carefully chronicled.

0847 Phillips, Richard B. "The Siege of Wonsan" Army Information Digest 8 11 (November 1953): 39-47.

Written before the seige was over but is very descriptive of what would turn out to be the longest blockade in American naval history.

0848 Plosz, A. J. "The Navy's Unorthodox War" Public Affairs 13 (Summer 1951): 25-32.

Looks at the unusual nature of the expectations placed on the Navy in Korea.

0849 Potter, Elmer B. The Naval Academy Illustrated History of the United States Navy. New York: Galahad Books, 1971.

A standard book included here because of the excellent sea maps and description of the navy role during the Inchon landing.

0850 Potter, Elmer B., editor. Sea Power: A Naval History. 2nd edition, Annapolis, Maryland: Naval Institute Press, 1981.

Interesting account of sea power which shows America in a comparison with the navies of other nations.

0851 Potter, Elmer B. and John R. Fredland. The United States and World Sea Power. Englewood Cliffs, New Jersey: Prentice-Hall, 1955.

A brief and general look at naval history as a focus of world power: includes the Korean War.

0852 Rairden, P. W., Jr. "The Junior Officer in Mine Warfare" United States Naval Institute Proceedings 79 9 (September 1953): 977-979.

Discusses the fact that so many minesweepers were commanded by officers who were gaining highly valuable sea combat experience. During the inter-war period mine sweepers were out of the main line of career growth.

0853 Ready Deck: This Is the USS Princeton, 1952. Tokyo: Toppan, 1952.

Daily account cruise book of carrier CV-37 during three cruises off Korean waters.

0854 Reilly, John C. Operational Experience of Fast Battleships: World War II, Korea, Vietnam. Washington, D. C.: Naval History Center, 1982.

Discusses the return of the battleship to operational command during the Korean War.

0855 Russell, Edward C. H.M.C.S Haida: A Brief History. Canada: no publisher, 1963.

A quick look at the service of the Canadian ship HMCS Haida.

0856 Ryan, Paul B. First Line of Defense: The U. S. Navy Since 1945. Stanford, California: Hoover Institution Press, 1981.

The Navy had to make some major adjustments after World War II, and was at a low ebb when called on for a quick response to needs in Korea.

0857 Salvo!: the USS New Jersey (BB62), November, 1950-December, 1951. no publisher, 1951.

Roster of officers and consideration of ship operations during the Korean War tour.

0858 Schratz, Paul R. Submarine Commander: A Story of World War II and Korea. Lexington, Kentucky: University Press of Kentucky, 1988.

While generally an account of the exploits of Captain Schratz during two wars, not unlike many memoirs available, it does introduce the interesting fact of submarine use in a ground war. The USS Pickerel was involved in some briefly related activities, and the author comments on the activities of other subs which were more directly involved with diversionary tactics, surveys, and secret landings.

0859 Scott-Moncrieff, A. K. "Navy Operations in Korean Waters" Journal Royal United Service Institution 98 (May 1953): 218-227.

Excellent account of the Commonwealth involvement associated with the United Nations command. The British response was very timely and significant.

0860 Shane, Patrick C. III "The 13 Wild Weeks of the USS Princeton" Saturday Evening Post 225 37 (1953): 28-29, 74-76, 80.

Tale of a carrier career from mothballs to combat duty in the Korean War.

0861 Smith, M. S. The Korea Cruise USS Philippine Sea CV-47. Berkeley, California: Lederer, 1951.

From July 1950 to June 1951 the USS Philippine Sea was one of the carriers operating off the coast, sailing in support of the ground troops and taking part in the Inchon landing.

0862 Tarpaulin (pseudonym). "His Majesty's Ship Ladybird" Naval Review (1992): 67-69.

A brief account of the ship which served as the headquarters for the British forces at Sasebo, Japan.

0863 Terzibaschitsch, Stefan. Aircraft Carriers of the U. S. Navy. New York: Mayflower Books, 1980.

Source book on the development of United States carriers and their wide use in Korea.

0864 Terzibaschitsch, Stefan. Cruisers of the U. S. Navy 1922-1962. Annapolis, Maryland: Naval Institute Press, 1988.

Traces the development of the cruiser with some brief coverage of Korea.

0865 Terzibaschitsch, Stefan. <u>Escort Carriers and Aviation Support Ships of the U. S. Navy</u>. Annapolis, Maryland: Naval Institute Press. 1981.
Traces the development of the escort carriers and includes some brief coverage of the Korean period.

0866 <u>"Theseus" Goes East, Being the Story of the Cruise of H. M. S. "Theseus" to the Far East for the Korean Operations, 1950/51, and an Account of Previous Ships of This Name</u>. Portsmouth: Acme Printing Company, 1951.
Brief account of British ships named <u>Theseus</u> and the role of the HMS <u>Theseus</u> during operations off Korean waters.

0867 <u>USS Bon Homme Richard CVA-31 Second Korean Cruise</u>. Tokyo: Toppan, 1952.
Narrative account of the carrier's second combat tour, yearbook variety.

0868 <u>U. S. S. Boxer: Korean Cruise, 1953</u>. Tokyo: Toppan, 1953
Narrative account of the United States carrier CVS-21 off Korean waters, yearbook variety.

0869 <u>USS Haven (AH-12), 1950-1951</u>. Berkeley, California: Lederer, Street & Zeus Company, Inc., 1951.
Narrative account of this major hospital ship which served in Korean waters during the first year of the Korean War.

0870 <u>U. S. S. Princeton, CV-37: Korea 1950-1951</u>. Berkeley, California: Lederer, 1951.
Tells of the activation of this mothballed ship in July 1950, and its service in Korea from December of 1950.

0871 <u>U. S. S. Wisconsin BB-64: Anniversary Edition 3 March 1951 (to) 3 March 1952</u>. Tokyo: Toppan, 1952.
Narrative and yearbook account of the battleship USS <u>Wisconsin</u> in Korean action.

0872 United States Navy, Pacific Fleet and Pacific Ocean Area. <u>CINCPACFLT Interim Evaluation Reports, Korea, 1950-1953</u>. Wilmington, Delaware: Scholarly Resources (Microfilm).
Valuable evaluation reports accompanied by temporary guide. Also microfilmed, six reels.

0873 United States Navy. U. S. S. Walke Korean Cruise, October 1950 to August 1951. Berkeley, California: Lederer, 1951.
    Narrative and yearbook account of the USS Walke's Korean service.

0874 Vernor, W. H., Jr. "Standby Squadron" United States Naval Institute Proceedings 78 7 (July 1952): 729-739.
    United States Navy Attack Squadron 702, a reserve outfit reviewed from training to assignment on the USS Boxer.

0875 Wages, C. J. "Mines. . .The Weapons that Wait" United States Naval Institute Proceedings 88 (May 1962): 103-113.
    Naval mines are the ideal weapon for "have-not" nations. And in the Korean War America lost control of the seas to a nation without a navy using pre-World War I weapons. The United Nations were not prepared for the North Korean and Russian use of mines, and it cost the United States temporary control of the sea.

0876 Weber, M. L. USS Rochester CA-124: Operation Korea, 1951-1952. San Diego, California: Book, 1952.
    Discusses naval fire support missions for ground troops performed by the fleet, and the Rochester.

0877 Worden, William L. "The Trick that Won Seoul" Saturday Evening Post 223 20 (1950): 29, 146-148.
    Discusses the role of the USS Collett (DD) and other ships involved in the attack on Wolmi-do Island prior to the Inchon invasion.

Marines

0878 Aguirre, Emilio. We'll Be Home For Christmas: A True Story of the United States Marine Corps in the Korean War. New York: Greenwich, 1959.
    The exploits of a marine from Company G, 3rd Battalion, 7th Marines who took part in the Inchon landing and went on to take part in the Chosin Reservoir retreat.

0879 Anderson, Burdon F. We Claim the Title. Aptos, California: Tracy Publication, 1994.
    A Marine's account of the 1st Division Marine campaigns and regimental histories of units in Korea.

0880 Bartlett, Tom. "The Fabulous, Frozen Fighting First" Leatherneck 63 (December 1980): 16-21.

Discusses the Inchon phases of the 1st Marine Division which was hastily reorganized and thrown into battle.

0881 Blakeney, Jane. Heroes, U. S. Marine Corps, 1861-1955. Washington, D. C.: Blakeney Publishers, 1957.
Primarily a biographical history of the development, and activities, of the Marine Corps including good Korean coverage.

0882 Braestrup, Peter. "Back to the Trenches" Marine Corps Gazette (March 1955).
A good look at the stalemate nature of the later war in Korea. Compared it to fighting in World War I.

0883 Brainard, Morgan. Then They Called For The Marines: A Marine Rifle Company in Korea, 1950-1951. Rutland, Vermont: Academy Books, 1989. 2nd edition. Formerly published as Men in Low Cut Shoes: A Marine Rifle Company in Korea.
A rather standard account of the men in a rifle company, from the marine landing past the Seoul campaign.

0884 Canzona, Nicholas. "Dog Company's Charge" United States Naval Institute Proceedings 82 7 (July 1956): 1203-1212.
An account of Company D, 2nd Battalion, 5th Regiment and the taking of Seoul following the Inchon invasion. The action, led by a rifle company, showed that five years into the atomic age, the work of clearing a city was still to be done by rifle squads. A point by point account of the action.

0885 Canzona, Nicholas A. "Marines Land at Pusan, Korea, August 1950" Marine Corps Gazette 69 (August 1985): 42-46+.
An interview with this famous military historian about the landings and early fighting of the marines who were first deployed at the Pusan Perimeter in Korea.

0886 Canzona, Nicholas A. "Reflections on Korea" Marine Corps Gazette 35 11 (1951): 56-65.
Focuses on shortages of equipment and the development of tactics during the early period of the war.

0887 Chung, Ul Mun. "Letter From Almond" Leatherneck 36 4 (1953): 34-35.
A Korean interpreter comments on his early months with the 7th Marine Regiment which arrived in time for the Inchon landing.

0888 Condit, Kenneth W. and Ernest H. Giusti. "Marine Air at the Chosin Reservoir" and "Marine Air Covers the Breakout" Marine Corps Gazette 36 6 (July-August 1952): 18-27.

Story of the 1st Marine Wing which provided primary air-ground support following the invasion at Inchon.

0889 Conner, John. "The New Breed" Collier's 126 (1950): 71-72.

Accounts for the 1st Marine Brigade during the first two months of the Korean War, including time along the defensive lines of the Pusan Perimeter, and prior to the pull-out for the Inchon landing.

0890 Davis, William J. "The Bloody Breakfast" United States Naval Institute Proceedings 79 7 (1953): 737-739.

Recounts the suffering of thosewho broke out of the Chosin trap in 1950 and made the difficult retreat and evacuation.

0891 Denson, John. "What Hurt Was to See Us Retreat" Collier's 126 10 (1950): 17, 58.

This is a description of the first contacts of United States forces with the North Korean Army, and of Sergeant Leonard Smith, one of the first Marines to be wounded. Expresses considerable shock over the retreat of Americans.

0892 Fenton, Francis I. "Changallon Valley" Marine Corps Gazette 35 (1951): 48-53.

Describes the activities of the men of Company B, 1st Marine Battalion, 5th Marines who fought a fierce battle during the ambush at Sachon on the 12th of August 1950.

0893 Geer, Andrew. The New Breed, The Story of the U. S. Marines in Korea. New York: Harper and Brothers, 1952.

This is the story of the United States Marines in Korea. While the Marines came reasonably late to the battle, early August 1950, their presence made a considerable difference both in terms of morale and in terms of available fighting men. The 1st Marine Brigade was pushed into battle almost immediately upon arrival, and held their section of the Pusan Perimeter during some of the heaviest fighting.

0894 Geer, Andrew. "Reckless, the Pride of the Marines" Saturday Evening Post 226 4 (1954): 31, 184-186.

Short narrative about "Reckless," a mule who carried ammo for the Marines of the 1st Division.

0895 Giusti, Ernest Henry. <u>The Mobilization of the Marine Corps Reserve in the Korean Conflict: 1950-1951</u>. Washington, D. C.: United States Marine Corps, G-3 Division Headquarters, 1953.

Marine Corps historical reference pamphlet which describes the recall of the Marine reservists who eventually formed the 1st Division.

0896 Hammel, Eric. "Hill 1282" <u>Leatherneck</u> 67 12 (December 1984): 26-31.

In November and December 1950, thousands of Communist People's Liberation Army soldiers waited to spring an awesome trap on the First Marine Division. Later known as Frozen Chosin.

0897 Heinl, Robert D. <u>Soldiers of the Sea: The United States Marine Corps, 1775-1962</u>. Annapolis, Maryland: United States Naval Institute, 1962.

An excellent one-volume history of the United States Marine Corps. Obviously written in support of the Marine Corps—and to defend their continued existence in the face of opposition—but nevertheless an informative account of the many actions successfully carried out. The author uses this work to accuse a wide variety of persons with trying to get rid of the marines, for a variety of political, as well as military reasons.

0898 Hicks, Norman W. "U.S. Marine Operations in Korea, 1952-1953" MA thesis, University of Maryland, 1962.

Discusses combat at an outpost manned by United States Marines the last year of the war.

0899 Johnstone, John H. <u>A Brief History of the 1st Marines</u>. Washington, D. C.: United States Marine Corps, Historical Branch G-3, 1968.

Short, semi-official account of the 1st Marine Division from conception to Korea.

0900 Klimp, Jack J. "The Battle for Seoul: Marine and MOUT (Military Operations in Urbanized Territory)" <u>Marine Corps Gazette</u> 65 (November 1981): 79-82.

Discusses the use of "Military Operations in Urbanized Territory" in the Seoul campaign, and makes the case for urbanized units in the Marine Corps.

0901 Krulak, Lt. Gen. Victor H., USMC Ret. <u>First to Fight: An Inside View of the U. S. Marine Corps</u>. Annapolis, Maryland: Naval Institute Press, 1984.

Good, but not such an insider view. Almost a public relations piece.

0902 Larkin, William T. <u>U. S. Marine Aircraft, 1914-1959.</u> Concord, California: Aviation History Publications, 1959.

Good detailed account of naval and marine aircraft used in the growing use of the Marine's air arm.

0903 "Marine Muscle Heads into War: 1st Division Men Sail for Korea" Life 29 (July 24, 1950): 28-29.
In fact it was a cover story as a quickly gathered band of Marines, the Provisional Brigade, headed for Korea. The rest of the Division came two months later.

0904 Martin, Harold H. "The Ordeal of Marine Squad 2" Saturday Evening Post 223 (1950): 24-25, 126-130, 133.
Martin follows the action of a marine rifle squad from mid July when they arrived, until 17 August 1950. Involved in heavy fighting the squad lost four who died and five who were seriously wounded.

0905 McClellan, Thomas L. "Operation Bumblebee: How the U. S. Marine Corps Developed Airmobile Tactics during the Korean War" United States Army Aviation Digest (June 1988): 38-44.
Well-prepared analysis of the development of airmobile tactics used in Korea, and later United States involvement.

0906 McDowell, Edwin. To Keep Our Honor Clean. New York: Vanguard, 1980.
A critical, loving account of a Marine recruit as he moves from basic training into combat.

0907 Mersky, Peter B. U. S. Marine Corps Aviation—1912 to the Present. Annapolis, Maryland: Nautical and Aviation Publishing Company of America, 1983.
A history of Marine aviation as it developed, and the growing role of the use of air support and the plane designed to be used in this fashion.

0908 Millett, Allan R. Semper Fidelis: The History of the United States Marine Corps. New York: Free Press, 1980, 1991.
Nicely researched and written one-volume work. Good strong chapter on the Korean period.

0909 Montross, Lynn. Cavalry of the Sky: The Story of U. S. Marine Combat Helicopters. New York: Harper and Brothers, 1954.
A brief history of the development of helicopter combat units, the training, and their deployment and use in Korea. Montross does his usual indepth research and is an excellent source of the use of helicopters for both combat and rescue. When MacArthur asked for the marines, he included in his request the first active helicopter unit.

0910 Montross, Lynn. "Fleet Marine Force Korea, I" United States Naval Institute Proceedings 79 8 (August 1953): 829-841. Part II in 79 9 (September 1953): 995.

First part of a two-part account of the marines in Korea. This first section contains a detailed account of the preparations for, and the execution of, the landing at Inchon and the Kimpo/Seoul campaign. Continues to Hungnam.

0911 Montross, Lynn and Nicholas A. Canzona. U. S. Marine Operations in Korea, 1950-1953. volume 1 "The Pusan Perimeter" Washington, D. C.: Historical Branch, Headquarters G-3, United States Marine Corps, 1954.

A detailed account of the United States Marine contribution to the Korean War from their first encounter with communist troops, until the second battle of the Naktong River. Operations of the 1st Provisional Brigade and Marine Air Group 33 from their landing 2 August 1950 until their withdrawal on 13 September 1950.

0912 Montross, Lynn and Nicholas A. Canzona. U. S. Marine Operations in Korea, 1950-1953. volume 2. "Inchon-Seoul Operation" Washington, D. C.: Government Printing Office, 1955.

A moment-by-moment narrative of the Marine landings at Inchon followed-up by the campaign against Seoul. An excellent account by two distinguished military historians. Appendix includes lists of units involved, officers, ships, etc.

0913 Murphy, Jack. History of the U. S. Marines. New York: Exeter Books, 1984. Revised and updated. Greenwich, Connecticut: Brompton Books, 1997.

A general illustrated history which deals with the Korean experience (chapter 5) and provides a very good description of the marine aspects of the Inchon landing, all supported with illustrations.

0914 Nicholson, Dennis D. "SOP: Night Raids" Marine Corps Gazette 39 3 (1955): 20-27.

A narrative and evaluation of Marine night raids on enemy positions, describes standard operating procedure.

0915 Owen, Joseph R. Colder Than Hell: A Marine Rifle Company Chosin Reservoir. Annapolis, Maryland: Naval Institute Press, 1996.

Owen describes the combat experiences during the early months of the Korean War. His descriptions of Chosin is long on Marine success and all but forgets the role of the Army 7th and 3rd Divisions in the success of the Chosin withdrawal.

0916 Parry, Francis F. "Marine Artillery in Korea: Part I, Ready or Not" Marine Corps Gazette 71 6 (June 1987): 47-52.

Brief memoirs of a man who was a battalion commander of a marine artillery outfit. Researchers often forget that the marines provided much of their own artillery support.

0917 Rawlins, Eugene W. Marines and Helicopters, 1946-1962. Washington, D. C.: History and Museums Division, Headquarters United States Marine Corps, 1976.

Describes the development of the helicopter and the innovations of air and ground combat uses from conceptualization through procurement to training in the Marine Corps.

0918 Reserve Officers of Public Affairs Unit 4-1. The Marine Corps Reserve: A History. Washington, D. C.: Division of Reserve, Headquarters, United States Marine Corps, 1966.

Chapter 8, "Korea," deals with the efforts to rebuild the Marine Corps in time to respond to General MacArthur's call for a Marine division. It was necessary to dig deeply into the reserve system to meet the demand for troops. The chapter on the recall for the Korean War, and the immediate involvement of reserves in combat, is a strong argument in favor of a ready reserve.

0919 Saluzzi, Joseph A. Red Blood . . . Purple Hearts: The Marines in the Korean War. Owings Mills, Maryland: Watermark Press, 1989; Brooklyn, New York: Eagle Productions, 1993.

Describes Marine activities and the Purple Heart, the medal which represents combat casualties.

0920 Senich, Peter R. U. S. Marine Corps Scout-Sniper: World War II and Korea. Boulder, Colorado: Paladin Press, 1993.

Interesting account of Marine snipers in World War II and Korea, dealing with equipment, supplies, and the rifles.

0921 Speights, R. J. Roster of the 1st Provisional Marine Brigade, Reinforced for August and September 1950, While in Action in Korea. Austin, Texas: R. J. Speights, 1990.

Personal roster of the catch-all Provisional Marine Brigade which was hastily formed for service in Korea.

0922 Stickney, William W. "The Marine Reserves in Action" Military Affairs 17 1 (Spring 1953): 16-22.

The Marine Corps had been allowed to be essentially dissolved so, when MacArthur called for the 1st Marine Division it was necessary to quickly rebuild the Corps. This is the story of that Marine Corps mobilization (including the recall) during the early stages of the Korean War. Nearly fifty percent of all officers and men recalled and mobilized were essentially combat ready, and 2,881 were immediately assigned to the 1st Marine Division.

0923 Thach, John S. "'Right on the Button': Marine Close Air Support in Korea" United States Naval Institute Proceedings 101 (November 1975): 54-56.

An account of UMF-214 (the Black Sheep Squadron) which was on the carrier USS Sicily.

0924 Third Marine Division. Fleet Marine Force Pacific. Dallas: Taylor, 1953.

Primarily a souvenir booklet, privately printed. Of little value to the serious researcher.

0925 3rd Marine Division Public Information Office. 3rd Marine Division. Dallas: Taylor, 1952.

Brief history of the division during the last two years of the war. A public relational tool of minimal value.

0926 United States Marine Corps. Marine Corps Aircraft, 1913-1965. Washington, D. C.: Historical Branch, 1967.

Historical reference pamphlet on Marine aviation. Useful but contains little detail.

0927 United States Marine Corps. Historical Branch, G-3. Our First Year in Korea. Washington, D. C.: Marine Corps Headquarters, 1953.

Reprints from the Marine Corps Gazette, 1950-1953, covering the period the Marines were in Korea.

0928 Wells, H. B. "They Double in Brass" Leatherneck 36 1 (1953): 26-29.

The duties of the 1st Marine Division band members when not performing.

Air War

0929 Air Power in Action: Korea 1950-51. New York: Fairchild Engine and Airplane Corporation, 1951.

Reprint of October, November, and December issues of Pegasus in which air action during World War II, the Korean War, and the Vietnam War is discussed.

0930 Air University Quarterly Staff. "The Bridges of Sinanju and Yongmidong" <u>Air University Quarterly Review</u> 7 1 (1954): 15-34.
Narrative of the 1953 air operations more than one hundred miles behind enemy lines.

0931 "The Air-Ground Operation in Korea" <u>Air Force</u> 34 (1951): 19-58.
Devoted to a consideration of the role played by the Air Force in flying the ground support missions during the first six months of the Korean War. The article fails to discuss the fact that, because of command difficulties, it was necessary to remove the Air Force from the Inchon plan.

0932 Albert, Joseph L. and Billy C. Wylie. "Problems of Airfield Construction in Korea" <u>Air University Quarterly Review</u> 5 (Winter 1951-1952): 86-92.
The lack of adequate supplies and heavy equipment made airfield construction very difficult; but it was made easier by using traditional constructive methods of the Koreans.

0933 Albright, Joseph G. "Two Years of MiG Activity" <u>Air University Quarterly Review</u> 6 (Spring 1953): 88-89.
Narrative and statistical information about results of combat in Russian-built planes. Lists more than 1,000 destroyed or damage to 115 American planes.

0934 Allsuip, Dan. "Robinson Risner: Korean War Ace" <u>Airman</u> 31 (September 1987): 34.
This account of aerial combat is part of the revival of interest in Air Force history, in the Korean War, which emerged in the 1980s.

0935 Amody, Francis J. "Skynights, Nightmares and MiGs" <u>American Aviation Historical Society Journal</u> 34 (Winter 1989): 308-313.
More on the combat experiences of Air Force jets during the Korean air war.

0936 Amody, Francis J. "We Got Ours at Night: The Story of the Lockheed F-94 Starfire in Combat" <u>American Aviation Historical Society Journal</u> 27 2 (1982): 148-150.
Experiences of the 319th Fighter Interceptor Squadron flying the Lockheed F-94 Starfire.

0937 Baer, Bud. "Three Years of Air War in Korea" <u>American Aviation</u> (July 6, 1953): 20-21.
Brief, and not very successful, effort to summarize the complexities of the air war in Korea.

0938 Barcus, Glenn O. "Tally for TAC" Flying 53 (July 1953): 17, 65.
   Discusses the effectiveness of Tactical Air Command during final phases of the war; includes destruction statistics.

0939 Bauer, Eddy. "Trial of Strength in Korea" Intervia 53 (1950): 567-573.
   Swiss expert concludes that American air power was all that kept North Korea from overcoming the South Koreans.

0940 Black, Charles. "The Truth about Air Support" Flying 48 2 (1951): 11-15, 57-59.
   Looks at all branches which provided air support for ground troops.

0941 Blunk, Chester L. "Every Man a Tiger": The 731st USAF Night Intruders over Korea. Manhattan, Kansas: Sunflower University Press, 1987.
   A popular, if less than objective, account of the role of night fighters during the war.

0942 Brooks, James L. "That Day (Over the Yalu)" Aerospace Historian 22 2 (June 1975): 65-69.
   F-86 pilot tells of the early engagements between United States and North Korean pilots.

0943 Brown, David. The Seafire: The Spitfire that Went to Sea. Annapolis, Maryland: Naval Institute Press, 1989.
   Covers, in part three, the British role in deception, bombardment, and spotting during the Inchon campaign when this ocean-going Spitfire saw considerable action.

0944 Butler, Howard K. Army Aviation Organization and Ordnance: Aircraft Supply and Maintenance in Korea, 1950-1952. St. Louis, Missouri: United States Army Aviation Systems Command, 1988.
   Outlines the organization and delivery systems of aviation equipment and supplies.

0945 Butler, Howard K. Organization of Army Aviation, 1942-1953. volume 1. "Wars and Interludes" St. Louis, Missouri: United States Army Aviation Systems Command, 1988.
   Administrative history of aviation organization and command through and between wars.

0946 Cable, Donald. "Air Support in the Korean War" Aerospace History 16 (Summer 1969): 26-29.
   This article reflects a renewed interest in the air war in Korea, and recounts the successful role of air power in holding the communist tide.

0947 Cagle, Malcolm W. "Carrier Jets Over Korea" <u>Skyways</u> 10 7 (July 1951): 10-12, 57.

A brief popularized version of his excellent longer and more serious work, with Frank A. Manson, on the naval war in Korea.

0948 Cagle, Malcolm W. and Frank A. Manson. "Post Interdiction Carrier Operations in Korea" <u>United States Naval Institute Proceedings</u> 83 (July 1957): 699-712.

A description of carrier planes in an interdiction model, taken from the book, <u>The Sea War in Korea</u>.

0949 Clark, Mark. <u>Air-Ground Operations</u>. APO: Headquarters, Far East Command, 1952.

Discusses the need for unified operations and close air support

0950 Clark, Mark W. "What Kind of Air Support Does the Army Want? An Interview with General Mark W. Clark" <u>Air Force</u> 33 (1950): 24-25, 52.

Discusses the need for close support between ground troops and air cover. It is of considerable value because of Clark's well-informed account of close air support activity during the first few months of the war.

0951 Cleveland, William M. <u>Mosquitos in Korea</u>. Portsmouth: Peter E. Randall Publisher, 1991.

Published by the historian of the Mosquito Association, it provides an interesting and detailed account of the daily operations of these valuable plans.

0952 Cline, Tim. "Forward Air Control in the Korean War" <u>American Aviation Historical Society Journal</u> 21 (Fall 1976): 257-262.

Good, but brief, discussion of the highly difficult role of the air controller in the Korean War.

0953 Cole, James L., Jr. "Lamplighters & Gypsies" <u>Aerospace Historian</u> 20 (March 1973): 30-35.

Describes the use of the C-47 "Gooney Bird" to drop illumination flares for the B-29 target drops. This proved very successful.

0954 Collins, William R. "The Helicopter in Marine Operations" <u>Army Information Digest</u> 6 6 (1951): 47-53.

Describes the growing value of helicopters in Korea as a reconnaissance and evacuation tool.

0955 Cooling, Benjamin F. Case Studies in the Development of Close Air Support. Washington, D. C.: Office of United States Air Force History, 1990.

Review of the development and execution of close air-ground support missions which include some insights into the problems of unified command and inter-service problems.

0956 Craigie, Laurence C. "The Air War in Korea" Aeronautical Engineering Review 11 (June 1952): 26-31.

Brief technical review of the first two years in the Korean air war.

0957 Crews, Thomas. Thunderbolt Through Ripper: Joint Operations in Korea, 25 January-31 March 1951. Carlisle Barracks, Pennsylvania: Army War College, 1991.

A narrative account of joint operations under Ridgway during the "settlement" period of the Korean War.

0958 Davis, Larry. MiG Alley: Air-to-Air Combat Over Korea. Carrollton, Texas: Squadron/Signal Publications, 1978.

Technical and data information as well as a narrative of air combat.

0959 A Day by Day History of the Far East Air Forces Operations. United States: Far East Command, 1951.

History of Air Force operations which was written too early to be of much use.

0960 DeGovanni, George. Air Force Support of Army Ground Operations: Lessons Learned during World War II, Korea, and Vietnam. Carlisle Barracks, Pennsylvania: Army War College, 1989.

Research analysis of air-ground support in Korea which compares support in each of these wars.

0961 Dews, Edmund and Felix Kozaczka. Air Interdiction: Lessons from Past Campaigns. Santa Monica, California: Rand Corporation, 1981.

Research efforts to evaluate logistical interference by air. This process was less effective than at first believed.

0962 Dockery, Charles L. "Marine Air Over Korea" Marine Corps Gazette 69 12 (December 1985): 38-50.

The Marine Aircraft Wing flew combat missions in support of ground troops both during the landing and during the rest of the war. The account covers the Marine air wing in general.

0963 Dolan, Michael J. "Mosquito and Horsefly" <u>Combat Forces Journal</u> 2
7 (February 1952): 35-37.
    Army spotter planes (L5) worked so well in directing ground support
that the Air Force sent out mosquito planes to replace them performing air
observation duties.

0964 Dolan, Michael J. "What's Right and Wrong with Close Air Support"
<u>Combat Forces Journal</u> 1 12 (July 1951): 24-30.
    Evaluates close air support and finds it successful yet is critical of
communication equipment and styles.

0965 Dorn, W. J. Bryan and O. K. Armstrong. "The Great Lessons of Korea"
<u>Air Force</u> 34 (May 1951): 24-30.
    The report of two Congressmen who toured Korea to see "what we
can do next time;" they were very impressed with the destructive use of air
power.

0966 Dorr, Robert F. <u>The Korean Air War</u>. Osceola, Wisconsin: Motorbooks
International, 1994.
    Popularized and well illustrated account of air operations during the
Korean War.

0967 Dorr, Robert F., Jon Lake and Warren Thompson. <u>Korean War Aces</u>.
London: Osprey Publishers, 1994, 1995.
    Documents the exploits of United States, and some Soviet Union,
fighter aces. Written for juvenile audience.

0968 DuPre, Flint O. "Night Fighters in MiG Alley" <u>Air Force</u> 36 (November
1953): 29-30, 70.
    Joint air operations and improved radar made night flights possible
and taught the Air Force some necessary lessons.

0969 Eighth Army, Fifth Air Force Joint Air Ground. "The Expanding Air
Force: 1 January to 1 August 1951" <u>Air University Quality Review</u> 4 (1951):
97-110.
    Traces the rapid expansion of the Air Force following the outbreak
of war, including the creation of new commands.

0970 Evans, Douglas K. <u>Sabre Jets over Korea: A Firsthand Account</u>. Blue
Ridge Summit, Pennsylvania: TAB, 1984.
    Part of the popular literature of the war, interesting but of little
scholarly value.

0971 Falls, Robert H. The Mighty Air Farce — Nothing Too Low for Honor; A Documentary History of the Air Force Reserve Call Up During the Korean War. no publisher, 1970.

A collection of documents and letters between author and others about the poor performance of reservists in Korea.

0972 Far East Air Force Bomber Command. "Heavyweights over Korea" Air University Quarterly Review 7 (Spring 1954): 99-115.

A resume of B-29 deployment, tactics, and achievements during the Korean War.

0973 Farmer, James A. and M. J. Strumwasser. The Evolution of the Airborne Forward Air Controller: An Analysis of Mosquito Operations in Korea. Santa Monica, California: Rand Corporation, 1967.

Account of the emergence of the highly successful Mosquito Operation.

0974 Farris, Phillip. "Jet War" Air Force Magazine 73 6 (June 1990).

The Korean War witnessed the full emergence of jet aircraft in combat. Good general account.

0975 Finletter, Thomas K. "Air Power in the Korean Conflict" Vital Speeches of the Day (September 15, 1950): 732-735.

More a defense of, rather than a description of, the volume of air power. At this stage (1950) it was yet to be proven.

0976 Fithian, Ben. "The F-94, First Kill in Korea" Navigator 28 (Winter 1981): 15-18.

Re-opened the post-war discussion of jet use and tactics, as well as providing a popular story of the F-94 Sabre.

0977 Fleming, Kenneth. "Hell Run Over Korea" Leatherneck 33 10 (1950): 18-20.

Marine Corps planes undertook photo missions to provide intelligence for the United States troops. Discusses the difficulty for carrier-based air photographers who risked life and limb to provide clear pictures of United Nations military movement.

0978 Foley, Edward D. Equitatus Caeli, 1952. Tokyo: Kasai, 1953.

History of Marine Helicopter Transport Squadron 161 in Korea.

0979 Folson, S. B. "Korea—A Reflection From the Air" United States Naval Institute Proceedings 82 7 (July 1956): 733-735.

Folson contends the United Nations could not claim to have total air superiority, primarily because of the North Korean ability to move supplies at night. The United Nations inability to hit the enemy, meant the job could not be accomplished. In a very real sense, the effectiveness of the air war was reduced because of lack of targets.

0980 Ford, W. W. "Direct Support Aviation" Combat Forces Journal 1 8 (March 1951): 13-14.
The author flew light planes, and argues for the close relations between air observation and artillery and ground support airfire.

0981 Fourth Aerial Photo Interpretation Company: Its History and Men, Korea 51-53. Korea: 67th Reconnaissance Technical Squadron, 1953.
A unit history with some excellent information available about photo aerial reconnaissance.

0982 Fricker, John. "Air Supremacy in a Limited War" Aerop 80 2074 (1951): 473-475.
Air power effectiveness like all military efforts, was greatly restricted by the concept of limited war, as well as by terrain.

0983 Futrell, Robert F. "Air War in Korea: II" Air University Quarterly Review 4 (Spring 1951): 108-109.
Series of articles by Air Force historians which describes the setting up of air operations in Korea.

0984 Futrell, Robert F. "A Case Study: USAF Intelligence in the Korean War" in Walter T. Hitchcock, editor. The Intelligence Revolution, A Historical Perspective, Proceedings of the Thirteenth Military History Symposium, U. S. Air Force Academy. Washington, D. C.: Office of Air Force History, 1991.
Intelligence in the war was less than successful, though Futrell's arguments raise some serious questions about what is known.

0985 Futrell, Robert F. Ideas, Concepts, Doctrine: Basic Thinking in the United States Air Force, 1907-1960. two volumes. Maxwell Air Force Base, Alabama: Air University Press, 1989.
Excellent consideration of jet war hostilities, it is very critical of the failure to draw experiential conclusions from their involvement, then to learn from experiences as the Marines and Navy had done.

0986 Futrell, Robert F. "Tactical Employment of Strategic Air Power in Korea" Airpower Journal 2 (Winter 1988): 29-41.

The successful integration of tactical and strategic aircraft was facilitated by changing operation control from Strategic Air Command to the FEAF commander.

0987 Futrell, Robert F. The United States Air Force in Korea, 1950-1953. New York: Duell, Sloan and Pearce, 1961. revised edition, 1983.

Considers the air war in Korea as an example of what not to do next time. Futrell, of the Air University, deals with the transition between more conventional warfare and jets. A good and factual history of the recreation of the Far East Air Force and its "decisive role" in Korea.

0988 Futrell, Robert F. United States Air Force Operations in the Korean Conflict, 25 June-1 November 1950. United States Air Force Historical Division, Historical Study, Number 71, 1952.

This department of the Air Force book is a limited introductory account of the role of the United States Air Force, from the day of America's involvement in Korea to the end of this period. Included are some "air operation" overlays that spell out different target (as well as command) areas. Futrell provides the reader with limited but good coverage.

0989 Futrell, Robert F. and Albert F. Simpson. "Air War in Korea" Air University Quarterly Review 4 2 (Fall 1950): 18-39; 4 3 (Spring 1951): 47-72; 4 4 (Summer 1951): 83-89.

Concerned initial reaction of the Far East Air Force and the use of air to support ground troops, and to provide strategic bombing. Material reappears in Futrell's longer history.

0990 Giusti, Ernest H. and Kenneth W. Condit. "Marine Air Over Inchon-Seoul" Marine Corps Gazette 36 (June 1952): 18-27.

During the Inchon-Seoul operation five squadrons were in action for eighteen days with thirty-two combat sorties averaged each day per squadron. The loss of eleven planes, six pilots, and one air crewman was remarkably low given the high degree of close ground support the planes provided.

0991 Goldberg, Alfred, editor. A History of the United States Air Force, 1907-1957. Princeton: D. Van Nostrand, Co. 1957.

Provides a clear and concise account of the growing influence of air action, with some account of action in Korea.

0992 Gray, Robert L., Jr. "Air Operations Over Korea" Army Information Digest 7 (January 1952): 16-23.

Gray looks at the first year of operations against North Korea and points out that much of the ability to provide group support was the lack of any significant aerial opposition. This made it possible for the Air Force to provide close support for ground troops almost at will, and to attack long range supply routes.

0993 Greenough, Robert B. "Communist Lessons from the Korean War" Air University Quarterly Review 5 (Winter 1952-1953): 22-29.
     American air success could change because the communists learned quickly and put the lessons into practice.

0994 Grogan, Stanley J., Jr. "Lightning Lancers: Combat Highlights of the 68th Squadron in Korea" Airplane History 9 (1962): 249-252.
     From their role as escort cover for the first flights of evacuees to the first use of night fighters, the 68th Squadron was early and heavily involved in the Korean War.

0995 Gunn, William A. A Study of the Effectiveness of Air Support in Korea. ORO-technical Memorandum, ORO-T-13. APO 500: Operations Research Office, Chevy Chase, Maryland: Johns Hopkins University, 1951.
     Interesting account which focuses on the United Nations, and to a lesser degree on the United States.

0996 Gurney, Gene. Five Down and Glory. New York: Ballantine, 1958.
     A not-very-useful history of World War II and the Korean War aerial operations.

0997 Halliday, Jon. "Air Operations in Korea: The Soviet Side of the Story" in William J. Williams, editor. A Revolutionary War: Korea and the Transformation of the Postwar World. Chicago: Imprint Publications, 1993.
     Despite their involvement in the air war, the Soviets were unable to stop the almost total destruction brought on by the United Nations air campaign. Anti-air war efforts were not very effective.

0998 Halliday, Jon. "A Secret War: U. S. and Soviet Air Force Clashed Directly in Korea" Far Eastern Economics Review (22 April 1993): 32-36.
     Halliday contends that the Soviets flying out of the Antung Air Base operated more than 150 planes against United States pilots.

0999 Hallion, Richard P. "Naval Air Operations in Korea" in William J. Williams, editor. A Revolutionary War: Korea and the Transformation of the Postwar World. Chicago: Imprint Publications, 1993.
     The Korean War was a major turning point for the United States Navy air units, which were in serious trouble and in danger of losing the autonomous status.

1000 Hallion, Richard P. The Naval Air War in Korea. Baltimore: The Nautical and Aviation Publishing Company of America, 1986.

Very interesting account of the naval air war. In particular, this work deals with the complicated air support system supplied by the navy before, during, and after the Inchon landing.

1001 Hightower, Charles D. The History of the United States Air Force Airborne Forward Air Controller in World War II, the Korean War, and the Vietnam Conflict. Fort Leavenworth, Kansas: Army Command and General Staff College, 1984.

The role of the airborne controller changed a great deal during the Korean War. A comparative study.

1002 Hill, A. S. "The Flight of the Filliloo Bird" United States Naval Institute Proceedings (January 1953): 45-49.

Observations of a B-29 tail gunner who flew missions over Korea during late 1950 and the early months of 1951.

1003 Hinkle, Charles. Air Sanctuaries in Limited War: A Korean War Case Study. Maxwell Air Force Base, Alabama: Air University, 1986.

The existence of sanctuaries to which Russian and Chinese planes could return, greatly aided the communist cause.

1004 Hirsch, Phil, editor. Fighting Aces. New York: Willow Books, 1956, 1971.

Accounts of Korean War aerial operations with more about the organization, planes, equipment, and tactics than about the aces.

1005 Holm, Skip. "Yalu River Raider" Air Progress 46 (September 1984): 41-49.

Interesting, but hardly new, account of the Air Force efforts along the communist border during the Korean War.

1006 Human Factors Affecting the Air War Effort; A Brief Summary of a Study of FEAF Personnel at a Critical Period in the Korean War: December 1950-January 1951. Maxwell Air Force Base, Alabama: Air University, 1951.

A study of morale and other human factors which affect aerial operations, based on early period operations, when joint operations were just getting started.

1007 Jabara, James. "Air War in Korea" Air Force 34 10 (October 1951): 53, 60.

Short personal commentary on the air war in Korea by the world's first air jet ace (six aircraft).

1008 Jackson, Robert. <u>Air War Over Korea</u>. New York: Scribner's, 1973.
An initial history of the role of air power in the opening days of the
Korean War. Well-defined, if essentially broad, coverage of the air war
which was so essential to delaying first the North Koreans, and then the
Chinese as they pushed the United Nations forces to the south. More a
popular account it lacks the depth to appeal to the scholarly audience.

1009 Jamison, Theodore. "Nightmare of the Korean Hills: Douglas B-26
Invader Operations in the Korean War, 1950-1953" <u>American Aviation
Historical Society Journal</u> 34 (Summer 1989): 82-93.
Technical narrative of B-26 special operations on bombing runs over
Korea.

1010 Jarnette, Thomas. "4th Fighter-Interceptor Group Operations in MiG
Alley" 17 June 1953, Records of the Fourth Fighter Wing, Washington,
D. C.: Center for Air Force History, no date.
Good account of this fighter wing, which operated against
communist pilots.

1011 Jessup, Alpheous. "Korea's Air Power Lessons. They Will Influence
Plans for the Future Planes, Equipment." <u>Aviation Week</u> 53 14 (October 2,
1950): 16-18.
Identifies lessons which can be learned about such things as tactical
air power, airfield construction, and air-ground operations.

1012 Johnson, James E. <u>Full Circle: The Story of Air Fighting</u>. London:
Chatto and Windus, 1964. London: Pan, 1968. <u>The Story of Air Fighting</u>.
revised and enlarged edition London: Arrow, 1985, 1987. London:
Hutchinson, 1985. New York: Bantam, 1986, 1987.
A fair view of air warfare in Korea, including a look at fighter pilots,
tactics, planes, and air operations.

1013 Johnson, Robert S. "Working on the Railroads" <u>Air Force Magazine</u> 35
3 (March 1952): 25-29
Discussion of air interdiction against the communist supply
routes—mostly railways—in North Korea.

1014 Johnston, Sidney F. <u>5th Air Force, 1950-1958, Korean War, Mosquitos,
Airborne and Ground Combat Controllers, 6147th TAC.CON.GP Korea:
1986 Directory</u>. Albuquerque, New Mexico: S. F. Johnston, 1986.
A rather ambitious look at some of the units which provided the
bulk of air control in Korea.

1015 Katzman, Jim. "To Stem the Tide" <u>Airman</u> 27 7 (1983): 24-30.

A well-written article on the role of airpower which focuses on key aircraft, tactics, statistics, and some political overview.

1016 Keenan, Richard M. "The Aircraft that Won a War: The Last of the Superfortresses" Aero History 17 1 (1970): 20-27.
The B-29s played an important role in Korea, but can hardly be identified as winning the war.

1017 Key, William G. "Air Power in Action: Korea, 1950-1951" Pegasus 17 (October 1951): 1-16.
Overview of the use of air power during the first year of the war, giving it more organization and significance than it deserved.

1018 Kirtland, Michael A. "Planning Air Operations: Lessons from Operation Strangle in the Korean War" Airpower Journal 6 (Summer 1992): 37-46.
Kirtland analyzed the effectiveness of the air war during Ridgway's campaign to restrict communist movement. The Americans underestimated the North Korean ability to rebuild.

1019 Knight, Charlotte. "Air War in Korea" Air Force 33 (1950): 21-25.
A war correspondent examines the United States air operations during the first few months of the war. She traces their efforts to halt the North Korean advance across the 38th Parallel.

1020 Knight, Charlotte. "The New Air War—Sabres vs MiGs" Collier's 127 (April 21, 1951): 26-27, 68-72.
A careful look at the use and effectiveness of the American jets which outflew and outfought the Russian and Chinese pilots and planes. More positive than her other works.

1021 Kohn, Richard H. and Joseph P. Harahan, editors. Air Interdiction in World War II, Korea, and Vietnam: Interviews with Gen. Earle E. Partridge, General Jacob E. Smart, and General John W. Vogt, Jr. USAF Warrior Series. Washington, D. C.: Government Printing Office, Office of Air Force History, 1986.
An interesting look at the poor combat conditions and command structures between the various services; all of which led to a lack of idea interdiction. Much of the problem lay with different methods of calling and regulating ground-air support, as well as the poor coordination between units.

1022 Kohn, Richard H. and Joseph P. Harahan, editors. Air Superiority in World War II and Korea: An Interview with Gen. James Ferguson, Gen.

Robert M. Lee, Gen. William Momyer, and Lt. General Elwood R. Quesada. USAF Warrior Series. Washington, D. C.: Government Printing Office, Office of Air Force History, 1983.

Good discussion of X Corps, brief control of, and desire to keep, operational control of the Marine Air Wing. The agreement imposed by MacArthur ran counter to the air coordination agreement between Army and Air Force which made the senior Air Force general the coordinator of air operations in the Korean theater. Considerable effort was expended to acquaint area and service contact over aircraft. The appendix outlines air command and employment of air power.

1023 Kohn, Richard H. and Joseph P. Harahan, editors. Strategic Air Warfare: An Interview with Generals Curtis E. LeMay, Leon W. Johnson, David A. Burchinal, and Jack J. Catton. Washington, D. C.: Government Printing Office, 1988.

Part of a series which compares aerial bombing in World War II, Korea, and Vietnam.

1024 Kropf, Roger F. "The US Air Force in Korea: Problems that Hindered the Effectiveness of Air Power" Airpower Journal 4 1 (Spring 1990): 30-46.

A rather ambitious attempt to deal with the problems which seemed to hinder a greater success for the Air Force in the Korean War. The author identifies the problems as poorly selected air bases, difficulty of the joint command structure, and poor air-to-ground coordination.

1025 Kuehl, Daniel T. "'Refighting the Last War': Electronic Warfare and the U. S. Air Force B-29 Operations in the Korean War, 1950-1953" Journal of Military History 56 (January 1992): 87-111.

A long and interesting account of the growth of electronic warfare, which identifies the United States effort as a responsive development. It was five years late, and had been forgotten again by Vietnam.

1026 Leaflet Drop Test from Army Aircraft: Report of AFF BD no. 1 Project no. AA 2951. Fort Bragg, North Carolina: Army Field Forces, 1953.

A look at propaganda and psychological warfare delivery system during the Korean War.

1027 Lobov, Georgi. "U. S. Air Actions in Korea Recalled." Moscow radio Broadcast in Korea, September 2, 1991, FBIS SOU-91-97, October 1991.

Lobov, who commanded Russia's air defense in Korea, identifies the Soviet's restricted ability to defend its targets as they desired.

1028 Marion, Forrest L. "The Grand Experiment: Detachment F's Helicopter Combat Operations in Korea, 1950-1953" Air Power History 40 (Summer 1993): 38-51.

Marion discusses a little understood part of the combat air war, good introductory material on helicopters.

1029 Mark, Eduard M. Aerial Interdiction: Air Power and the Land Battle in Three American Wars. Washington, D. C.: Government Printing Office, 1994.

A broad look at interdiction and an effort to compare the use of airpower in this very different war.

1030 Marshall, Chester. B-29 Superfortress. Osceola, Wisconsin: Motorbooks International, 1993.

Superficial look at the role of this major bomber during World War II and Korea.

1031 Martin, Harold H. "How Our Air Raiders Plastered Korea" Saturday Evening Post 223 (1950): 26-27, 88-90.

Considers the different Far East Commands operating in the early war period, 25 June to 4 July 1950. Deals with the various roles of air and naval flight operations in Korea during this week of the early fighting.

1032 Matt, Paul R., compiler. United States Navy and Marine Corps Fighter, 1918-1962. Los Angeles: Aero Publishers, 1962.

Photos, descriptions, and narratives of fighters in a long history which culminated in the Korean War effort.

1033 McCaffery, Dan. Air Aces: The Lives and Times of Twelve Canadian Fighter Pilots. Toronto: Lorimer, 1990.

Short biographies describing the heroics of Canadian fighter pilots during World War II and Korea.

1034 McLaren, David. "Air Support in Korea: Mustang Style" Aerospace Historian 33 (June 1986): 74-66.

Less an analysis than might be expected, it is primarily a popular account of aerial combat.

1035 McLaren, David. "Mustangs in Aerial Combat: The Korean War" American Aviation Historical Society Journal 30 (Summer 1985): 94-101.

More mileage out of well-used materials, this account of aerial combat is more descriptive than analytical.

1036 McMaster, Donald W. "The Evolution of Tactical Airpower: With Particular Emphasis Upon Its Application by the U. S. Navy and U. S. Marine Corps in the Korean War, June 1950-July 1953" MA thesis, University of Maryland, 1959.
    MA: airpower

1037 McNitt, James R. "Tactical Air Control in Korea" Air University Quarterly Review 6 (Summer 1953): 74-86.
    The "Mosquitos" planes and air control system worked well in Korea despite obsolete equipment.

1038 Merrill, Frank. A Study of the Aerial Interdiction of Railways During the Korean War. Fort Leavenworth, Kansas: Army Command and General Staff College, 1956.
    Research study of the effectiveness of railway interdiction. Merrill found the military was overly optimistic about their success.

1039 Millett, Allan R. "Korea, 1950-1953" in Benjamin Franklin Cooling, editor. Case Studies in Development of Close Air Support. Washington, D. C.: Office of Air Force History, 1990.
    Well-respected historian looks at the growth of close air support in combat, discovered it continued to be a problem late into the Korean War.

1040 Milton, T. R. "The Equalizer in Korea" Air Force Magazine 74 (October 1991): 72-76.
    The Allies were in trouble, the ground war in balance, if it were not for the 5th Air Force, North Korea might have been victorious.

1041 Momyer, William W., Arthur J. C. Lavalle and James C. Gaston. Air Power in Three Wars. Washington, D. C.: Government Printing Offices, 1978, 1983, 1986. Arno Press, 1978, 1980.
    Addresses the continued failure to consider policy and doctrine changes necessary to provide essential command and control for air power.

1042 Monat, Pawel. "Russians in Korea: the Hidden Bosses" Life 48 25 (June 27, 1960): 76-102.
    On the tenth anniversary of the invasion of South Korea, a Polish author explains how the Russians ran the show in Korea, both before and during the war.

1043 Moore, Dermot M. and Peter Bagshawe. South Africa's Flying Cheetahs in Korea. Johannesburg: Ashanti Publishing, 1991.
    An account of the South African Air Force Squadron which served in Korea, losing thirty-four pilots and two members of the ground crew.

1044 Mossman, Billy C. "The Effectiveness of Air Interdiction During the Korean War" Center for Military History, Draft Study No. 2-27 (AD.H) Washington, D. C.: Office of the Chief of Military History, Department of the Army, 1966.

Contains a great deal of useful information on the methods of air interdiction, and its effectiveness. Not an optimistic view.

1045 Newman, Stanley F. H. Oklahoma Air National Guard Pilots in the Korean War. Oklahoma City, Oklahoma: 45th Infantry Division Museum, 1990.

A useful unit history about the 185th Fighter Squadron, including personal narratives.

1046 North Korean Air Force: NK Control of Occupied Areas, North Korean 6th Infantry Division, North Korea: 9th Infantry Division. Manila, General Headquarters, Far East Command, 1951.

Analysis of North Korean air, control, and dispersion in occupied areas.

1047 159th Fighter Bomber Squadron, Florida Air National Guard. St. Augustine, Florida: State Arsenal, 1988.

Useful unit history of this air reserve unit called in action.

1048 Owen, Elmer G. and Wallace F. Veaudry. "Control of Tactical Air Power in Korea" Combat Forces Journal 1 9 (April 1951): 19-21.

Praises use of pilots as ground control officers in the development of air-ground support systems in Korea.

1049 Park, Sun E. "Operation Dragonfly" US Army Aviation Digest 27 (1981): 7-9.

The aviation section of the United States 24th Infantry provided the first use of air reconnaissance for ground troop in July of 1950. The effort was so successful it became the model for the creation of an operational unit, known as the Mosquitos, in August of 1950.

1050 Parker, Gary W. A History of Marine Medium Helicopter Squadron 161. Washington, D. C.: Marine Corps History and Museums Division, 1978.

Unit history, including discussion of technical data and equipment. The helicopter came into its own during the Korean War.

1051 Parker, Gary W. and F. M. Batha, Jr. A History of Marine Observation. Carrollton, Texas: Squadron/Signal Publications, 1982.

Squadron yearbook history.

1052 Partridge, Earle. Air Interdiction in World War II, Korea, and Vietnam. Washington, D. C.: Office of Air Force History, 1986.

A series of operational interviews with Generals Partridge, Smart, and Vogt concerning the value of air interdiction and its use in war.

1053 Physical and Psychological Effects of Interdiction Air Attacks as Determined by POW Interrogation. Washington, D. C.: Center for Air Force History, Records of Fifth Air Force, 1951.

An attempt, from interviews of POWs, to determine the effectiveness of air attacks on supply and operations.

1054 Poe, Bryce. "Korean War Combat Support: A Lieutenant's Journal" Air Force Journal of Logistics 13 (Fall 1989): 3-7.

Deals with the complexities, and occasional dangers, of logistic support, cargo, and passenger movement.

1055 Politella, Dario. Operation Grasshopper. Wichita, Kansas: Robert R. Longo Co., 1958.

The story of army light aviation in Korea from aggression to armistice.

1056 Prasad, Sri Nandan and B. Chakravorty. History of the Custodian Force (India) in Korea, 1953-54. New Delhi: Government of India, 1976.

The role of India's forces which served a major role in the POW exchange and the early phases of the armistice.

1057 Putt, Donald L. "Air Weapons Development Systems" Army Intelligence Digest 8 8 (1953): 8-13.

Claims kill superiority was the result of the American's balanced weapons systems and training.

1058 Questions Pertaining to Air-Ground Operations for OCAFF Observer Team no. 7. no publisher, 1953

Antiaircraft artillery operations, standard operating procedure, for use of 116.10 mc (White Channel) between Army and Air Force.

1059 Ragle, George L. "Dragonflies Over Korea" Combat Forces Journal 1 4 (November 1950): 32-33.

The small observer planes used by the army (L4 in this case) played a series of significant roles in addition to their assigned observation duties. During the early days of fighting the 24th Infantry, used them for carrying ammo, wounded, fire direction, supplies to cut off units, and for various commander's direct observation of troop displacement.

1060 Ransom, Frank E. Air Sea Rescue, 1941-1952. U. S. Air Force Historical Study #95. Washington, D. C.: U. S. Air Force, 1953.

One of the significant lessons learned in Korea was advanced rescue techniques, which were highly developed during the Korean War.

1061 Reid, William M. "Tactical Air in Limited War" Air University Quarterly Review 8 (Spring 1956): 40-48.

Air superiority was possible in Korea, but the essential success of the United States Air Force was greatly restricted by "limited war" decisions.

1062 Reinburg, J. Hunter. "Night Fighter Squadron" Ordnance 49 268 (1965): 416-418.

Night flying operations are discussed by a Marine Corp pilot involved in air support.

1063 Risedorph, Gene. "Mosquito" American Aviation Historical Society Journal 24 1 (Spring 1979): 45-51.

Discusses the development of the T-6 trainer into tactical airborne coordinators in developing ground support fire.

1064 Roberts, Wayne K. "Early Evolution of Helicopter Tactics" Vietnam 9 1 (June 1996): 18-24.

The helicopter saw service in Korea and was useful, but was used in Vietnam where it was vital. Good brief history of the helicopter in Korea provided in a sidebar.

1065 Scholin, Allan R. "On the Graveyard Shift" Air Force Magazine 56 9 (September 1973): 102-106.

Discusses the role of B-26 bombers used to hit supply dumps, convoys, and railways to prevents North Koreans from supplying their troops.

1066 Schuetta, Lawrence V. Guerrilla Warfare and Airpower in Korea, 1950-53. Maxwell Air Force Base, Alabama: Air University, 1964, 1970, 1988.

Consideration of interplay between undercover activities and air interdiction.

1067 Sherwood, John D. Officers in Flight Suits. the Story of American Air Force Pilots in the Korean War. New York: New York University Press, 1996.

Interesting and well-constructed account of the United States Air Force in the Korean War.

1068 Shrader, Charles R. "Air Interdiction in Korea" Army Logistician (March-April 1992): 11-13.

Basically shows why air interdiction was less than successful, discusses the Korean War in counterpart to the Gulf War.

1069 Silber, J. and M. Astrachan. History of Bombing Accuracy During the Korean War. Headquarters: Fifth Air Force, 1953.
    Data on 5th Air Force bombing successes, a questionable record.

1070 Simpson, Albert F. "Tactical Air Doctrine: Tunisia and Korea" Air University Quarterly Review 4 4 (Summer 1951): 5-21.
    Lessons of air command learned in campaigns in Tunisia were applied to problems of air operations in Korea and found to be useful, Discusses "defensive umbrella" doctrines being changed in favor of air commanders.

1071 Simpson, Albert F. Historical Research Center USAF Credits for the Destruction of Enemy Aircraft, Korean War. Maxwell Air Force Base, Alabama: Air University, 1963.
    Identification of communist air losses created by the United States Air Force in Korea.

1072 Sleeper, Raymond S. "Korean Targets for Medium Bombardment" Air University Quarterly Review 4 3 (Spring 1951): 21.
    Story of the early air attacks by B-29s, the difficulty of finding targets for the massive bombers, and the use of the heavy bombs during the early battles in July and August of 1950.

1073 Spick, Mike. Jet Fighter Performance: Korea to Vietnam. London: Ian Allen, 1986.Osceola, Wisconsin: Motorbooks International, 1986.
    An analysis of jet performance from Korea through Vietnam: 1950-1973 operations.

1074 Stanglin, Douglas and Peter Craig. "Secrets of the Korean War" U. S. News & World Report (August 9, 1993): 45-47.
    After forty years the reports of pilots show that Stalin was involved in launching the war, and sending Russian pilots.

1075 Stewart, James T. Airpower: The Decisive Force in Korea. Princeton, New Jersey: D. Van Nostrand Co., 1957.
    Twenty-five articles which hold that airpower played the decisive role in the fighting in Korea. Various chapters of this book were published as articles in the Air University Quarterly Review.

1076 "The Story of 'Operation Strangle'" Air Intelligence Digest 5 1 (January 1952): 4-10.

Discusses the United Nations command use of air interdiction during periods of intensive aggression, as in the pursuit of Operation Strangle.

1077 Strain, Joseph H. "Cavalry of the Air" Marine Corps Gazette 36 3 (1952): 30-35.
        Discusses "Operation Summit," the first use of the helicopter to move combat troops, on 9 September 1951.

1078 Strawbridge, Dennis and Nannette Kahn. Fighter Pilot Performance in Korea. Chicago: University of Chicago Press, 1955.
        A fairly standard look at pilots, performance, and events in the air war in Korea.

1079 Sugar, Jim. "Korea: 35 Years After MIG Alley" Flying 113 (December 1986): 60-68.
        A recounting of the Air Force first response to the North Korean invasion, and the difficulties of reactivation.

1080 Sullivan, Jim and Don Greer. F4U Corsair in Action. Carrollton, Texas: Squadron/Signal Publications, 1977, 1981, 1994.
        Technical data and illustrations of the F4U Corsair as it saw action in World War II and Korea.

1081 Sutton, George M., Alan P. Knight, William R. Wilcox and Edgar H. Steeg. Helicopters in Korea: 1 July 1951-31 August 1953. no publisher, 1953.
        A popularized look at the helicopter in action.

1082 "Tactical Air Rescue in Korea" Air University Quarterly Review 6 (Fall 1953): 120-123.
        One of the great lessons learned in Korea was air rescue, including use of helicopters. Based on 3rd Air Rescue Group.

1083 Tactical Air Support, 10 May-5 June 1951. X Corps, 1951.
        Useful information dealing with aerial operations, 10th Army Corps.

1084 Taylor, Roger C. MiG Operations in Korea. Maxwell Air Force Base, Alabama: Air University, 1986.
        Data and analysis of MiGs operating in North Korea and with Chinese forces.

1085 Teschner, Charles G. "The Fighter-Bomber in Korea" Air University Quarterly Review 7 2 (Summer 1954): 71-80.

The fighter-bomber was a primary weapon used by all the services during the last two years of the war.

1086 "Three Very Long Minutes" United States Naval Institute Proceedings 76 12 (December 1950): 1365-1369.
    A photographic essay of naval aircraft from Task Force 77 in support of the Inchon landing. Korea reaffirmed the value of the aircraft carrier in support of land operations. Includes one of the first photos of a helicopter air-sea rescue.

1087 Thyng, Harrison R. "Air-to-Air Combat in Korea" Air University Quarterly Review 6 2 (Summer 1953): 40-45.
    The sixteenth jet ace in Korea describes the air sweep to the Yalu River, and talks about the shortcomings of the Sabre jet.

1088 Tilford, Earl H. "A History of the United States Air Force Search and Rescue Operations in Southeast Asia, 1961-1975" Ph.D. thesis, George Washington University, 1984.
    A look at the expanding rescue operation during World War II, the Korean War, Vietnam, and the Mayaquez crisis in May 1975.

1089 Tillman, Barret. Corsair: The F4U in World War II and Korea. Annapolis, Maryland: Naval Institute Press, 1979.
    Describes the Corsair and its role in air combat and ground support in Korea.

1090 Tormoen, George E. "'Political Air Superiority' in the Korean Conflict" Air University Quarterly Review 6 (Winter 1953-54): 78-84.
    The decision to prevent American airmen from crossing the Yalu River provided the Red Chinese with "air superiority."

1091 Torrance, E. Paul. Factors in Fighter-Interceptor Pilot Combat Effectiveness. San Antonio, Texas: Lackland Air Force Base, 1957.
    Complex look at piloting, combat psychology, aggressive behavior, and psychological issues related to combat air war.

1092 Turner, Richard E. Mustang Pilot. London: W. Kimber, 1970.
    The 354th Fighter Group during World War II and the Korean War.

1093 Ulanoff, Stanley M., editor. Fighter Pilot. Garden City, New York: Doubleday, 1962.
    Basic look at the role of the fighter pilot during World War II and the Korean War.

1094 United States Aerospace Studies Institute Concept Division. Guerrilla Warfare and Airpower in Korea 1950-53. Maxwell Air Force Base, Air University: Aerospace Studies Institute, 1964.

A brief survey of interdiction in Korea, primarily during the "stalemate" period of the war.

1095 USAF Credits for Destruction of Enemy Aircraft, Korean War. USAF Historical Study 81. Washington, D. C.: Government Printing Office, 1963.

A list of those aircraft "officially" destroyed by United States (United Nations) planes during the Korean War.

1096 "United States Air Force Operation in the Korean Conflict, 25 June-1 November 1950" United States Air Force Historical Study, Number 71. Washington, D. C.: Operational Research Office, 1952.

A restricted monograph written to show the extent and success of the Air Force. The account is overly optimistic. It was later expanded and published in book form by Robert Futrell.

1097 United States Army Command and General Staff College. Theater Air: Modern Case Studies in Military Planning and Evaluation. Fort Leavenworth, Kansas: Army Command and General Staff College, 1994-1995.

Interesting study of theater-wide air consideration presented as a case study program.

1098 United States Department of Defense. Air Craft Recognition Manual, Supplement, 4 June 1953. Washington, D. C.: Government Printing Office, 1953.

Includes markings on United States, United States Navy, Royal Air Force, Royal Canadian Air Force, Royal Swedish Air Force, Air Force France, and others.

1099 United States Secretary of Defense. "Air War in Korea" Air University Quarterly Review 4 (1950): 19-39.

An official assessment of United States Air Force operations in Korea, 25 June to 1 November 1950. The not-too-surprising conclusion is that the Air Force did well. Despite the somewhat self-serving attitude this is an excellent source for statistics on sorties flown, targets, when delivered, and how they related to the ground war.

1100 Vandenberg, Hoyt S. "The Truth about Our Air Power" Saturday Evening Post 17 (February 1951): 20-21.

The Korean War Air Force Chief of Staff compares the various capacities of American and Soviet planes, as well as discussing the overall value of the air war in Korea.

1101 Wallrich, William. "Bedcheck Charlie Flies Again" Air Force (September 1953): 110-113.
　　　　Every war seems to create its "bedcheck" incidents. In this case the trials of troops dealing with a light flying North Korean plane that came to harass the troops at night. Talks about the difficulties of catching or destroying the slow-moving plane.

1102 Waterhouse, Fred J. The Rakkasans: Airborne. Paducah, Kentucky: Turner Publishing Company, 1991.
　　　　Brief institutional history of 187th Airborne Infantry Regiment in World War II, Korea, Vietnam, and the Persian Gulf War: "The Steel Berets."

1103 Watson, Mark. "Tactics for Limited Conflict" Saturday Review 45 (January 27, 1962): 19.
　　　　A review of Futrell's book, stresses the conflict between Futrell and Appleman's South to the Yalu.

1104 Weyland, Otto P. "The Air Campaign in Korea" Air University Quarterly Review 6 3 (Fall 1953): 3-28.
　　　　This brief account presents an overly optimistic view of the success of both air-to-ground support and strategic bombing. A major problem was that North Korea targets did not present themselves in a manner that allowed the Air Force the full use of its bombing power. Air-to-ground support was not as successful, especially at the beginning of the war, because of command limitations.

1105 Wheeler, Gerald. "Naval Aviation in the Korean War" United States Naval Institute Proceedings 83 7 (July 1957): 767-777.
　　　　There is no substitute for control of the sea and the sky, and fairly quickly, this was accomplished. But if there is no strong air support of troops this is not fully effective. Wheeler discusses the way in which naval-ground support was a major contribution to that control.

1106 Winchester, James H. "Report on Korean Air Losses" Aviation Age 16 5 (November 1951): 38-39.
　　　　Compares the win and loss record between F-84 and F-86 and the Russian-built MIG-15 during the first year-and-a-half of the war.

1107 Winnefeld, James A. and Dana J. Johnson. <u>Joint Air Operations: Pursuit of Unity in Command and Control, 1942-1991</u>. Annapolis, Maryland: Naval Institute Press, 1993.

An excellent study of the failure of command between services. The command question grew to dangerous dimensions especially at this time when pre-war battles were still remembered.

1108 Wykeham-Barnes, P. G. "Air Power Difficulties in the Korean Conflict" <u>Military Review</u> 33 (April 1953): 73-81.

A repeat of the author's <u>Journal Royal United Service Institute</u> article.

1109 Wykeham-Barnes, P. G. "The War in Korea with Special Reference to the Difficulties of Using Our Air Power" <u>Journal Royal United Service Institution</u> 97 586 (May 1952): 149-163.

Problems of the Royal Air Force in action in Korea, written by a staff officer who saw it happen. Imposing a limit on crossing the Yalu River was against all theories of military policy.

1110 Yool, W. M. "Air Lessons from Korea" in <u>Brassey's Annual: The Armed Forces Year-Book</u>. New York: Macmillan, 1951.

Criticizes the role of strategic air power by showing it did not have the decisive effect envisioned. Written early and the author did not have the advantage of late operational appraisals.

1111 Zaloga, Steven. "The Russians in MiG Alley" <u>Air Force Magazine</u> 74 2 (February 1991): 74-77.

An attempt to identify the Russian role in air combat.

1112 Zimmerman, Don Z. "FEAF: Mission and Command Relationships" <u>Air University Quarterly Review</u> 4 (Summer 1951): 95-96.

The author looks at the changing mission of the Far East Air Force during the first six months of the war.

MILITARY OPERATIONS

Battles

1113 Alexander, Nicholas. <u>Rakkasans: Those Men Who Fell From the Sky with Umbrellas</u>. Sacramento, California: Dramco Publishers, 1982, 1988.

An account, later revised, of efforts to use airborne troops for special duties in Korea. Focuses on the 187th Airborne Regimental Combat Team.

1114 Alsop, Joseph. "Matter of Fact" <u>Leatherneck</u> 33 12 (1950): 33.

An accurate and interesting account of the Inchon to Seoul campaign by Alsop, a well-known reporter, who was covering Korea.

1115 Appleman, Roy E. "The Bowling Alley Fight" <u>Army</u> 11 9 (April 1961): 44-49.

An account of the Wolfhounds, 27th Infantry Regiment, 25th Infantry Division, who held the line for seven days during a North Korean infantry and armor attack near the village of Sio-ri.

1116 Banks, Charles L. "Inchon To Seoul: Service In Action" <u>Marine Corps Gazette</u> 35 5 (May 1951): 20-21.

Supporting and supplying the 1st Marine Division in its landing at Inchon, and in the eighteen-mile drive to Seoul, created significant problems for the division's service units. The speed of assembly and the rapid movement toward Seoul, made the job even more difficult. Many new techniques and doctrines were tested in battle for the first time and found successful.

1117 Barker, A. J. <u>Fortune Favours the Brave—The Battle of the Hook, Korea, 1953</u>. London: Leo Cooper, 1974.

The story of the Duke of Wellington Regiment in the battle of the Hook. Popular history.

1118 Barth, George B. "The First Days in Korea" <u>Combat Forces Journal</u> 2 8 (March 1952): 21-24.

The overconfidence suffered by so many United States troops when they first entered Korea was quickly replaced by stubborn determination.

1119 "Battle of Korea: Over the Beaches" <u>Time</u> 56 (September 25, 1950): 25-31.

An indepth reporting of the Inchon landing with selected coverage of MacArthur and the naval officers responsible for landing the troops. The brief article compares Inchon with the island hopping of World War II.

1120 <u>Battle of Maryang San: 3rd Battalion, The Royal Australian Regiment, Korea 2-8 October 1951</u>. Balmoral, New South Wales, Australian Army, 1991.

Personal narratives and a description of campaigns fought by this Australian regiment in Korea.

1121 Bell, James A. "The Brave Men of No Name Ridge" <u>Life</u> 29 9 (1950): 34.

An account of United States troops at the first battle of the Naktong River in August of 1950.

1122 Blair, Clay, Jr. "Robinson Crusoe of Schinz-do" <u>Life</u> (July 28, 1952): 95-107.

Adventure of Colonel Albert W. Schinz who, shot down over Korea, spent thirty-seven days on a North Korean-held island.

1123 Blumenson, Martin. <u>Withdrawal from Taejon, 20 July 1950: After Action Interview 1950</u>. Archive/Manuscript Control, 1950.

Interviews with Robert L. Herbert, Joseph S. Szito, Robert E. Nash, and George L. Wilcox of the 19th Infantry Regiment, 24th Infantry Regiment, in a review of the battle of Taejon.

1124 Breen, Bob. <u>The Battle of Kapyong</u>. Sydney, Australia: Army Training Command, 1992.

Author tries to work out the sequence of events at this battle, often confused by authors, and blames failure of radio communications for the difficulties, because it required forward unit commanders to take responsibility.

1125 Cagle, Malcolm W. "Errors of the Korean War" United States Naval Institute Proceedings 84 1 (March 1958): 31-35.

After accepting Inchon as a valid effort, this Navy historian identified several errors; 1) the decision to land at Wonsan 2) retreating too far after China entered the war 3) the failure to coordinate aerial interdiction at the theater level, and 4) failure to adopt the Navy "close air support system." But the greatest failure overall was timidity, the unwillingness to win.

1126 Campbell, David R. "Fighting Encircled": (A Study in Leadership). Washington, D. C.: Center of Military History, 1987.

Comparisons of leadership during desperate battles—Argonne 1918, Ardennes 1944-45, Korea 1950-53 (Chosin), and Vietnam. Very informative study.

1127 Cannon, Michael. "Task Force Smith: A Study in (un)Preparedness and (ir)Responsibility" Military Review 68 2 (February 1988): 63-74.

Task Force Smith was the first American unit in combat in the Korean War. They suffered heavy losses due to the outdated nature of their equipment, the poor quality of ammo, and the unrealistic nature of their peace-time training.

1128 Canzona, Nicholas A. "A Hill Near Yongsan" Marine Corps Gazette 39 (1955): 55-59.

Accounts of the 1st and 2nd Battalion, 5th Marines during the bloody Second Naktong River campaign in September of 1950.

1129 Carpenter, John L. "Marching Through the Valley of Death: The United States Marines in the Battle for the Chosin Reservoir During the Korean War." MS thesis, Illinois State University, 1994.

MS: Chosin

1130 Chen, Wen-Hui C. Wartime "Mass" Campaigns in Communist China: Official Country-wide "Mass Movements" in Professional Support of the Korean War. Lackland Air Force Base, Texas: Air Research and Development Command, 1955.

Looks at country-wide appeals in China, seeking popular support for the Korean War.

1131 Chilcote, Ted C. The Battle of the Twin Tunnels, Korea, 1 February 1951. Carlisle Barracks, Pennsylvania: United States Army War College, 1988.

Combat action narrative on the 23rd Regimental Combat Team at this significant battle.

1132 Chong, Anson and Charles Joseph Hilton. Chosin, The Untold Story. Honeoye, New York: International Association, 1993.

One of the few works on the Army at Chosin. This traces the role of the 7th Infantry Division.

1133 Chosen [sic] Reservoir: A Battlebook. Fort Leavenworth, Kansas: United States Command and General Staff College, 1983.

A look at the 1st Marine Division winter warfare campaigns, and losses, in the Korean winter of 1950-51.

1134 Cleaver, Frederick W. UN Partisan Warfare in Korea, 1951-1954 Chevy Chase, Maryland: Johns Hopkins University, 1956.

Overly dramatic account of commando operations, guerilla warfare, and underground efforts in Korea. Informative but too early to be helpful.

1135 Colon, William. "Task Force Smith" Infantry 70 (January-February 1980): 35-37.

Short account of the formation and deployment, as well as the costs, of the first American unit to face the North Koreans.

1136 Cowart, Glenn C. Miracle in Korea: The Evacuation of X Corps from the Hungnam Beachhead. Columbia: University of South Carolina Press, 1992.

The story of how the 3rd Infantry Division entered the war in Korea, held their ground at Chosin, and saved thousands of American lives during the evacuation.

1137 Cowings, John S. and Kim Nam Che. Twelve Hungnam Evacuees. Headquarters: 8th United States Army, 1975.

Useful discussion of refugee dispersal from the Hungnam withdrawal and evacuation.

1138 Craig, Berry. The Chosin Few: North Korea, November-December 1950. Paducah, Kentucky: Turner Publishing Company, 1989.

Yearbook variety account of the 10th Corps Army, includes personal narratives and individual records.

1139 Davies, William J. Task Force Smith: A Leadership Failure? Carlisle Barracks, Pennsylvania: United States Army War College, 1992.

Task Force Smith may have been a political necessity but it was also a military disaster. Davies asks the question if leadership, at some level, was the problem.

1140 <u>Delay and Withdrawal, Task Force Smith and the 24th Division, 5-9 July 1950</u>. APO: Eighth United States Army, 1990.

Packet designed for a "staff ride" dealing with action of the Task Force, and is very informative.

1141 Department of the Army, FM 31-21. "Organization and Conduct of Guerilla Warfare" Washington, D. C.: Government Printing Office, 1951.

Discusses projection policy for, and about, guerilla warfare. Very early offering and many theories changed a good deal during the war.

1142 De Reus, C. C. "The Perimeter Pays Off" <u>Combat Forces Journal</u> 3 5 (December 1952): 31-34.

Excellent account of patrol action while serving with the 3rd Battalion, 7th Regiment, 3rd Infantry Division, during the perimeter period.

1143 Dill, James H. <u>Sixteen Days at Mungol-Li</u>. Fayetteville, Arkansas: M & M Press, 1993.

Very well-written narrative of the Korean War which describes the days when the United Nations took a stand along the main line of resistance and held against the Chinese

1144 Dill, James H. "Winter of the Yalu" <u>American Heritage</u> 34 (1982): 33-48.

A member of the Army 7th Division the author recounts the landing at Inchon in September, then to the Yalu and back. One of the few commentaries on the 7th Division at Inchon.

1145 Edwards, James. "Action at Tongmyongwon" <u>Infantry School Quarterly</u> 38 1 (1951): 66-83.

The 2nd Battalion, 23rd Infantry, 2nd Division held the enemy from 21-24 August 1950, thus avoiding a bridgehead across the Naktong River.

1146 Edwards, James. "Naktong Defense" <u>Infantry School Quarterly</u> 38 2 (1951): 77-92.

Account of the 2nd Battalion, 23rd Infantry, 2nd Division which held 18,000 yards of front, and partially destroyed two North Korean Divisions, which were in the attack from 31 August to 16 September 1950.

1147 Eldredge, Jim. "End of the Beginning" <u>Soldiers</u> 40 (September 1985): 6-8.

A general account of the Inchon landing which claims that it was the turning point of the war. "The gamble paid off—in aces."

1148 "The Fall of Seoul: US Marines in Street Fighting Proceeding September 28" London News 217 (October 7, 1950): 556-557.

Focuses on the house-to-house nature of the fighting in the campaign to retake Seoul. This sort of fighting was a new form for the Marines, and required some adaptation of procedures.

1149 Foster, Simon. Hit the Beach!: Amphibious Warfare from the Plains of Abraham to San Carlos Water. London: Arms and Armour, 1995. Distributed by Sterling Publishing Company in New York.

An interesting history of amphibious landings which include a good account of the landing at Inchon.

1150 Fowle, Barry C. "Civil Works and Military Construction" Engineers 5 (January 1991): 48-49.

The story of the 14th Engineer Combat Battalion (ECB) of the 1st Cavalry Division which arrived in Korea in July of 1950. The battalion served as infantry during much of this time, but also worked on the destruction of key bridges across the Naktong River. A short but excellent piece about combat engineers at Pusan.

1151 Green, Carl R. The Korean War Soldier at Heartbreak Ridge. Mankato, Minnesota: Capstone Press, 1991

A young person's look at war in Korea based on the experiences of William R. Sanford who fought on the Ridge.

1152 Greenwood, C. I. Once Upon a Time. Springfield, Illinois: Phillips, 1989.

This is a privately printed account of the battle action of Marine Gunnery Sergeant C. I. Greenwood who landed with the marines at Inchon. A highly personal, but very informative, account of the "troops" side of the landing. Manages to avoid much analysis and blame.

1153 Griffin, Harry K. "Typhoon at Kobe" Marine Corps Gazette 35 9 (September 1951): 60-65.

With the Inchon invasion locked into a September 15, 1950, landing date Lieutenant Colonel R. L. Blust, commanding the port of Kobe in southern Japan, was given the job of loading the troops and their supplies. Faced with this task he worked through unbelievable, if normal, difficulties but had his greatest challenge with the arrival of typhoon "Jane." Time was lost and ships damaged, but they managed to sail on schedule.

1154 Grodecki, Thomas S. From Powser River to Soyang: The 300th Armored Field Artillery in Korea: A Case Study of the Integration of the

Reserve Component Into the Active Force. Washington, D. C.: Center of Military History, 1989.

Interesting account of reservist outfit, the Wyoming National Guard, and its integration into established and regular army forces.

1155 Gugeler, Russell A. "Attack Along a Ridgeline" Combat Forces Journal 4 10 (May 1954): 22-27.

Naktong River, 15 August 1950, 2nd platoon, Company A, 1st Battalion of the 34th Infantry Regiment conducted a disastrous attack, which led to the death of over half the members. Gugeler describes the role of the 34th Infantry, fighting along the ridge after a break in the central section of the Pusan Perimeter near the Naktong River on 6 August 1950, where a hard-driving North Korean force was stopped.

1156 Gugeler, Russell A. "The Defense of a Battery Position" Combat Forces Journal 4 11 (June 1954): 35-37.

The North Koreans made an art out of hitting artillery positions in the dark of night. Gugeler urges the development of a policy of defense.

1157 Halloran, B. F. "Inchon Landing" Marine Corps Gazette 56 9 (September 1972): 25-32.

A very supportive statement concerning the planning and execution of the Inchon landing which the author felt was not only "masterful," but was accomplished in record time.

1158 Hammel, Eric M. Chosin: Heroic Ordeal of the Korean War. New York: Vanguard Press, 1981.

More a history of the development of marine forces in Korea, the early chapters provide background, and throughout there is steady reference to events prior to and during the Chosin Reservoir campaign. Well-indexed.

1159 Harris, Richard. Korean Conflict: Rear Area Security, IX (US) Corps, 25th Infantry Division, 35th Infantry Regiment: October 1950. Fort Leavenworth, Kansas: United States Army Command and General Staff College, 1984.

Communist tactics were such that "rear" areas were more combat vulnerable than in previous wars. This is an area plan for security.

1160 Heasley, Morgan B. "Mountain Operations in Winter" Military Review 32 3 (June 1952): 11-18.

The American infantry is capable of conducting mountain operations in winter with only minor substitution in weapons and equipment.

1161 Heilbrunn, Otto. Partisan Warfare. New York: Frederick A. Praeger, 1962. London: Allen & Unwin, 1962.

Interesting, but limited, story of national involvement in guerilla warfare. Does not have the advantage of later monographs.

1162 Heinl, Robert D. "Inchon" Marine Corps Gazette 51 (September 1967): 20-28, (October 1967): 45-50.

A two-part indepth account of the planning for Inchon, including Marine preparation and shipments as well as the landing. Center to this study is the author's wonder at MacArthur's division of the landing to a morning attack on Wolmi-do and an afternoon attack on Inchon. Must be considered a masterpiece of planning. An analysis of the materials which he would later publish in considerably more detail in book form.

1163 Heinl, Robert D. "The Inchon Landing: A Case Study in Amphibious Planning" Naval War College Review 39 9 (Summer 1967): 51-72.

Heinl includes some materials which would later be published in his very fine book-length study. A good account by this top historian on the full range of planning and execution of Operation Chromite. He supports Admiral W. F. Halsey's statement "the Inchon landing is the most masterly and audacious strategic stroke in all history."

1164 Heinl, Robert D., Jr. Victory at High Tide: The Inchon-Seoul Campaign. New York: J. B. Lippincott, 1968.

MacArthur was not convinced that the landing at Inchon would be sufficient for the Eighth Army to break out of Pusan and move north. He felt that General Walker and the defenders of Pusan had been retreating so long they might be unable to take the offensive even if the Inchon attack was successful. MacArthur suggested other possible landings to break the hold, the replacement of Walker as Army Commander as well as lack of confidence in Eighth Army in general. Events were to prove him wrong.

1165 High, Gil. "Never Again" Soldiers 45 9 (September 1990): 24-25.

Discusses the failures imposed on Task Force Smith, and yet acknowledges the significant role played by this small group of men.

1166 Hinshaw, Arned L. Heartbreak Ridge: Korea, 1951. New York: Praeger, 1989.

Identifies army operations during the hill war and reports on one of the most desperate fights of all.

1167 Hittle, J. D. "Korea: Back to the Facts of Life" United States Naval Institute Proceedings 76 12 (December 1950): 1289-1298.

The author is concerned with protecting the "balanced fleet concept" and uses the successful attack on Inchon as an example of the cooperation between the Marines and the United States Navy.

1168 Hopkins, William B. <u>One Bugle, No Drums: The Marines at Chosin Reservoir</u>. Chapel Hill: Algonquin Books, 1986.
     Hopkins provides essentially a book about the fight at Chosin and contains a very good account of the formation of the marine units which landed at Wolmi-do and then Inchon.

1169 Hoyt, Edwin P. <u>On To the Yalu</u>. New York: Stein and Day, 1984.
     Good history of the "turn-around" at Inchon and the push north to the Yalu River. His treatment is one of the few which deals with the KATUSA (Korean Army Troop Augmentation to United States Army) troops who made up a good portion of the 7th Infantry (Army) Division.

1170 Hoyt, Edwin P. <u>The Pusan Perimeter: Korea, 1950</u>. New York: Stein and Day Publishers, 1984.
     One of the few full-length study of the Pusan Perimeter which concentrates on the amazing defense that was conducted there. This narrative, told by a popular and respected historian, follows from the invasion, through the first efforts to delay the North Koreans, the retreat to Naktong, the formation of the first and second defense line for the Perimeter, and the many efforts to break the United Nations defense.

1171 Ickes, Harold L. "Once More We Fight For Time" <u>New Republic</u> 123 (July 31, 1950): 17.
     The United States has been pushed into a beachhead with no place else to go, trading men for time while the "corrupt police state of South Korea" crumbled.

1172 "Inchon: The Beachhead for Professionals" <u>Marine Corps Gazette</u> 69 (September 1985): 3-6.
     When MacArthur planned the Inchon landing he determined he had to have the 1st Marine Division to spearhead the landing. The reason the landing appeared so well-planned and executed, General O. P. Smith said, was "that professionals did it."

1173 "The Inchon Landings" <u>The American Legion</u> (July 1993): 24-27, 61.
     A short well-developed account of the landing at Inchon. It supports the belief that the amphibious assault is "the most powerful tool we have." Attributes the surprisingly low casualty rate to the successful planning and execution of the assault.

1174 Johnson, Ellis A. <u>Armored Warfare in the Eighth Army in Korea</u>. Fort Monroe, Virginia: Chief of Army Field Forces, 1951.

Early, and sometimes misinformed, account of the combat uses of tanks in Korea.

1175 <u>Kansas and Wyoming Lines Report, 1952</u>. Headquarters: 10th Engineer Combat Battalion, 3rd Infantry Division, 1952.

The development of battle lines, sometimes very much like World War I, were constructed at these two major battle lines.

1176 Karig, Walter, Malcolm W. Cagle and Frank A. Manson. <u>Battle Report: The War in Korea</u>. volume 6. New York: Rinehart and Company, Inc., 1952.

This is an added sixth volume in what was to be a five-volume account of World War II by three well-qualified historians. Appendix contains names of killed and wounded, medals received, and other pertinent information.

1177 Karig, Walter, Malcolm W. Cagle and Frank A. Manson. "The Man Who Made Inchon Possible" in Donald B. Robinson. <u>The Dirty Wars: Guerrilla Actions and Other Forms of Unconventional Warfare</u>. New York: Delacorte Press, 1968.

An eye-witness account of Lieutenant Eugene Franklin Clark, United States Navy, who lived behind enemy lines at Inchon to map items of land, tides, weather, and enemy positions to make possible the landing at Inchon.

1178 Keighley, Larry. "Four Dead—Three Wounded" <u>Saturday Evening Post</u> 223 17 (October 21, 1950): 32-33, 157.

Account of LCVP (Landing Craft, Vehicle and Personnel) during the attack on Red Beach at Inchon. In this first-time landing against a large city, four were killed and three hit in the first minutes.

1179 Kemp, Robert F. <u>Combined Operations in the Korean War</u>. Carlisle Barracks, Pennsylvania: United States Army War College, 1989.

The most difficult problem the United Nations forces faced was the frustrations of varied languages, systems, equipment, and supply differences. Combined operations grew significantly in Korea.

1180 <u>Key Korean War Battles Fought in the Republic of Korea</u>. APO, San Francisco: Headquarters, Eighth United States Army, 1972.

A short and limited account of the battles fought by Eighth Army and X Corps during the Korean War. Very one-sided and of limited value, but good bibliography source.

1181 "The Korean War" <u>Newsweek</u> 36 13 (September 25, 1950): 21-30.
　　　　Claims that the Inchon landing, which was outlined and analyzed in the article, was "the most telegraphed Sunday punch in military history" but was still successful. Provides an excellent source on diversion efforts at Kunsan, Mokpo, Samchok, Yongdok, and Pohang. Contains some very fine detailed maps for the landing, including the various beaches.

1182 Langley, Michael. <u>Inchon Landing: MacArthur's Last Triumph</u>. New York: Times Books, 1979.
　　　　A British account of the preparations for, and execution of, the Inchon landing. Brief and overly simple at times, it nevertheless is strongly supportive of MacArthur and the landing that was "an amazing example of planning, luck, courage, and leadership."

1183 Larew, Karl G. "Inchon Invasion Not a Stroke of Genius or Even Necessary" <u>Army</u> 38 (December 1988): 15-20.
　　　　Larew contends that the strike at Inchon did not save the Eighth Army, for it was not in danger. It would have been better to use the 1st Marine Division to support the Eighth. The decision at Inchon put Pusan in danger as they pulled troops out. The victory at Inchon led to the invasion of the North because it made Truman and MacArthur think they could not be beaten. Larew contends that the President should have stopped MacArthur's plan.

1184 Lavine, Harold. "Inchon: 'A HelluvaGamble' that Paid Off" <u>Newsweek</u> 36 13 (September 25, 1950): 25.
　　　　Lavine, one of the first reporters to land with the Marines, describes the high risks involved in making the landing at all and expresses amazement at the early success.

1185 Leckie, Robert. <u>Great American Battles</u>. New York: Random House, 1968.
　　　　A collection of accounts of major American battles which includes the Inchon-Seoul campaign. Leckie, a well-known military historian, tries to explain how Americans fought. There is little new information here.

1186 Lichterman, Martin. "To the Yalu and Back" in Harold Stein, editor. <u>American-Civil-Military Decisions: A Book of Case Studies</u>. Birmingham: University of Alabama Press, 1963.
　　　　Study of the civilian and military consideration behind putting limits on the advance on the United Nations troops in the winter 1950-1951.

1187 Maddox, Robert. "War in Korea: The Desperate Times" <u>American History Illustrated</u> 13 4 (1978): 26-38.

Describes the initial actions in July of 1950, primarily the role of "Task Force Smith" (which suffered fifty percent casualties), and the 24th Division which, short of weapons and ammunition, suffered great losses of men and land.

1188 Mainard, Allen G. "Sea Wall" in Karl Schuon, editor. The Leatherneck: An Informal History of the U. S. Marines. New York: Franklin Watts, Inc., 1993.

An excellent (and personal) account of the Marines hitting the sixteen-foot harbor sea wall which protected Inchon and which had to be scaled by the landing troops. It marked a historic moment for the Marines. Original article located in Mainard, Allen G. "Sea Wall" Leatherneck 40 9 (1957): 42-45.

1189 Mamaux, David H. Operation CHROMITE: Operational Art in a Limited War. Fort Leavenworth, Kansas: United States Army Command and General Staff College, 1987.

Study of the operational plans put together under MacArthur for the invasion at Inchon.

1190 Mann, Frank L. "Operation 'Versatile'" Military Engineers 44 299 (May-June 1952): 168-173.

The 2nd Engineer Special Brigade went ashore with the Marines and were in operation, and by D+1 provided port operation as well as emergency construction.

1191 Marshall, S. L. A. Battle at Best. New York: Morrow, 1964.

A series of short narratives of men involved in small-unit action in World War II and Korea. The author's theme is their brave action and overall ability to fight under the worst of conditions.

1192 Marshall, S. L. A. Notes on Infantry Tactics in Korea. Chevy Chase, Maryland: Johns Hopkins University, 1951.

This exceptional historian comments on what he witnessed in Korea, and is optimistic about the American fighting soldier.

1193 Marshall, S. L. A. Operation Punch and the Capture of Hill 440: Suwon, Korea, February 1951. Chevy Chase, Maryland: Johns Hopkins University, 1952.

Strong military historian provides a sound analysis of infantry action during the heart of the war.

1194 Marshall, S. L. A. Pork Chop Hill: The American Fighting Man in Action, Korea, Spring, 1953. New York: Morrow, 1956, 1968; Nashville:

Battery Press, 1986; New York: Jove Books, 1986; Norwalk, Connecticut: Easton Press, 1993.

Excellent account of the United States Army forces who fought, and refought, this bitter battle. Despite careful attention it is hard to hide the overall failure of United States military/political policy.

1195 Marshall, S. L. A. The River and the Gauntlet: Defeat of the Eighth Army by the Communist Chinese Forces, November 1950, in The Battle of the Chongchon River, Korea. New York: Morrow, 1953.

Describes the longest retreat in American history as the United Nations forces basically disintegrated as they were pushed south before the Chinese Army. Yet the author is very supportive of the Army and its weapons and equipment.

1196 Marshall S. L. A. "This Is the War in Korea" Combat Forces Journal 1 11 (June 1951): 15-22.

A hard look at the first few months of the war where many mistakes were made, troops and equipment limited, but Eighth Army fought well.

1197 Martin, Harold H. "The Colonel Saved the Day" Saturday Evening Post 223 11 (1950): 32-33, 187, 189-190.

Lieutenant Colonel John Michaelis, 27th Infantry Regiment Commander, held his assigned defense position in the face of heavy North Korean infantry action near Chindong-ni.

1198 Martin, Harold H. "The Epic of Bloody Hill" Saturday Evening Post 223 (1950): 50-54, 59-60.

Describes the bitter fighting at Bloody Hill where the men of the 1st Provisional Marine Brigade made a significant stand near the crossing of the Naktong River.

1199 McGovern, James. To the Yalu: From the Chinese Invasion of Korea to MacArthur's Dismissal. New York: Morrow, 1972.

A highly critical analysis of MacArthur's decision to push to the Yalu River. Holds the view that the Joint Chiefs of Staff did not have the power to stop him.

1200 Montross, Lynn. "The Capture of Seoul—Battle of the Barricades" Marine Corps Gazette 35 8 (August 1951): 26-37.

A continuation of Montross' excellent accounts of the Inchon landing and the battle for Seoul. In this segment he deals with the assault by Marine infantry, the crossing of the Han River, and the final assault on Seoul. Supported by excellent maps.

1201 Montross, Lynn. "Fleet Marine Force Korea, I" <u>United States Naval Institute Proceedings</u> 79 8 (August 1953): 829-841. II 79 9 (September 1953): 995.

    First part of a two part account of the marines in Korea. This first section contains a detailed account of the preparations for, and the execution of, the landing at Inchon and the Kimpo/Seoul campaign. Second part continues to Hungnam.

1202 Montross, Lynn. "The Inchon Landing: Victory Over Time and Tide" <u>Marine Corps Gazette</u> 35 7 (July 1951): 26-35.

    This is a very significant article. It deals with the reversal in Marine Corps history, when MacArthur requested a Marine division. This necessitated the call-up of troops, organization for reservists, transportation of whole units to Japan and Korea, the planning and supply of a division.

1203 Montross, Lynn. "The Pusan Perimeter: Fight For a Foothold" <u>Marine Corps Gazette</u> 35 (June 1951): 30-39.

    Montross, in making the case for the 1st Provisional Marine Brigade serving from 7 August to 7 September 1950, tends to forget the harsh and desperate fighting of United States, Republic of Korea, and some United Nations troops which held the line for months. Follows operations of 1st Provisional Marines from 7 August to 7 September 1950 which helped to establish and hold the United Nations defense command at the Pusan Perimeter.

1204 Montross, Lynn and Nicholas Canzona. <u>The Chosin Reservoir Campaign</u>. Washington, D. C.: U. S. Marines Corps Headquarters, 1957.

    A good look at the Marine role at Chosin, but as is usual, this account tends to ignore the other military services.

1205 Montross, Lynn and Nicholas A. Canzona. "Large Sedentary Targets on Red Beach" <u>Marine Corps Gazette</u> 44 9 (September 1960): 44-50.

    Part of the "audacious gamble" at Inchon was the beaching of eight LST's (Landing Ship Tanks) at H hour plus 1 hour. In this way much needed supplies were available for landing—tanks, rations, gas, ammo, water—as well as four surgical teams for immediate medical care. The officers and crews are listed.

1206 Mortensen, Roger. <u>Inchon and the Strategy of the Indirect Approach</u>. Air Command and Staff College, Research Report, Maxwell Air Force Base, Alabama, 1977.

    A student special project report from the command classes at the Air Command and Staff College, responding to the question of interdiction.

A copy is available at the Air University Library, but only to qualified scholars and with special permission from the staff.

1207 Murray, R. L. "The First Naktong" Marine Corps Gazette 49 (November 1965): 84-85.
Brief account of the fighting between the North Koreans and the Marines along the Naktong River during the bloody days from 17-19 August 1950. Reminds the reader that the Marines were fighting along the Naktong River in the early 1950s.

1208 Nearing, Scott. Operation Killer. Washington, D. C.: World Events Committee, 1951.
Brief analysis of Ridgway's offensive designed to kill communist soldiers rather than take land.

1209 "New Troops Bolster Battered GI's" Newsweek 36 (August 7, 1950): 15-17.
A steady stream of men and equipment arriving in Pusan supported the United Nations forces there, as Walker held the North Koreans and protected the Pusan Perimeter.

1210 Noble, Harold Joyce. Embassy at War. Seattle: University of Washington Press, 1975.
Harold Noble was an expert on Korean affairs, and First Secretary of the American Embassy at the time of the North Korean invasion. He recounts the period from 25 June 1950 to 29 September 1950 during which the Americans, as well as the Republic of Korea, suffered defeat, retreated, and finally took a stand at Pusan. His background and insights paint an interesting picture of the early days.

1211 Paschall, Rod. "Special Operations in Korea" Conflict 7 2 (1987): 155-178.
One of the few articles to discuss North Korean partisans who, during the early months, inflicted nearly 70,000 casualties among the North Korean troops. The United Nations did not make the most of these partisans because they were considered disorganized.

1212 Paschall, Rod. A Study in Command and Control: Special Operations in Korea, 1951-1953. Carlisle Barracks, Pennsylvania: United States Army Military History Institute, 1988.
Commando operations, underground, and guerrilla warfare all created their own problems of command and control.

1213 Pirnie, Bruce R. "The Inchon Landing: How Great Was the Risk?" Joint Perspectives 3 1 (Summer 1982): 86-97.

The author gives an excellent review of the landing at Inchon, then concludes that it was not really much of a gamble. The situation was such that there was "periculum in mora" (danger in delay).

1214 Pittman, Phill. The Battle of Sukchon-Sunchon: Defensive, Encircled Forces: Allied Forces, 187th Airborne RCT: Enemy Forces, North Korea 239th RGT, 20-25 October, 1950. Fort Leavenworth, Kansas: United States Army Command and General Staff College, 1984.

A study in combat as an encircled force—the 187th chasing North Koreans in northern Korea.

1215 Pratt, Sherman W. Decisive Battles of the Korean War: An Infantry Company Commander's View of the War's Most Critical Engagements. New York: Vantage Press, 1992.

Hard to distinguish between narrative and commentary. Certainly an interesting and informative view of the war from the company level.

1216 "President" Department of State Bulletin 23 (October 9, 1950): 586.

The text of President Harry Truman's message of congratulations to MacArthur on the Inchon success, and General MacArthur's reply to the President.

1217 Pusan Perimeter, Naktong River Bulge, August-September 1950. APO: Eighth United States Army, 1991.

Covers the 24th Infantry Division and the 1st Provisional Brigade (Marine), at the battle of Naktong Bulge.

1218 Quinn, Joseph M. "Catching the Enemy Off Guard" Armor 60 4 (1951): 46-48.

Describes the 89th Tank Battalion (Task Force Dolvin) which led the breakout of the Pusan Perimeter in September 1950.

1219 Report of the Subcommittee on Internal Security; Subcommittee to Investigate the Administration of the Internal Security Act and Other Internal Security Laws to the Committee on the Judiciary. part 25, Senate, 84th Congress, 1st Session, January 21, 1955. Washington, D. C.: Government Printing Office, 1955.

Lieutenant General Edward Almond's testimony tries to explain the purpose of Inchon and the value of the divided command which created X Corps.

1220 Rice, Earle. The Inchon Invasion. San Diego, California: Lucent Books, 1996.
     Juvenile literature which is basically the "story" of Inchon.

1221 Robinson, William G. "Counterattack on the Naktong, 1950" Leavenworth Papers No. 13. Fort Leavenworth, Kansas: United States Army Command and Staff College, 1985.
     Sets the stage for the Pusan Perimeter and for counterattacks along the "bulge line" as North Korean forces push the last desperate attacks.

1222 Rogers, John S. The Battle for Seoul: An Overview of Marine and Enemy Forces Used. no publisher, 1982.
     A quick look at the fifteen-day battle from Inchon to the conquest of Seoul. Primarily Marine, little on the 7th Infantry Division. The author identifies enemy units.

1223 Russell, George H. "Defense On An Extended Front" Infantry School Quarterly 43 2 (1953): 60-64.
     The 23rd Infantry Regiment defended a 16,000 yard front on the Taegu-Pusan Perimeter during August and September of 1950, and did it successfully. This article tries to explain how it was possible.

1224 Russell, William C. Stalemate & Standoff: The Bloody Outpost War. DeLeon Springs, Florida: W. Russell, 1993.
     Standard account of war, made valuable by its look at the final years, not the more dramatic early war.

1225 Russell, William C. Ten Days at White Horse. Arlington, Virginia: no publisher, 1988.
     Remembrances of the prolonged Battle of White Horse Mountain (1952) as seen by the author/participant.

1226 Schnabel, James F. "The Inchon Landing: Perilous Gamble or Exemplary Boldness?" Army 9 (May 1959): 50.
     An excellent account of the planning, risks, evaluation of the Inchon landing, which is generally supportive of General MacArthur, his planning staff, and the decisiveness of the battle which led to eventual victory.

1227 Schott, Joseph L. Above and Beyond. New York: G. P. Putnam's Sons, 1963.
     One hundred and thirty-one Medals of Honor were awarded during the Korean War. There are several accounts of Korean War recipients and their activities leading to the heroism during this campaign.

1228 Seibert, Donald A. The Regulars. Carlisle Barracks, Pennsylvania: United States Army Military History Institute, no date.

Manuscript which looks at the cadre Army available when war broke out, and on which the Korean Army was built.

1229 Sheldon, Walt. Hell or High Water: MacArthur's Landing at Inchon. New York: The Macmillan Company, 1968.

An excellent and detailed study of the Inchon landing from conception to the wrap-up. The success was the result of MacArthur's determination. Never the secret it was claimed (called "Operation Common Knowledge" by many of the press) it was the result of one man's determination. Despite the opposition of the president, Pentagon, typhoons, and high water the carefully planned attack was all MacArthur promised.

1230 Simmons, Edwin H. "War-Gaining Inchon" Fortitudine (Fall 1987): 3-6.

Describes Inchon as a war-game exercise in naval training where the risks increased the level of success.

1231 Smith, Lynn D. "A Nickel After a Dollar: MacArthur's Daring Plan for the Invasion of Inchon" Army 20 (September 1970): 24.

Discusses MacArthur and the invasion of Inchon, on the basis that it was only a small risk compared to the risk of an involvement in Korea.

1232 Smith, Oliver P. "Inchon Landing" Marine Corps Gazette 44 (September 1960): 40-41.

Written by the commanding general of the 1st Marine Division and his only comment on the war. He indicated amazement at the ability of the navy and marines to land a combat-ready division on the beaches in such a short time with so little difficulty. Provides details of 1st Marine Division Operation order (02-50) the Inchon Landing Operational Plan.

1233 Stanford, N. R. "Road Junction" Marine Corps Gazette 35 9 (September 1951): 16-21.

At the crossing of the Han, and in the middle of Seoul, a rifle company commander discovers that there are times when you have to throw away the book. This article is a vivid account of small-unit action and tense command decisions during the battle for Seoul.

1234 Stanton, Shelby L. America's Tenth Legion: X Corps in Korea, 1950. Novato, California: Presidio Press, 1989.

A better-than-average look at X Corps, its commander, its assignments, and the difficulties raised by the complicated command and unusual assignments. The creation of the independent body, and its separate existence on the drive north, was one of the more controversial issues of MacArthur's command.

1235 Stelmach, Daniel S. "The Influence of Russian Armored Tactics on the North Korean Invasion, 1950" Ph.D. dissertation, Washington University, St. Louis, 1973.
     Russian tanks maneuvered by North Korean tankers, using Russian tactics, proved ruthless and efficient and when used in the triangular fashion armor-infantry-artillery, were almost impossible to stop.

1236 Summerby, Janice. Native Soldiers: Foreign Battlefields. Ottawa, Canada: Government of Canada, 1993.
     Makes a rather exaggerated case for North American Indians who fought with Canadian forces in World War II and Korea.

1237 Tallent, Robert W. "Inchon to Seoul" Leatherneck 34 1 (1951): 12-17.
     An enlisted man's account of the drive from Inchon to Seoul which, at least from his perspective, was not the easy task sometimes described.

1238 Tallent, Robert W. "Pusan—A Stop Enroute" Leatherneck 33 (1950): 14-17.
     Traces the pull-out of the 1st Provisional Marines who in the midst of a desperate fight to save Pusan were pulled out to prepare for the Inchon landing. At a time when the success of the defense was in serious question, and against Walker's requests, MacArthur pulled the Marines out, regrouped, and went on to the invasion.

1239 Tallent, Robert W. "Street Fight in Seoul" in Karl Schuon, editor. The Leatherneck: An Informal History of the U. S. Marines. New York: Franklin Watts, Inc., 1993.
     The 7th Regiment, 1st Marine Division, missed the landing but the unit arrived from the United States in time to participate in the advance against Seoul. This is an excellent account of urban warfare, a somewhat unusual fighting arena for the Marines.

1240 Tapplet, R. D. and R. E. Whipple. "Darkhorse Sets the Pace" Marine Corps Gazette 37 6 and 7 (June-July 1950): 14-23, 44-50.
     The United States 1st Marine Division carried the landing at Inchon. The spearheaded group was the Third Battalion, Fifth Marines Regiment. This is an account of the combat activities of the Third Battalion at the Inchon landing.

1241 Tate, James H. "The First Five Months" Army Information Digest 6 3 (March 1951): 40-48.

This is the first of a long series on the fighting of the war, and covers the details of the battle fought by United Nations troops from the initial invasion to the perimeter at Pusan.

1242 Thompson, Milton R. "Employment of Armor in Korea, The First Year: A Research Report" Fort Knox, Kentucky: Armored School, 1952.
     An early, and incomplete, look at the limitations of tank warfare in Korea.

1243 Thompson, Reginald. Cry Korea. London: MacDonald and Company Ltd., 1951.
     British correspondent who went along on the Inchon landing, considered the whole effort to be over-kill, too much force for too little target. Thompson found the Marines to be less humane than he expected. An interesting affirmation of the British view that they were fighting in Korea, but not for Korea.

1244 Tomlinson, H. Pat. "Inchon: The General's Decision" Military Review 47 (April 1967): 28-35.
     This article centers on the Joint Chiefs of Staff debate over approval of the landing, the alternative landings suggested (one site suggested was Kunsan), and relates the landing to Wolfe at Quebec, a concept which appears with great regularity. The Joint Chiefs of Staff were overwhelmed by MacArthur who outranked and out demanded them all.

1245 Totten, James P. "Operation Chromite: A Study in Generalship" Armor 85 (November-December, 1976): 33-38.
     The entire operation at the Inchon landing was conceived, staffed, and executed within ninety days. In order to put the plan into operation, foreign nationals serving in the United States 7th Infantry Division, untrained ship captains and inexperienced crews, Japanese nationals and their landing craft were involved in pulling it off. The author argues that the operation was unjustified on every grounds but imagination. But, once it was decided, an amazing job was performed.

1246 "Turning of the Tide in Korea and the Meeting of 'a New Foe'" United Nations Bulletin 9 10 (November 15, 1950): 528-530.
     Excerpts from MacArthur's report to the United Nations on the landing at Inchon, and the successful campaign for Seoul. Somewhere between the tide tables and his own "sense" of timing it was generally accepted that . . . "had the landing been delayed so much as a month, it would have been too late."

1247 United Nations Command. <u>One Year in Korea, A Summary: 25 June 50-25 June 51</u>. Tokyo: Far East Command, 1951.

Command reports to the United Nations about the first year of combat. Not much help.

1248 <u>UN Partisan Forces in the Korean Conflict, 1951-1952: A Study in their Characteristics and Operations</u> Tokyo: Military History Detachment-3, 1954.

A generally unsuccessful attempt to define the nature of partisan activities, including the 8086th group. Partisan warfare was never fully utilized.

1249 United States. <u>Report of Army Field Observer Team No. 5</u>. Far East Command, 1951.

Formal and technical field reports (team 5) established by Far East Command concerning the first year of combat. Technical data.

1250 United States. <u>Report of Army Field Observer Team No. 6</u>. Far East Command, 1952.

Formal and technical field reports (team 6) established by Far East Command concerning the second year of the war.

1251 United States. <u>Report of Army Field Observer Team No. 7</u>. Far East Command, 1952.

Formal and technical field reports (team 7) established by Far East Command concerning the second year of the war.

1252 United States. <u>Report of Army Field Observer Team No. 8</u>. Far East Command, 1953.

Formal and technical field reports (team 8) established by Far East Command concerning the third year of the war.

1253 United States. <u>Special After Action Report, Hill 395 (White Horse Mountain) 6-15 October 1952</u>. APO: IX United States Corps, 1952.

After action report of the IX Corps action during the prolonged battle at White Horse Mountain commissioned by the Corps.

1254 United States Army Corps, 10th. <u>Battle of the Soyang-River (Special Report)</u>. Headquarters: X Corps, 1951.

After-action report, commissioned by the Corps, of X Corps action at the Battle of Soyang River.

1255 United States Army Corps, 10th. <u>Special Report on Chosin Reservoir, 27 November-10 December 1950</u>. Headquarters: X Corps, 1951.

After-action special report dealing with the forced retreat at Chosin, and the successful action involved in the evacuation.

1256 United States Army Corps, 10th. Special Report on Hungnam Evacuation, 9-24 December 1950. Headquarters: X Corps, 1950.
Field report on the evacuation of United States and Republic of Korea troops from Hungnam following the retreat at Chosin.

1257 United States Army Winter Environmental Team. Winter Combat Problems, Korea, Dec. 1951-Feb. 1952. Washington, D. C.: Department of the Army, 1952.
Research report on the effect of winter on combat, following the second desperate winter in the Korean War. The United States was not well prepared in 1950 for winter combat.

1258 United States Military Academy, Department of Military Art and Engineering. Operations in Korea. West Point, New York: United States Military Academy, 1956.
Brief account of American military units in Korea, and of those in operation during the war. Excellent source.

1259 Utz, Curtis A. Assault From the Sea: The Amphibious Landing at Inchon. Washington, D. C.: Naval History Center, Department of Navy, 1994.
Short, but very helpful account of the landing at Inchon, tracking the roles of the various units involved. Primarily a naval approach.

1260 Walker, Hank and Carl Mydans, photographer, editor. "The Invasion: The Pattern of the War is Changed As U. N. Forces Strike the Red Rear" Life 29 14 (October 2, 1950): 23-32.
A photo essay of the invasion which contains a good "I was there" report on the landing. The wide angle picture of the landing beaches is worth ten maps in understanding the landing difficulties. The essay covers through the fall of Kimpo airfield and the attack on Seoul.

1261 "War in Asia" Time 56 (July 17, 1950): 17-18.
Reports that failures are forcing the United States troops (United Nations) into an ever-tightening perimeter around the port of Pusan. Discusses weapons available for the defense of the perimeter.

1262 "War in Asia" Time 56 (July 24, 1950): 20-21.
Warns that communist forces are threatening to cut the rail line, and to encircle and destroy the forces of the United States on their first line of defense at the Pusan Perimeter.

1263 "War in Asia" <u>Time</u> 56 (July 31, 1950): 15-17.
  While the United States troops steadily retreated toward the built-up area around Pusan, there is no reason to believe that the communists are not planning to expand the war into Indo-China.

1264 "War in Asia" <u>Time</u> 56 (August 7, 1950): 18-20.
  Reports that General Walker had issued a "stand-or-die" order as the United Nations moves into some hastily developed lines of defense around Pusan. MacArthur estimates 90,000 North Korean troops are ready to attack.

1265 "War in Asia" <u>Time</u> 56 (August 21, 1950): 18-22.
  The perimeter has held and the communists have been stopped. The United States will soon begin counterattacks against North Korean forces.

1266 "War in Asia" <u>Time</u> 56 (August 28, 1950): 21-23.
  Discusses the choice faced by United Nations forces, to attack or move back into a defense perimeter. The decision to move into a perimeter definitely saved the situation.

1267 "War in Asia" <u>Time</u> 56 (September 4, 1950): 20.
  The perimeter defense is holding as United Nations forces continue to gather soldiers and supplies. Command is now voicing concern about over-confidence. This seems to be the extreme of "morale-building" articles.

1268 War in Asia" <u>Time</u> 56 (September 25, 1950): 25-32.
  In reporting, the landing at Inchon was described as being in the "American tradition." Maps and descriptions are very good, particularly of Wolmi-do Island and a good account of three leaders; General Almond, Admiral Struble, and Admiral Doyle: the X Corps and 7th Task Force commanders.

1269 Williams, John H. "Stand or Die" <u>Army</u> 35 8 (August 1985): 56-68.
  Deals with the fighting during the early phase of the war, and at the Pusan Perimeter. North Korean commanders had been ordered to conquer all of South Korea by 15 August 1950 and they were running out of time. The United Nations troops were running out of space. By early August the fighting had become desperate and troops were aware that there was no where else to run.

1270 Zaloga, Steven J. and George Balin. <u>Tank Warfare in Korea, 1950-53</u>. Hong Kong: Concord Publishing Company, 1994.
  Short technical display of equipment with some narrative about tank tactics.

Special Operations

1271 Beaumont, Roger A. Military Elites. Indianapolis, Indiana: Bobbs-Merrill, 1974. London: R. Hale, 1976.
    Excellent early account of specialized troops in several wars. Some coverage of Korea.

1272 Black, Robert W. Rangers in Korea. New York: Ivy Books, 1989.
    A popular but very good look at Rangers in Korea. Ridgway did not like the concept of special forces, but they were put to good use.

1273 Breuer, William B. Shadow Warriors: The Covert War in Korea. New York: Wiley, 1996.
    Based on interviews this covers covert maneuvers, secret missions, and propaganda campaigns conducted by the United States and South Korea. These actions were directed by Joint Service Operations, which included intelligence and counter-intelligence operations.

1274 Cooper, Paul L. Weekend Warriors. Manhattan, Kansas: Sunflower University Press, 1996.
    An account of reservists as citizen/sailors who flew in Reserve Fighter VF-871 off the USS Princeton.

1275 Davison, W. Phillips and Jean Hungerford. North Korean Guerrilla Units. Santa Monica, California: Rand Corporation, 1951.
    Not very useful study of North Korean insurgents. Too early and of questionable value.

1276 Day, James S. "Partisan Operations of the Korean War" MA thesis, University of Georgia, 1989.
    MA: partisans

1277 Dockery, Kevin. SEALS in Action. New York: Avon Books, 1991.
    Popularized history of Seals including Underwater Demolition Teams—as they were called then—in Korea.

1278 Evanhoe, Ed. Darkmoon: Eighth Army Special Operations in the Korean War. Annapolis, Maryland: Naval Institute Press, 1995.
    Account of USEA G-3 miscellaneous group, which took forays into Korea as special operations agents.

1279 Gray, David R. "Black and Gold Warriors: US Army Rangers During the Korean War" Ph.D. dissertation, Ohio State University, 1992.

The Rangers, recreated in Korea, were designed as light infantry to off-set the North Korean infiltration units, and were used to provide short-range penetration forces.

1280 Haas, Michael E. and Dale K. Robinson. Air Commando! 1950-1975: Twenty-Five Years at the Tip of the Spear. Hurlburt Field, Florida: Air Force Special Operations Command, 1994.
A useful narrative of so-called "air commando" operations during Korea and Vietnam.

1281 Knox, Robert R. A Study of Ranger Units in World War II and Korea: An Analysis of Their Successes and Failures. Fort McClellan, Alabama: United States Army Chemical Corps School, 1960.
This book sees more success than failure in the use of Rangers in Korea, but is a good first look.

1282 Malcolm, Ben S. White Tigers: My Secret War in North Korea. Washington, D. C.: Brassey's, 1995.
First book available about the American-led guerilla war deep behind enemy lines in Korea, using previously unavailable classified materials. Combines firsthand information and knowledge of intelligence operations to provide this excellent study.

1283 Mark, Ray. Sugar Cain's Young Lions: A Story of the 6th Ranger Infantry Company (Airborne) of the Korean War Era. Seattle, Washington: no publisher or date.
A regimental history privately printed; useful but limited.

1284 Nelson, Robert B. Unit History, 6th Ranger Infantry Company Airborne. Carlisle Barracks, Pennsylvania: Archive/Manuscript Control, 1951.
A short (sixteen page) regimental history of a ranger company in active duty.

1285 Stubbe, Ray W. Aarugha! Report to Director, Historical Division, Headquarters, Marine Corps, On the History of Specialized and Force-Level Reconnaissance Activities and Units of the United States Marine Corps, 1900 to 1974. Great Lakes, Illinois: Stubbe, 1981. Washington, D. C.: United States Marines, 1990.
The work is not much longer than the title, but contains a lot of useful and interesting material.

Strategies and Tactics

1286 Anderson, Kenneth. U. S. Military Operations: 1945-1983. New York: The Military Press, 1984.

General illustrated history with good, well-defined maps of a variety of operations, including Korea.

1287 Blumenson, Martin. "MacArthur's Divided Command: An Assessment in the Light of Army Doctrine" Army 7 (November 1956): 38-44.

In dividing command MacArthur violated a principle of war long followed. It was done because of the communication problems caused by the Taebaek Mountains which would separate the command, and the general problem of communication. Yet as the United Nations troops moved north each appeared ignorant of the other. The decision, however important to MacArthur, caused trouble for Walker at Pusan, and a later disharmony in command.

1288 Brodie, Bernard. A Guide to Naval Strategy. Princeton: Princeton University Press, 1958.

A very general work which contains a good chapter on the naval strategy of the Korean War.

1289 Doughty, Robert. "The Evolution of U. S. Army Tactical Doctrine, 1946-1976" Leavenworth Papers: Combat Study Series Institute. Fort Leavenworth, Kansas: United States Army Command and General Staff College, 1979.

Discusses the development of tactical doctrines through the post-World War II era. Chapter seven deals with the Korean period, and is primarily concerned with shortages in unit size and limited supply and equipment.

1290 Falls, Cyril. "A Window on the World: Still Delaying-actions in Korea" The Illustrated London News 217 (July 29, 1950): 172.

General MacArthur was defeated at the battle of Kum River, the line where he assumed he could finally stop the North Koreans. He retreated into a defense perimeter to fight for time.

1291 Johnson, Dana J. Roles and Missions for Conventionally Armed Heavy Bombers: An Historical Perspective. Santa Monica, California: Rand Corporation, 1994.

Describes the uses, and defines the roles of non-nuclear bombing in World War II, Korea, and Vietnam, claiming a serious role remains for the heavy bombers.

1292 Kaufmann, William W. <u>Policy Objectives and Military Action in the Korean War</u>. Santa Monica, California: Rand Corporation, 1956.

An attempt to understand the relation between policy and military activity in Korea. Presented to the American Political Science Association in 1956. Primarily dated.

1293 Kleinman, Forrest K. "The Tactician of Danger Forward" <u>Army</u> 9 (November 1958): 26-29.

Short supportive article which acknowledged General John Church, of the 24th Division, as a major tactician in this bewildering period of the Korean War.

1294 Koh, Byung Chul. "The Korean War as a Learning Experience for North Korea" <u>Korea and World Affairs</u> 3 3 (Fall 1979).

Putting the best face on difficult period, the author suggest lessons which can be learned from the years of war.

1295 Marshall, Thomas L. "The Strategy of Conflict in the Korean War" Ph.D. dissertation, University of Virginia, 1969.

Looks at Red China and the United States and their ability to fight a limited war, recognizing that armed conflict was a part of their policy.

1296 Miller, Robert E. "Separate Tank Battalion versus The Tank Regiment: A Research Report" Fort Knox, Kentucky: Armored School, 1952.

This report compares tactics and finds fault with methods of World War II and Korea.

1297 Nicholson, Dennis D. "Creeping Tactics" <u>Marine Corps Gazette</u> 42 (1958): 20-26.

Describes the tactics of the first few months of the war as North Koreans crept into American positions and launched devastating attacks from all directions.

1298 Ohn, Chang-Il. "The Joint Chiefs of Staff and U. S. Policy and Strategy Regarding Korea, 1945-1953" Ph.D. dissertation, University of Kansas, 1983.

Ohn holds that the Joint Chiefs of Staff could not relate what was happening in Korea to the larger strategic interests for America, and thus waffled in their policy and actions during the Korean War. Such lack of clarity, especially in the beginning, made the war very costly.

1299 <u>The Relationship of Casualties to Tactics and Ammunition Expenditure: 2nd U. S. Infantry Division, Korea, 1 February 1953-31 March 1953</u>. no publisher, 1953.

Interesting study which again supports the fact that in combat only a small percentage of soldiers actually use their weapons, and when they do, they are generally ineffective.

1300 Sherry, Mark D. "The United States Strategy for Containing China, 1949-1953" Ph.D. dissertation, Georgetown University, 1993.
Outlines the overall strategy for containing communist China, discussed in the light of the "strategic defense" compromise.

1301 Temple, Charles E. "Should Tank Units Be Trained in Indirect Fire?: A Research Report" Fort Knox, Kentucky: Armored School, 1952
A look at tactics as gunnery and tank warfare is discussed. The review leaves the reader without a definite answer.

1302 United States Policy in the Korean Conflict, July 1950-February 1951. Washington, D. C.: Government Printing Office, 1951, 1983.
Collection of materials dealing with American involvement, which relates general policy at the beginning of the Korean War.

1303 United States Policy in the Korean Crisis. Washington, D. C.: Government Printing Office, 1950, 1972, 1983.
Collection of materials dealing with foreign relations in the early Korean period. Includes reference to the Voice of America.

1304 Waldman, Michael. "Why to the Yalu? Foreign Policy Aims, Military Objectives, and Government Decision Making in the Advance of American Troops to the Yalu River in 1950" AB thesis, Harvard University, 1982.
AB: war expansion

Logistics, Troops, Weapons, Decorations

1305 Ammunition Shortages in the Armed Services. Congressional Record, Senate, 83rd Congress, 1st session, 1953.
A look at the early shortages of appropriate ammunition for the Armed Forces. The problem was getting the correct ammo, not the amount available.

1306 Arrington, Leonard J. and others. "Sentinels on the Desert: The Dunway Proving Grounds (1942-1963) and the Desert Chemical Depot (1942-1955)" Utah Historical Review 32 1 (1964): 32-43.
A short history of the Dunway Center for chemical warfare research shows how the outbreak of war in Korea led to reactivation and expansion of the facilities. Became a problem when charges of chemical warfare were leveled against the Americans.

1307 Arrington, Leonard J. and Thomas G. Alexander. "Supply Hub of the West: Defense Depot Ogden" Utah Historical Quarterly 32 2 (1964): 99-121.

An account of the impact of the Korean War on the Defense Depot at Ogden, Utah, where in 1950 125,093 tons of material was shipped to the front.

1308 Atkins, E. L., H. P. Griggs and Roy T. Sessums. North Korean Logistics and Methods of Accomplishment. Chevy Chase, Maryland: Johns Hopkins University, 1951.

An early, but still helpful, look at North Korea supply and distribution—less dependent on the road or cities.

1309 Barker, E. L. "The Helicopter in Combat" United States Naval Institute Proceedings 77 11 (November 1951): 1207-1222.

Excellent account of the expanding use of choppers in the Korean War, providing special examples of military value.

1310 Bell, E. V. H. "The 4.2 Mortar in Korea" Combat Forces Journal 3 5 (December 1952): 27-29.

An exchange of letters between General Bellene and Lieutenant Colonel Bell, Chemical Mortar Battalion, on the use of the 4.2 mortar in Korea.

1311 Bellene, E. F. "Wonder Weapon" Combat Forces Journal 3 4 (November 1952): 28-30.

The use of napalm in Korea, especially in the "iron triangle," proved to be a highly effective anti-personnel weapon.

1312 Benson, Lawrence R. "The USAF's Korean War Recruiting Rush... and the Great Tent City at Lackland Air Force Base" Aerospace Historian 25 2 (1978): 61-73.

Discusses the effort to get nearly 70,000 airmen trained, equipped, and ready for the service.

1313 Berebitsky, William. A Very Long Weekend: The Army National Guard in Korea 1950-1953. Shippensburg, Pennsylvania, White Mane Publishing Company, 1996.

Lists and discusses the contributions of the forty-three national guard units that served in Korea.

1314 Black, Richard B., W. A. Taylor and William Neilson. An Evaluation of Service Support in the Korean Campaign. Chevy Chase, Maryland: Johns Hopkins University, 1951.

A consideration of the use of napalm, supply/logistics, and equipment provided by support groups during the Korean War.

1315 Boettcher, Thomas D. First Call: the Making of the Modern U. S. Military, 1945-1953. Boston: Little, Brown and Company, 1992.
    Armed forces history that traces involvement from the need to provide an army of occupation, and the peace-time problems which came to light at the outbreak of war in Korea.

1316 Borts, Lawrence H. and Frank C. Foster. Medals of America Presents United States Military Medals, 1939 to Present. Fountain Inn, South Carolina: Medals of America Press, 1995.
    Covers awards available for the Army, Navy, Air Force, Marines, Merchant Marines, and Coast Guard in World War II, Korea, Vietnam, and the Gulf War.

1317 Bowers, Ray. "Korea: Proving Ground in Combat Air Transportation" Defense Management Journal 12 (July 1976): 62-66.
    From the beginning the organization and effectiveness of air support transport proved the value of learning from experience.

1318 Boyd, Ralph C. and John G. Westover. "Truck Platoon—Withdrawal from Taejon" Combat Forces Journal 3 2 (September 1952): 26-27.
    Deals with the difficulty of supply and transport during the early days of the war. During July and August of 1950, trucks running out of Pusan harbor were used to move retreating men and equipment and to deliver much needed supplies.

1319 "Building Our Military Power" Army Information Digest 5 9 (1950): 3-10.
    Describes events and actions taken to meet the staffing needs of the Korean War.

1320 Bunker, William B. "Organization for an Airlift" Military Review 31 (April 1951): 25-31.
    Considers the development and deployment of airlift activities conducted by the United States Air Force out of Japan.

1321 Burke, Ronald R. Troopship: The Story of the James O'Hara and Her Times. Seattle, Washington: R. R. Burke, 1992.
    A personal narrative of transportation during World War II and the Korean War, using the O'Hara as an example.

1322 Burnham, P. "Rearming for the Korean War: The Impact of Government Policy on Leyland Motors and the British Car Industry" Contemporary Record 9 2 (1995).
　　　Interesting account of British logistic and production efforts and the effect on a major industry.

1323 Bykofsky, Joseph. Battlefield Mobility: Pooled Motor Transport in a Combat Support Role. Washington, D. C.: Department of the Army, 1958.
　　　Short research paper on the valuation of pooled transport, along with recommendations for improving support functions.

1324 Chester, David J. and Niel J. Van Steenberg. "Effects on Morale of Infantry Team Replacement and Individual Replacement Systems" Sociometry 18 4 (August 1955): 587-597.
　　　Compares the morale of replacements assigned as individuals, with the four-man-team replacements which proved more effective.

1325 Cocklin, Robert F. "Artillery in Korea" Combat Forces Journal 2 1 (August 1951): 22-27.
　　　Considers the role of artillery in support of infantry in firing six battery units. But the advantage was weakened by poor supplies of materials and equipment.

1326 Coggins, Thomas M. "Replacements are Coming" Marine Corps Gazette 37 6 (1953): 50-54.
　　　Looks at the processing of the Marines at Camp Pendleton for service in Korea. When the Korean War broke out the marines were in what amounted to a layoff. The sudden call for the 1st Marine Division reserve, the recall to Camp Pendleton, California, turned it into a beehive of replacement and training.

1327 Collier, Harry H. and Paul Chin-Chih Lai. Organizational Changes in the Chinese Army, 1895-1950. Taipei: Office of the Military Historian, 1969.
　　　Defines some major changes in the command structure and training programs within the Chinese military.

1328 Copsey, Robert L. "The Air Force Reserve" Journal of Military History 17 1 (Spring 1953): 11-16.
　　　Looks at the impact of the Korean War on the Air Force Reserve program where eighty percent of the officers were in the reserve program.

1329 Correa, Edward L. Logistics and the Chinese Communist Intervention During the Korean Conflict (1950-1953). Carlisle Barracks, Pennsylvania: United States Army War College, 1986.

A research study on the logistical nature of the Chinese commitment to Korea, and the preparation for involvement.

1330 Cox, William W. Report on the Use of Body Armor in Combat, Korea, February 1952-July 1952. Washington, D. C.: Government Printing Office, 1952.

Strong on the success of body armor and the health value in the use of protective clothing in Korea.

1331 Crossland, Richard B. and James T. Currie. Twice the Citizen: A History of the United States Army Reserve, 1908-1983. Washington, D. C.: Office of the Chief, Army Reserve, 1984.

A useful history of the Army Reserves and how the citizen soldiers were put to use (1908-1983) in four major wars.

1332 Davidson, B. "Why Half Our Combat Soldiers Fail to Shoot" Collier's 130 (November 8, 1952): 16-18.

Based on an interview with historian S. L. A. Marshall who says failure of aggression on the battlefield can be traced to early training. During World War II there were cases where only thirty-seven men out of 1,000 fired their weapons. During the Korean War it was about one out of two.

1333 Dougherty, Jack D. "Logistical Support of Armored Units in Korea: A Research Report" Fort Knox, Kentucky: Armored School, 1952.

Short report on supply problems of armor units fighting in Korea. Tanks were never considered very successful there.

1334 Dowling, Patrick M., Thomas H. Tudor and Theodore G. Schad. The Vulnerability of Army Supply to Air Interdiction. Chevy Chase, Maryland: Johns Hopkins University, 1953.

This study focuses on the United Nations but provides valuable information on the North Korean People's Army countermeasures.

1335 Drummond, J. E. "A Supply Officer's Report" The Supply Mercury (March 1952): 10-22.

Rather detailed account of the supply level and the difficulties of maintaining the necessary supplies.

1336 Dunstan, Simon. Armour of the Korean War 1950-1953. London: Osprey Publishing, 1982.

Brief illustrated history of the heavy armor used by both the United States and the North Koreans (Soviets) during the war. The static nature of the war, toward the end, limited tanks but it was such armor that moved the North Koreans rapidly south. Illustrations are excellent.

1337 Enakiev, O. The Foreign Armies: The Morale of American Troops in Korea. no publisher, 1959.

This short (sixteen page) study, translated from Russian, addresses the psychological aspects of the American fighting man.

1338 Flanagan, William J. "Korean War Logistics: The First Hundred Days" Army Logistics 18 (March-April 1986): 34-38.

Takes a brief look at the problems with supply and distribution during the first three months of the war. Not only were there limited supplies in Japan, there were few supplies anywhere. What army logistics was able to accomplish was not far short of a miracle.

1339 Flynn, George Q. "The Draft and College Deferments During the Korean War" Historian 50 (May 1988): 369-385.

When the Korean War broke out the army was depleted. Peace efforts and reorganization had limited the size of the military and when it became evident that troops were going to be needed the draft went into action. Though the need was great, the system was poorly staffed and many young men avoided the draft with a series of deferments.

1340 Fogleman, Ronald R. "Modernization for Korean War Stopped Post-WWII Reduction, Made Us Ready" Officer 68 (December 1991): 28-30, 41-42.

Calls for more interpretation of the transformation brought on by airpower's holistic imprint on warfare.

1341 Forney, James I. "Logistics of Aircraft Maintenance During the Korean War" MS thesis, Air Force Institute of Technology, 1988.

Looks at the specialized nature of aircraft weapons system maintenance and repair during the Korean War.

1342 Garn, Phil R. "75 mm Recoilless Rifle in Korea" Combat Forces Journal 2 9 (April 1952): 23-25.

The 75 mm recoilless rifle was first introduced in Korea in August 1950 and was used at Tongmyongwon where it was proved to be very effective. The 75 mm was one of the most powerful infantry-support weapons available, and gave the troops a new response to North Korean tanks. The difficulty of the mountainous terrain in Korea made it necessary to provide a large number of support troops for this crew served weapon.

1343 General Headquarters, Far East Command, Intelligence Section, General Staff. Logistical Capability of Communist Forces in Korea To Support a Major Offensive. APO: General Headquarters, Far East Command, Intelligence Section, General Staff, 1953.

Very important source for information about communists and North Korean logistics efforts.

1344 General Headquarters, Far East Command, Intelligence Section, General Staff. <u>Materials in the Hands of or Possibly Available to the Enemy in Korea</u>. APO: General Headquarters, Far East Command, Intelligence Section, General Staff, 1951.

Contains discussion and illustrations of most of the communist weapons and vehicles used in Korea.

1345 General Headquarters, Far East Command, Intelligence Section, General Staff. <u>Order of Battle Information, Chinese Communist Regular Ground Forces (China, Manchuria, and Korea)</u>. Tokyo: General Headquarters, Far East Command, Intelligence Section, General Staff, 1951.

A compilation of materials on the communist "Order of Battle." Very early report which has since proven to be inaccurate at places.

1346 General Headquarters, Far East Command, Intelligence Section, General Staff. <u>Order of Battle Information, Chinese Communist Third Field Army</u>. Tokyo: General Headquarters, Far East Command, Theatre Intelligence Division, Operations Branch, 1950.

"Order of Battle" for the very active 3rd Field Army.

1347 General Headquarters, Far East Command, Intelligence Section, General Staff. <u>Uniform, Insignia, Equipment— North Korean Army</u>. Tokyo: General Headquarters, Far East Command, Intelligence Section, General Staff, 1950.

Standard work for identifying and describing most communist items of issue.

1348 Gimbert, Robert A. <u>X Corps Logistics during Eighth Army Offensive of 1950</u>. Carlisle Barracks, Pennsylvania: United States Army War College, 1986.

Logistical problems at the Corps level were magnified by the rapid movement north in 1950, and the diversity of command.

1349 Gleim, Albert F. <u>Navy Cross Awards for the Korean War</u>. Fort Meyer, Virginia: Planchet Press, 1995.

Biographical notes about recipients, and a description of the events for those receiving the Navy Cross Awards in Korea.

1350 Gleim, Albert F. and Charles P. McDowell <u>The United Nations Korean Service Medal</u>. Fort Myer, Virginia: Foxfall Press, 1990.

Illustrations of service medals.

1351 Gough, Terrence J. U. S. Army Mobilization and Logistics in the Korean War: A Research Approach. Washington, D. C.: Center of Military History, 1987.

Discusses the difficulty of initial mobilization and logistical support during the early and middle period of the Korean War. Considers military commanders lack of respect for logistical problems.

1352 Giusti, Ernest H. The Mobilization of the Marine Corps Reserve in the Korean Conflict. Washington, D. C.: Historical Branch, G-3, Division Headquarters, U. S. Marine Corps, 1967.

Excellent account of the re-creation of the Marines out of reservists. The formation of the 1st Division was a sign of the success of the program.

1353 Hampson, Gary. Strategic Sealift Lessons Learned: A Historical Perspective. Fort McNair, D. C.: Industrial College of the Armed Forces, Executive Research Project, 1988.

An excellent analysis of the size and effectiveness of the logistical problem involved in fighting a war 4,000 miles form the resources.

1354 Harris, Frank J. Training the Combat Rifleman in the Chinese Communist Forces and North Korean Army. Operations Research Office-Training Manuel, T-52, FEC. Chevy Chase, Maryland: Johns Hopkins University, 1954.

Considers the training as well as the political indoctrination received by soldiers of the communist forces.

1355 Headquarters, Department of the Army Forces, Office of the Assistant Chief of Staff, G-2. North Korean Order of Battle. Intelligence Research Project No. 5942. Washington, D. C.: Headquarters, Department of the Army, Office of the Assistant Chief of Staff, 1959.

Intelligence report on, and an analysis of, the North Korean People's Army "Order of Battle."

1356 Headquarters, Eighth United States Army. Combat Information Bulletin No. 1, Korea. Headquarters, Eighth United States Army, 1950.

Material primarily provided on the logistics systems of resupply for the North Korean People's Army and the Chinese Communist Forces.

1357 Headquarters, Eighth United States Army. Intelligence Estimates 27 June 1953. APO: Headquarters, Eighth United States Army, 1953.

Intelligence report considers the state of communist logistics at the time of the armistice.

1358 Headquarters, Eighth United States Army, United States Fifth Air Force, Assistant Chief of Staff, A-2. Supply and Transportation Systems of the Chinese Communists and North Korean Forces in Korea. Tokyo: Headquarters, Eighth United States Army, United States Air Force Assistant Chief of Staff, A-2, 1951.

Excellent source on how the communists supplied their troops, but some early information has proven to be inaccurate.

1359 Headquarters, Eighth United States Army in Korea. Armor Bulletin No. 5. Korea: Headquarters, Eighth United States Army in Korea, 1952.

Important materials on the design of equipment, and the tactics of armor in the North Korean People's Army forces.

1360 Headquarters, Eighth United States Army in Korea, Historical Section and Eighth Army, Historical Service Detachment (Provisional). Logistical Problems and Their Solutions. APO: Headquarters, Eighth United States Army Korea, 1952.

Strong focus on the United States but provides a wide look at the difficulties supplying diversified commands; more about problems than solutions.

1361 Headquarters, Eighth United States Army in Korea, Office of the Assistant Chief of Staff, G-2. Periodic Intelligence Report. Irregular, June 1950-September 1953.

Important source on North Korean and Chinese Communist Forces logistical needs and supply potential.

1362 Headquarters, United States Army Forces, Far East (Advanced), Office of the Assistant Chief of Staff, G-2. "Chinese Communist Army Develops into Effective Force of 3,500,000" USAFFE Intelligence Digest 201 (February 1953): 86, 95.

Intelligence estimates about the rapid expansion of the Chinese army in the field. The United Nations was always concerned about the Chinese manpower potential.

1363 Headquarters, United States Army Forces, Far East (Advanced), Office of the Assistant Chief of Staff, G-2. "The Communist Forces' Logistic Movement in Korea" USAFFE Intelligence Digest 191 (April 1952): 16-17.

Intelligence estimates of the potential movement of supplies and equipment in North Korea.

1364 Headquarters, United States Army Forces, Far East (Advanced), Office of the Assistant Chief of Staff, G-2. "Enemy Motor Transport in North Korea" USAFFE Intelligence Digest 1 9 (2 May 1953): 29-49.

Intelligence estimates and evaluations of potential motor transport available to the North Koreans at the period of the Korean War.

1365 Headquarters, United States Army Forces, Far East (Advanced), Office of the Assistant Chief of Staff, G-2. Estimates of the North Korean Capability to Reinforce Their Organized Forces by the Spring of 1951. Intelligence Staff Study No. 6018. Washington, D. C.: Headquarters, Department of the Army, Office of the Assistant Chief of Staff, G-2, 1950.
Intelligence estimates of the potential for an organized redevelopment which would put a North Korean army in the field by spring of 1951.

1366 Headquarters, United States Army Forces, Far East (Advanced), Office of the Assistant Chief of Staff, G-2. "Far East Trends, January-June 1955" USAFFE Intelligence Digest 5 7 (July 1955): 17-20.
Intelligence estimates of future trends in North Korea and Chinese forces and political overtures.

1367 Headquarters, United States Army Forces, Far East (Advanced), Office of the Assistant Chief of Staff, G-2. "Food Supply in the Communist Far East" USAFFE Intelligence Digest 6 1 (January 1956): 13-16.
Intelligence estimates of food supplies and the distribution of food in China and North Korea.

1368 Headquarters, United States Army Forces, Far East (Advanced), Office of the Assistant Chief of Staff, G-2. "Individual Histories, Chinese Communist Support and Service Units" USAFFE Intelligence Digest 2 6 (2 October 1952): 46-54, 45.
Intelligence narratives of a variety of specialized support and supply units among communist Chinese forces.

1369 Headquarters, United States Army Forces, Far East (Advanced), Office of the Assistant Chief of Staff, G-2. "Logistical Capability of the Chinese Communist Ground Forces on the Offshore Front" USAFFE Intelligence Digest, 5 11 (November 1955): 8-14.
Intelligence estimates on the ability of the Chinese to provide off-shore logistic support to their troops in the field. Despite naval superiority the United Nations was aware of the communist ability to land supplies along the coast.

1370 Headquarters, United States Army Forces, Far East (Advanced), Office of the Assistant Chief of Staff, G-2. Logistical Data for the Chinese Communist Army. Intelligence Research Project No. 6231. Washington,

D. C.: Headquarters, Department of the Army, Office of the Assistant Chief of Staff, G-2, 1959.

Very useful on the availability of materials in 1950 and their potential availability to communist forces.

1371 Headquarters, United States Army Forces, Far East (Advanced), Office of the Assistant Chief of Staff, G-2. "Manpower in North Korea" USAFFE Intelligence Digest 5 4 (April 1955): 11-18.

Intelligence estimates of potential manpower for North Korean troops are considered, as well as the possibility of volunteer troops joining them.

1372 Headquarters, United States Army Forces, Far East (Advanced), Office of the Assistant Chief of Staff, G-2. "Medical Support in North Korea" USAFFE Intelligence Digest 2 11 (17 December 1953): 7-47.

Intelligence estimates of the medical supplies and personnel available for field operations in North Korea.

1373 Headquarters, United States Army Forces, Far East (Advanced), Office of the Assistant Chief of Staff, G-2. "Military Supply in North Korea" USAFFE Intelligence Digest 5 10 (October 1955): 40-44.

Intelligence estimates of general/miscellaneous military supplies which would be available for North Korean forces.

1374 Headquarters, United States Army Forces, Far East (Advanced), Office of the Assistant Chief of Staff, G-2. "Munitions Production in Communist China" USAFFE Intelligence Digest 184 (September 1951): 47-49.

Intelligence estimates on production and dispersion of munition supplies in Red China.

1375 Headquarters, United States Army Forces, Far East (Advanced), Office of the Assistant Chief of Staff, G-2. "North Korean Railroad Security Division" USAFFE Intelligence Digest 1 2 (17 January 1953): 25-29.

Intelligence estimates on the dispersion of, and abilities of North Korean railroad security in light of partisan activities.

1376 Headquarters, United States Army Forces, Far East (Advanced), Office of the Assistant Chief of Staff, G-2. "North Korean Underground Industry" USAFFE Intelligence Digest 2 5 (17 September 1953): 1-2.

Intelligence estimates on the production rates and division in North Korean underground facilities.

1377 Headquarters, United States Army Forces, Far East (Advanced), Office of the Assistant Chief of Staff, G-2. The Pre-Inchon North Korean People's

Army. Intelligence Research Project No. 6231. Washington, D. C.: Headquarters, Department of the Army, Office of the Assistant Chief of Staff, G-2, 1950.

An important analysis of the North Korean People's Army on the eve of the Inchon Landing. By this time the North Korean forces were stretched about as far at they could go.

1378 Headquarters, United States Army Forces, Far East (Advanced), Office of the Assistant Chief of Staff, G-2. "Railroads and Highway Transport in North Korea and Their Impact on Enemy Logistics" USAFFE Intelligence Digest 1 13 (2 July 1953): 25-45.

Intelligence estimates of transportation potentials in North Korea via rail and road and impact on the enemy.

1379 Hershey, Lewis B. "Mobilization of Manpower" Quartermaster Review 30 (1950): 4-5, 144-147.

The Director of Selective Service explains the problems in raising a force of three million from veterans, reservists, and new recruits.

1380 Hospelhorn, Cecil W. "Aerial Supply in Korea" Combat Forces Journal 1 10 (May 1951): 28-30.

An account of the 2348th Quartermaster Aerial Supply Company during the first six months of the war, including the 1950 airdrop to the Marines at the Chosin Reservoir.

1381 Huston, James A. Guns and Butter, Powder and Rice: U. S. Army Logistics in the Korean War. Selinsgrove, Pennsylvania: Susquehanna University Press, 1989.

The abrupt nature of the Korean invasion, and America's response made it particularly hard on those responsible for supply. The first hundred pages of this work explains how it was possible to deliver a troop build-up of nearly 100,000 men and to provide two million tons of supplies prior to the Pusan breakout. For the first three months of the war in Korea it was fought with World War II supplies, a good portion of it considered obsolete at the time of its use.

1382 Huston, James A. "Korean Logistics" Military Review 36 2 (February 1957): 18-32.

Focuses on United States logistics in responding to the special needs of American forces in Korea.

1383 Huston, James A. The Sinews of War: Army Logistics. Washington, D. C.: Government Printing Office, 1966.

An early account of the development of army logistics during the Korean War.

1384 Identification of Shells and Shell Fragments Used by the United States Forces, North Korean Army and Chinese Communist Forces in Korea. APO: United States Armed Forces Far East, 1954.
    Primarily this is a manual for identification, but it contains a great deal of technical information.

1385 Investigation of the Ammunition Shortages in the Armed Services; Report of the Preparedness Subcommittee No. 2. Washington, D. C.: Government Printing Office, 1954.
    A look at why America ran out of ammunition in Korea. One point was not that ammunition was short, rather that it was the wrong ammunition.

1386 Jacobs, Bruce. Korea's Heroes: The Medal of Honor Story. New York: Lion, 1958.
    A view of Medal of Honor winners in Korea, from privates to generals, showing what they have in common.

1387 Johnson, Robbie. Canadian War Service Badges 1914-1954. Surrey, British Columbia: Johnson Books, 1995.
    Covers the military decorations offered by the Canadian government from 1914 through 1954 with a section on Korea.

1388 Jones, James C. "Recall" Leatherneck 34 11 (1951): 14-21.
    When the call went out for the 1st Marine Division, the best hope lay in the qualified reserves who could be, and were, recalled for immediate active duty.

1389 Jordan, Kenneth N. Forgotten Heroes: 131 Men of the Korean War Awarded the Medal of Honor, 1950-1953. Atglen, Pennsylvania: Schiffer Publications, 1995.
    Biographies and exploits of the Medal of Honor winners from the Korean War. Well written.

1390 Karsten, Peter. "The American Democratic Citizen Soldier: Triumph or Disaster?" Journal of Military History 30 1 (Spring 1966): 34-40.
    Considers the citizen soldier and his performance, good and bad, during the Korean War. Says they have been more a triumph than a disaster.

1391 Kendall, John M. "An Inflexible Response: United States Army Manpower Mobilization Policies, 1945-1957" Ph.D. dissertation, Duke University, 1983.

An extension of Kendalls's MA thesis, expanding the coverage of draft and mobilization.

1392 Kendall, John M. "The Inflexible Response: United States Army Mobilization Doctrine, 1945-1951" MA thesis, Duke University, 1979.

A critical look at America's inability to launch a military response to the threat of foreign involvement.

1393 Key, William G. "Combat Cargo: Korea, 1950-1951" Pegasus 17 5 (November 1951): 1-16.

The operation and deployment of airlifting combat supplies to active zones in Korea.

1394 Kitchens, John W. "Cargo Helicopters in the Korean Conflict" parts 1 and 2. United States Army Aviation Digest 41 10 (October 1992) and 41 11 (November 1992).

The 6th Transportation Helicopter Company was activated on a April 1951 and sent to Korea where they supplied troops and removed the wounded at "Old Baldy."

1395 Korea: The Names, the Deeds. New York: Dell Publishing, 1987.

Biographies of men who won the War Medal of Honor in combat during the Korean War. Jordan (listed previously) is a better source.

1396 Larson, Zelle A. "An Unbroken Witness: Conscientious Objection to War, 1948-1953" Ph.D. dissertation, University of Hawaii, 1979.

Provides a history of American attitudes toward "Conscientious Objection" status from the Berlin Crisis to the end of the Korean War.

1397 Launius, Roger. "MATS and the Korean Airlift" Airlift 12 (Summer 1990): 16-21.

Brief history by NASA historian concerning Military Air Transport System during the Korean War; the prolonged need to move staff and equipment in and out of Korea.

1398 Launius, Roger D. Significant Airlift Events of the Korean Conflict, 1950-1953: A Brief Chronology. Scott Air Force Base, Illinois: Office of Historical Military Airlift Command, 1990.

A listing, with annotation, of MATS activities during the Korean War. Very helpful.

1399 "Logistics: By Sea and Air to Korea" Combat Forces Journal 1 3 (October 1950): 46.

A reply to comments in Life (September 1950) which expressed amazement at the amount of supplies reaching Pusan. The article provides statistics on the large amounts of supplies provided and comments on the excellent manner in which they were delivered. The response to logistic needs is one of the great success stories of the war.

1400 Lord, Lewis. The Medal of Honor. no publisher or date.

Two Korean War heroes, John Page and Charles Loring, are honored in this account of the early war and what it means to perform deeds of heroism.

1401 Marshall, S. L. A. Infantry Operations and Weapons Usage in Korea (Winter 1950-51). Boston: Johns Hopkins University, 1953. London: Greenhill Books, 1988.

Discusses the operations of Eighth Army during the winter of 1950 by looking at the behavior of soldiers, the use of weapons and the nature of the infantry tactics. Not very complimentary of any of the areas discussed.

1402 Marston, Anson D. "Wartime Role for Colleges and Universities" Journal of Military History 18 3 (Fall 1954): 131-144.

Discusses the role of colleges and universities in preparing troops for the Korean War, suggesting that the educational centers did not have the information needed to be really effective. Author advocates change.

1403 Martin, John G. It Began at Imphal: The Combat Cargo Story. Manhattan, Kansas: Sunflower University Press, 1988.

An interesting and informative account of a little known aspect of warfare. It traces the air combat cargo aspect of fighting in World War II and Korea. The work includes the account of an emergency delivery of a pontoon bridge, left behind by mistake and needed in the advance from Inchon.

1404 McFalls, Carroll, Jr. "Armor in Korea: The Maintenance Platoon" Combat Forces Journal 2 11 (June 1952): 38-39.

Discusses the mission of a tank repair outfit, the 70th Tank Battalion.

1405 McQuiston, I. M. "History of the Reserves Since the Second World War" Journal of Military History 23 1 (Spring 1959): 23-27.

Discusses the impact of the Korean War on the Armed Services Reserve, still an essential force.

1406 Mesko, Jim. <u>Armor in Korea: A Pictorial History</u>. Carrollton, Texas: Squadron/Signal Publications, 1983.

     Illustration of tanks used during the Korean War. Beautifully detailed drawings and discussion of early availability and tactics.

1407 <u>The Military Ribbons of the United States Army, Navy, Marines, Air Force, and Coast Guard: A Complete Guide to Correct Ribbon Wearing</u>. Fountain Inn, South Carolina: Medals of America Press, 1995.

     Covers medals, ribbons, awards offered by the American government during World War II, Korea, Vietnam, and the Gulf War.

1408 Miller, W. L., Jr. "The Use of Flame in Korea" <u>Combat Forces Journal</u> 4 8 (March 1954): 37-39.

     Discusses the wide use of flame, in throwers and in bombs, in both offensive and defensive war.

1409 Moakley, G. S. <u>U. S. Army Code of Conduct Training: Let the POW's Tell Their Stories</u>. Fort Leavenworth, Kansas: United States Army Command and General Staff College, 1976.

     The Army quickly provided a code behavior for those in prisoner-of-war camps, and developed a training program to prevent a reoccurrence of Korean War problems.

1410 <u>Mobilization in the Korean Conflict</u>. Dunn Loring, Virginia: Historical Evaluation and Research Organization, 1982.

     A fair look at the recruitment and mobilization of troops in the Korean War.

1411 <u>Mobilization of the Marine Corps Reserve in the Korean Conflict 1950-1951</u>. Washington, D. C.: History Branch G-3 Division, United States Marine Corps, 1967.

     A short history of the identification, and call-up, of marine units and individuals, plus the movement of marine troops to fill existing combat groups, and shipment.

1412 Moenk, Jean R. <u>Training During the Korean Conflict, 1950-54</u>. Fort Eustis, Virginia: United States Army Transportation Training Center, 1962.

     Account of Army training mission, particularly of the transportation corps, during the Korean War.

1413 Murphy, Edward F. <u>Korean War Heroes</u>. Novato, California: Presidio Press, 1992.

     An account of the 131 Medal of Honor winners during the Korean War. Provides some excellent insights to life on the line.

1414 Nigro, Edward. "Early Troop Carrier Operations in Korea" Air University Quarterly Review 7 (Spring 1954): 86-89.

Discusses the use of a variety of carrier aircraft which were used in the rapid distribution of ground troops.

1415 O'Brien, M. J. Trans-Pacific Airlift in Support of Army Operations, July 1950-June 1952. Chevy Chase, Maryland: Johns Hopkins University, 1955.

The army in Japan was not well-equipped enough to supply either American or Republic of Korea troops. The initial supply came from the United States via airlift. During the conflict, airlift operations continued to be highly significant.

1416 "Operation Load-Up" Quartermaster Review 30 3 (1950): 40-41, 109-110.

An interesting account of the joint Army, Navy, and Marine Corps efforts to load the lst Marine Division at Kobe Base, Japan. This twelve-day ordeal was a major accomplishment not only of supply, but of cooperation.

1417 Ostrom, Barbara K. "Logistics of Ammunition in Korea" MS thesis, Massachusetts Institute of Technology, 1978.

MS: ammunition

1418 Owens, Richard W. "AA Makes the Team" Combat Forces Journal 3 10 (May 1953): 27-29.

This AA outfit (quad fifties) drew the first enemy blood as they downed a plane on the fourth day of battle. These quad fifties were put on the bed of the "Duce-and-a-Half" trucks and were moved easily. While also available as antiaircraft many AA units were assigned as self-propelled support units with the infantry. In this role they proved to be very effective against massed troops.

1419 Pack, Harry S. A Survey of Helicopter Operations, Maintenance, and Supply in Korea. Chevy Chase, Maryland: Johns Hopkins University, 1954.

Helicopters, which found use in Korea, were both a supply element and a logistical problem of their own. The helicopter proved to be very effective in troop supply.

1420 Perry, K. A. "Logistics in the Far East" The Supply Mercury (June 1951): 8.

Short article on the difficulties of supply in the Far East, a full fourteen sailing days from the West Coast.

1421 Preston, R. T. "Flame Thrower Fuel—Its Use in Korea" Canadian Army Journal (July 1955): 149-153.

Contends that fuel was available on a division level, but admits supplies were very low at local commands because no one anticipated the degree of mobility of the early war.

1422 Quartermaster Activities Relating to the Korean War, June 1950-September 1951. no publisher, 1951.

The set-up of quartermaster lines in joint and divided command is discussed.

1423 Reeder, William R. The Korean Ammunition Shortage. Syracuse, New York: Syracuse University, 1954.

The question of ammunition shortages became a major concern both as a combat and supply question. The problem was often related to types of ammo rather than simply needs.

1424 Rivera, Margarita. "Airlift of Cargo and Passengers in the Korean War" Air Force Journal of Logistics 13 (Fall 1989): 8-11.

A serious look at the logistical problems in keeping the supplies moving as the demands grew. The United States was not ready for this war and took some time catching up.

1425 Ruestow, Paul E. "Air Force Logistics in the Theater of Operations" Air University Quarterly Review 6 (Summer 1954): 45-46.

Discusses the growth of Air Force logistical support and shows how training and communication was accomplished.

1426 Seals, Billy R. Evolution of Military Manpower Policy: The Korean War. Maxwell Air Force Base, Alabama: Air War College, 1975.

The rapid reversal of manpower needs between 1945 and 1953 required a whole new look at the problems of supplies.

1427 Shrader, Charles. Communist Logistics in the Korean War. Westport, Connecticut: Greenwood Press, 1995.

An excellent work on the complicated system of the North Korean and Chinese logistics during the Korean War.

1428 Shreve, Robert O. Combat Zone Logistics in Korea. Chevy Chase, Maryland, Johns Hopkins University, 1951.

This account focuses on the United Nations logistical problems, dealing with problems of multiple sources and disposal. Early, and incomplete, effort to define and analyze the procurement and logistics situation in Korea.

1429 Skroch, Ernest J. "Quartermaster Advisors in Korea" Quartermaster Review 31 (1951): 8-9, 118-123.

Describes the activities of the Quartermaster section of the Korean Military Advisory Group. This section was responsible for establishing the ROK systems for the development of food supplies during the early war.

1430 Snodgrass, Raymond J. History of Ordnance Activities Relating to the Korean Conflict, June 1950-September 1951. Office of the Chief of Ordnance, 1951.

A technical and narrative account of the ordnance needs and a specific evaluation of how well it worked.

1431 Stanton, Shelby. US Army Uniforms of the Korean War. Harrisburg, Pennsylvania: Stackpole, 1992.

Identification of uniforms available during early months, the difficulty of supply, and the inappropriateness of what was available. Supply problem considered on pages 1-17.

1432 Stickney, William W. "The Marine Reserves in Action" Journal of Military History 17 1 (Spring 1953): 16-22.

The impact of the Korean War on the Marine Reserve program. By the end of March 1951 thirty-eight percent of officers and forty-eight percent of enlisted men came from the reserves.

1433 Tactical and Logistical Employment of the M-39 and T18E1 Armored Personnel Carriers During the Battle for Outpost Pork Chop, Vicinity Chorwon, North Korea, 6-11 July 1953. APO: 7th Infantry Division, 1953.

The title promises more than it delivers; basically a look at the suggestion of personnel carriers during the Pork Chop campaign. This study was commissioned by the 7th Division.

1434 Thebaud, Charles C. Problems in the Airdrop of Supplies and Personnel. Washington, D. C.: Government Printing Office, 1952.

Korea did not prove to be a good place for air drops and the airborne units did not fare all that well. Supply, however, was a different situation.

1435 Thompson, Annis G. The Greatest Airlift: The Story of Combat Cargo. Tokyo: Dai-Nippon Printing Company, 1954.

Primarily a report of the role of the 315th air division supplying troops early in the war. A remarkable achievement well documented.

1436 United States. Japan Logistical Command Activities Report, 25 August-30 September 1950. no publisher, 1950.

Japan was the prime logistical support base; its activities were highly significant. This study however fails to provide much help in understanding the role Japan played in logistics.

1437 United States Army, Far East Command, Uniform, Insignia, Equipment (of the) North Korean Army. Tokyo, Far East Command, 1950.
Basic text in how to recognize the enemy. Provides good information on the standard issue.

1438 United States Committee on Armed Services. Ammunition Supplies in the Far East: Hearings Before the Committee on Armed Services. Washington, D. C.: Government Printing Office, 1953.
Testimony of General James A. Van Fleet and others on the shortage of small arms armament in Korea during the first year.

1439 United States Department of the Navy, Office of Naval Intelligence. Port Logistics Summary, Korea. no publisher, 28 June 1950.
Considers the vital role played by ports in logistics efforts; a very significant part of the supply service.

1440 United States Selective Service System. "Orientation Kit" Washington, D. C.: Government Printing Office, 1966.
A collection of pamphlets dealing with the background and laws of the "draft" during World War II and Korea.

1441 Urquhart, G. A. "Diplomats and Drivers—Support in the Rear of 25 Canadian Infantry Brigade Group During the Korean War" Canadian Defence Quarterly 10 2 (Autumn 1980): 41-47.
The Korean War enhanced Canadian identity and stresses the profession of arms, diplomatically as well as militarily, in Canada.

1442 Van Vechten, Marie-Louise. "Narrative Report: K-19, Canteen, Pusan, Korea, 30 April 1951" no publisher or date.
A less-than-helpful survey of a highly over-rated experience; the canteens at Pusan.

1443 Walker, Adrian. A Barren Place: National Servicemen in Korea, 1950-1954. London: Leo Cooper, 1994.
Those responding to the British draft (national service) found Korea an unusually difficult place to be. Some accounts and narratives.

1444 Walker, Stanley L. "Logistics of the Inchon Landing" Army Logistician (July-August 1981): 34-38.

Logistics support planning, preparation, and execution of the 15 September 1950 amphibious landing of the 1st Marine Division at Inchon was accomplished in less than thirty-three days, including Marine equipment moved from Barstow, California.

1445 Westover, John. Combat Support in Korea. Washington, D. C.: Combat Forces Press, 1955. Reissued by Center of Military History, 1987.
Deals with logistics at lower levels where problems were persistently faced; shortages, wrong materials, etc. Getting the materials was not so much a problem as moving them around to the right places.

1446 Young, H. N. "Fragment of the Recent History of the Organized Service" Journal of Military History 19 3 (Fall 1955): 137-144.
A discussion of the criticism caused by the call-up of reserves, as well as the impact of the Korean War on them. and, the effect of the Korean War in preventing extended reserve commitments.

1447 Zimmerman, LeRoy. "Korean War Logistics: Eighth United States Army, 19 September 1950 to 31 December 1950" Carlisle Barracks, Pennsylvania: United States Army War College, 1986.
A survey of logistical problems on the army level, especially during the break-out period of the Korean War.

SPECIAL TOPICS

Armistice

1448 Armstrong, W. B. "The Armistice in Korea" <u>Canadian Army Journal</u> (October 1955): 57-62.
    Brief history of the armistice, and the Canadian role in "Operation Glory," the recovery of bodies buried in enemy territory, resulting in the exchange of more than 20,000 bodies.

1449 Bailey, Sydney D. <u>The Korean Armistice</u>. New York: St. Martin's Press, 1992.
    This study is about the convoluted processes by which the Korean War ended short of victory. It takes a very detailed look at the fighting of the war as each action, advance, and retreat was measured against the undecided factor of victory or negotiation.

1450 Bernstein, Barton J. "The Struggle over the Korean Armistice: Prisoners of Repatriation" in Bruce Cumings, editor. <u>Child of Conflict: The Korean-American Relationship, 1943-1953</u>. Seattle: University of Washington Press, 1983.
    Describes the problem of the POW issue and how it played out in the armistice agreement.

1451 Bernstein, Barton J. "Syngman Rhee: The Pawn as Rook—The Struggle to End the Korean War" <u>Bulletin of Concerned Asian Scholars</u> 10 1 (January-March 1978).

Discusses the difficulty presented by President Rhee who opposed the armistice and took unauthorized action in releasing POWs.

1452 Bernstein, Barton J. "Truman's Secret Thoughts on Ending the Korean War" Foreign Service Journal 57 (November 1980): 31-33, 44.
    Truman thought if an armistice could not be achieved, the Korean War might expand into China, and that might well mean nuclear weapons.

1453 Bogenberger, D. "A Study of the Tactics and Strategy Used by the Negotiations During the Korean Truce Talks" MA thesis, San Francisco State College, 1957.
    MA: negotiations

1454 Brazda, Jaroslav J. "The Korean Armistice Agreement: A Comparative Study" Ph.D. dissertation, University of Florida, 1956.
    Finds that the changing nature of the concept of armistice was in partial to blame for the length of time needed to arrange a cease-fire in Korea. Yet, it admits the armistice negotiations in Korea were delayed, primarily by Cold War tensions.

1455 Bullen, Roger. "Great Britain, the United States and the Indian Armistice Resolution on the Korean War, November 1952" in Aspects of Anglo-Korean Relations, International Studies London: International Centre for Economics and Related Disciplines, London School of Economics, 1981.
    Both India and the British government made several efforts to arrange a cease-fire in Korea. Often these were supportive of one another; sometimes not supportive. The 1952 effort was a major move.

1456 Chung-kuo jen. . . . The Struggle for Peace in Korea: Selected Documents. Chinese People's Committee for World Peace, 1953.
    Well-selected documents and material on the Chinese effort to create peace. Significant materials for one seeking a clearer picture.

1457 Dille, John. Substitute for Victory. Garden City, New York: Doubleday, 1954.
    Makes the claim that the United States (United Nations) acceptance of an armistice was justified, and that it made excellent political sense which would produce lasting good in the Cold War. The idea of victory had become "archaic."

1458 Farrar, Peter N. "Britain's Proposal for a Buffer Zone South of the Yalu in November 1950" Journal of Contemporary History 18 (1983): 327-351.

Discussion of a neglected opportunity for a peace settlement proposed by the British government early in the Korean War.

1459 Farrar, Peter N. "A Pause for Peace Negotiations: The British Buffer Zone Plan of November 1950" in James Cotton and Ian Neary, editors. The Korean War in History. [Studies on East Asia]. Atlantic Highlands, New Jersey: Humanities Press International, Inc., 1989.

Part of a collection of revisionist interpretations which sees the Korean War in terms of domestic actions, and which saw the Inchon landing and drive toward China as the essential end of the Korean War. Failure to consider the British plan seriously led to a whole new war.

1460 Foot, Rosemary. "Anglo-American Relations in the Korean Crisis: The British Effort to Avert an Expanded War, December 1950-January 1951" Diplomatic History 10 (Winter 1986): 43-58.

United States and Great Britain remained far apart on China, but British pressure aided Truman's negotiation openers.

1461 Foot, Rosemary. A Substitute for Victory: The Politics of Peacemaking at the Korean Armistice Talks. Ithaca: Cornell University Press, 1990.

Discusses not only the agreement, but the four major missed opportunities. Foot treats the communists very well, and identifies the United States as villain. Excellent research.

1462 Goldhamer, Herbert. The 1951 Korean Armistice Conference: A Personal Memoir. Santa Monica, California: Rand Corporation, 1994.

A personal account of the first, and early, phases of the armistice efforts, by one who was involved.

1463 Joy, Charles Turner. How Communists Negotiate. New York: Macmillan, 1955.

An eyewitness account of the Korean truce talks by the United Nations chief representative.

1464 Joy, Charles Turner. "My Battle Inside the Korean Truce Tent" Collier's 130 (August 16, 23, 30, 1952): 36-43, 26-31, 70-73.

Material concerning Chief of United Nations Armistice Team. Good insights into the mindset of the communists across the table.

1465 Joy, Charles Turner. Negotiating While Fighting: The Diary of Admiral C. Turner Joy at the Korean Armistice Conference. Allen E. Goodman, editor. Stanford, California: Hoover Institute, 1978.

The negotiating diary of the United Nations chief armistice representative, Admiral Joy.

1466 Kahn, Lessing A. and Florence K. Nierman. A Study of Chinese and North Korean Surrenderers. Chevy Chase, Maryland: Johns Hopkins University, 1953.

A survey of why Chinese and North Korean soldiers surrender, as determined by a series of interviews of POWs. Part of Project POWOW.

1467 Kim, Hyun Choong. "The Korean Armistice Negotiations and Syngman Rhee's Policy" MA thesis, University of Washington, 1960.

MA: armistice

1468 Kinter, W. R. "Making an Armistice Work" Combat Forces Journal 4 6 (January 1954): 14-17.

Focuses on the negotiations which took part during most of the Korean War, and finally led to an armistice.

1469 Kriebel, P. Wesley. "Korea: The Military Armistice Commission 1965-1970" Journal of Military History 36 3 (October 1972): 96-99.

Discusses the continued tension in Korea and the failure of the Armistice Commission to carry out the 1953 agreement. The cease-fire was a military agreement, not a political one.

1470 Lazar, Isador. Daily Diary. no publisher, 1953.

One volume typescript account of the United Nations Military Armistice Commission escort officer who investigated POW camp Koje-do, 25 August to 3 September 1953.

1471 Lewane, Leonard L. "Fighting and Negotiating Against the Communists!" MA thesis, George Washington University, 1969.

MA: negotiating

1472 Matray, James I. "Truman's Plan for Victory: National Self-Determination and the Thirty-Eighth Parallel Decision in Korea" Journal of American History 66 2 (September 1979): 314-333.

Holds the view that the invasion was part of the overall plan to expand, by war if necessary, Russia's political influence in Asia.

1473 Matray, James I. "Villain Again: The United States and the Korean Armistice Talks" Diplomatic History 16 3 (Summer 1992): 473-480.

Review of Substitute for Victory which challenges Rosemary Foots' view on communist good intentions, and supports the United States' effort.

1474 Newbold, Alan L. "Panmunjom and Warsaw: A Study of Subdiplomatic Frustration" MA thesis, St. Louis: Washington University, 1967.

MA: diplomatic frustration

1475 Niksch, Larry A. The Korean Armistice Negotiations. Washington, D. C.: Library of Congress, 1967.
A fairly detailed account of the inner workings of the team responsible for the armistice negotiations.

1476 Operation Little Switch. four volumes. Seoul, Korea: 1953
Account of the exchange of sick and wounded POWs which marked the first break in a long stalemate.

1477 Simon, Ernest A. "The Operation of the Korean Armistice Agreement" thesis, Charlottesville, Virginia: Judge Advocate General's School, 1969.
Thesis: armistice

1478 The Team Behind the Armistice: The Story of the Support Group, UNCMAC, Munsan-ni, Korea. United States: Support Group, TI&E Office, 1954.
Account of the Eighth Army group which provided support facilities for the negotiating team.

1479 The Truth of the Panmunjom Incident. Pyongyang, Korea: Foreign Languages Publication House, 1976.
North Korean view of the Korean Military Archives Group (KMAG) and the armistice.

1480 Vatcher, William H., Jr. Panmunjom: The Story of the Korean Military Armistice Negotiations. New York: Frederick A. Praeger, Inc., 1958.
This story of the negotiations is told by an academic member of the United Nations team who observed the tactics on both sides of the table.

1481 Winnington, Alan. Plain Perfidy: The Plot to Wreck Korean Peace. Peking: no publisher, 1954.
Discusses the effort by communist prisoner to wreck the armistice talks and the peace.

1482 Yang, Dae-hyun. "Korean Truce Talks: Multi-dimensional Situational Analysis" Ph. D. dissertation, Munich University, 1982.
An effective analysis of the numerous nations, agents, and diplomatic expectations involved in the effort to arrive at an armistice. Early, but informative.

1483 Yi, Chong-gun. Panmunjom. Pyongyang, Korea: Foreign Languages Publishing House, 1986.
A discussion of the armistice process and the formation of the Demilitarized Zone (DMZ), presented from the communist side.

1484 Young, Kenneth. Negotiating with the Chinese Communists: The United States Experience 1953-1957. New York: McGraw-Hill, 1968.
Analysis of how the communists negotiated to bring an end to the Korean War and beyond.

Prisoner-of-War: Accounts, Brainwashing, Atrocities

1485 Adam-Smith, Patsy. Prisoners of War: From Gallipoli to Korea. Ringwood, Victoria, Australia: Viking, 1992.
A chronicle and commentary about Australian prisoners-of-war from World War I, World War II, and Korea.

1486 Biderman, Albert D. "Communist Attempts to Elicit False Confessions from Air Force Prisoners of War" Bulletin New York Academy of Medicine 33 (1957): 616-625.
Depicts the use of communist brainwashing efforts and describes them as being more painful and effective than older methods.

1487 Biderman, Albert D. "Effects of Communist Indoctrination Attempts: Some Comments Based on Air Force Prisoner of War Study" Social Problems 6 4 (1959): 304-313.
An analysis of communist brainwashing attempts, especially against 235 Air Force POWs who were repatriated in 1953. The attempts were generally ineffective.

1488 Biderman, Albert D. Further Analysis of POW Follow-up Study Data. Alexandria, Virginia: DDC, 1965.
More information based on the same data as his earlier work. Not all that helpful.

1489 Biderman, Albert D. "The Image of Brainwashing" The Public Opinion Quarterly 26 (Winter 1962): 547-563.
A long analysis of the facts and fears of brainwashing, concluding that much of the problem was one of image which requires more study.

1490 Biderman, Albert D. March to Calumny: The Story of American POWs in the Korean War. New York: Macmillan, 1963.
Harsh treatment and torture was responsible for the breakdown of Americans in captivity. The author's views are as onesided in favor of the POWs as others are against them.

1491 Bluth, Thomas D. "Long Range Consequences of the POW Treatment in Korea: An Analysis of the Mayer-Kinkead and Biderman-Monroe Interpretation of Korea" MA thesis, Georgetown University, 1964.

A study which compares POW treatment by the United States and North Korean governments, and tries to determine the effect.

1492 Bradbury, William C. Determinants of Loyalty and Disaffection in Chinese Communist Soldiers During the Korean Hostilities: An Explanatory Study. Washington, D. C.: Georgetown University, 1956.
Research project which attempts to deal with why some communists rejected their government and came over to the West.

1493 Brown, Wallace L. The Endless Hours: My Two and a Half Years As a Prisoner of the Chinese Communists. New York: Modern Literary Edition Publishing Company, 1961. W. W. Norton, 1961.
Popular narrative of life as a prisoner-of-war with wide comment on the nature of communist prisons.

1494 Bunker, Gerald E. The Question of Repatriation of Prisoners of War and the Korean Peace Talks: Historical, Political, and Legal Aspects. Harvard: Harvard University, 1963.
Problems surrounding the question of repatriation of prisoners came from Truman's feelings that America had mistreated refugees during World War II. This study looks at the history and legality of the question.

1495 Burchett, Wilfred G. and Alan Winnington. Koje Unscreened. London: Britain-China Friendship Association, 1953.
An account of prisoners and prison atrocities through which the authors accuse the United States (United Nations) of poor treatment of prisoners at the Koje prisoner compound.

1496 Carmelite Nuns, Seoul. Carmel and the Korean Death March. Flemington, New Jersey: St. Teresa's Press, 1984.
Careful narrative of the famed disaster.

1497 Clarke, Conley. Journey Through Shadow: 839 Days in Hell: A POW's Survival in North Korea. Gaffney, South Carolina: C. Clarke, 1988
Personal narrative of life in the prisoner-of-war camps.

1498 Cole, Paul M. POW/MIA Issues. volume 1. "The Korean War" Santa Monica, California: Rand Corporation, 1994.
Concern over missing prisoners-of-war and those listed as missing-in-action, who still remain unaccounted produces a dark cloud of concern over the war, and American concern for its troops still hangs over the Korean War.

1499 Communist Utilization of Prisoners of War. Tokyo: Headquarters, Far East Command, 1953.

Analysis of the use the communists made of prisoners, particularly Americans, both for labor and propaganda.

1500 "The Conduct of Prisoners of War" Columbia Law Review 56 5 (May 1956).

Concerned with the "illegal" activities of POWs and the control of camps, especially by the Chinese prisoners.

1501 Crosbie, Philip. March Till They Die. Dublin: Browne and Nolan, Limited, 1956. Westminster, Maryland: Newman Press, 1956.

A rather dramatic account of prisoner movement.

1502 Crosbie, Philip. Pencilling Prisoner. Melbourne: Hawthorn Press, 1954.

Elaborate narrative describing life in the prisoner-of-war camps.

1503 Davies, Stanley J. In Spite of Dungeons: The Experiences as a Prisoner-of-War in North Korea of the Chaplain to the First Battalion, the Gloucestershire Regiment. London: Hodder and Stroughton, 1955.

Raises the questions of the religious issues of being a prisoner-of-war as well as the difficulties faced by the chaplain himself.

1504 Enoch, Kenneth L. and John S. Quinn. Statements by Two Captured U. S. Air Force Officers on Their Participation in Germ Warfare in Korea. Peking: Chinese People's Committee for World Peace, 1952.

Statements and comments about Air Force officers who provided the communist "confessions" about germ warfare.

1505 Felton, Monica. What I Saw in Korea. London: M. Felton, 1951.

Brief (eleven-page) account of atrocities witnessed by the author, a member of a British women delegation who traveled to North Korea at the communist's request.

1506 Friedrich, Alexandra M. "POWs: Victims of the Cold War?: A Comparative Analysis of the Prisoner of War Issue in the Korean and Vietnam War Armistice and Peace Negotiations: A Thesis" MA thesis, University of New Orleans, 1993.

MA: prisoners-of-war

1507 Frohock, Fred M. "The Korean War Prisoner Exchange" MA thesis, University of Florida, 1961.

MA: prisoners-of-war

1508 Gaston, Peter. Korea, 1950-1953, Prisoners of War, The British Army. London: Stamp Exchange, 1976.

The British view of prisoners-of-war. Britain had about one thousand men who were held by the communists during the war.

1509 Goldich, Robert L. POW and MIAs in Indochina and Korea: Status and Accounting Issues. Washington, D. C.: Library of Congress, 1991.

The difficulty of accounting for prisoners-of-war and those missing-in-action after the primary war years had passed.

1510 Great Britain. The Experience of British Prisoners of War in Korea. London: Her Majesty's Stationary Office, 1953.

A semi-official account of the behavior of British prisoners-of-war, most who had a good record while in prison.

1511 Gruenzner, Norman. Postal History of American POWs: World War II, Korea, Vietnam. State College, Pennsylvania: American Philatelic Society, 1979.

Interesting account of postal communication and commemoration of prisoners during the wars mentioned.

1512 The Handling of Prisoners of War During the Korean War. San Francisco, California: United States Army, 1960, 1974.

The United States Army policies for handling communist prisoners taken during the Korean War.

1513 Hansen, Kenneth K. Heroes Behind Barbed Wire. Princeton, New Jersey: D. Van Nostrand, 1957.

Identifies thousands of Chinese and North Korean POWs who defied the communists and refused to return. Lacking in objectivity.

1514 Harrison, Thomas D. with Bill Stapleton. "Why did Some G.I.'s Turn Communist? Collier's 132 13 (1953): 25-28.

Gives one of the more realistic accounts of life in the prison camps and estimates that ninety-five percent or more of the United Nations prisoners resisted the communist effort to sway their loyalty.

1515 Harvey, Alton H. "Captive vs. Captor: The Maintenance of Control over Communist Prisoners of War" thesis, Charlottesville, Virginia: Judge Advocate General's School, 1962.

Thesis: prisoner control

1516 Hearings on Cold War, Korea, WWII, POWS. Washington, D. C.: Government Printing Office, 1993.

Congressional hearings on the prisoner question which compares prisoner reaction during World War II, Korea, and Vietnam.

1517 "How Reds Tortured U. S. Prisoners" U. S. News & World Report 39 10 (September 2, 1955): 26-27.
A rather dramatic account of the Chinese practice of torturing United States soldiers in a way as to leave no physical signs.

1518 Hunter, Edward. Brainwashing in Red China: The Calculated Destruction of Men's Minds. New York: Vanguard Press, 1951.
Discusses treatment of POWs in communist hands. This work is based on interviews taken from refugees from the mainland.

1519 Hunter, Edward. Brainwashing: The Story of the Men Who Defied It. New York: Farrar, Strauss, 1956.
More on brainwashing and the techniques used which Hunter traces back to Lenin. Rather dramatic narration of cases when men held out.

1520 Hunter, Edward. "Our POWs Are Not Traitors" Combat Forces Journal 4 3 (October 1953): 36-37.
Claims that men who give in are sick, not traitors, and should be treated as persons who have no control over their conditions.

1521 Jolidon, Laurence. Last Seen Alive: The Search for the Missing POWs from the Korean War. Austin, Texas: Ink-Slinger Press, 1995.
A rather exaggerated look at the prisoners from the Korean War who remain unaccounted for.

1522 Kahn, Lessing A. A Preliminary Study of Chinese and North Korean Soldier Reactions to UN Weapons in the Korean War. Chevy Chase, Maryland: Johns Hopkins University, 1952.
This is a part of project POWOW, which was an effort to judge the effectiveness of United Nations weapons, military tactics, and propaganda on communist soldiers, by interviewing prisoners.

1523 Kahn, Lessing A. A Preliminary Study of North Korean and Chinese Surrenders. Chevy Chase, Maryland: Johns Hopkins University, Operations Research Office, 1951.
A technical memorandum (ORO-T-2) dealing with communist prisoners.

1524 Kim, Myolng Whai. "Prisoners of War as a Major Problem of the Korean Armistice" Ph.D. dissertation, New York University, 1960.

An argument for not forcing POWs to return home, if they do not want to do so. The analysis looks at the question of prisoner return as a drag on the armistice process.

1525 Kinkead, Eugene. In Every War But One. New York: W. W. Norton, 1959, 1982.
        Kinkead claims that the lack of discipline among American troops led to their inability to deal with the communist techniques.

1526 Kinkead, Eugene. Why They Collaborated. New York: Longman, 1960.
        Puts the worst possible case forward, claiming men were dying because of their own lack of discipline. The author's interpretation of collaboration was so broad as to make the inquiry nearly meaningless.

1527 Lech, Raymond B. Broken Soldiers: American Prisoners of War in North Korea. Chelsea, Michigan: Scarborough House, 1991.
        The supposed account of American prisoners-of-war in North Korea who gave in and helped the communist cause in some fashion.

1528 Loosbrock, John F. "Confess, Yankee, Confess!" Air Force 1 (November 1953): 25-28.
        Some men confessed to real or imaginary charges. The reasons they did were varied, but this article states that new factors must be designed to prevent Americans from being so easily influenced in any future wars.

1529 MacDonald, James A. "The Problems of U. S. Marine Corps Prisoners at War in Korea" MA thesis, University of Maryland, 1961.
        Compares the role of United States Marine prisoners to that of other American troops. Claims training helped the Marines remain unaffected by the communist methods.

1530 Manley, Omer L. Hands Up. New York: Carlton Press, 1978.
        A personal narrative of this Sacramento, California, author who was captured, escaped, and was recaptured.

1531 Mayer, William E. "Why Did So Many G. I. Captive Gives In?" U. S. News & World Report 40 (February 1956): 56-62, 64-72.
        Mayer, an Army psychiatrist, explains the view that the poor conduct of American POWs was caused by a flaw in the American character and the failure to teach Americans the value of their nation.

1532 Meerloo, Joost A. M. "The Crime of Menticide" American Journal of Psychiatry 107 (1951): 594-598.

Meerloo is concerned about the deaths which he believed were caused by mental anguish.

1533 Meyers, Samuel M. and William C. Bradbury. The Political Behavior of Korean and Chinese Prisoners of War in the Korean Conflict: A Historical Analysis. Washington, D. C.: George Washington University, 1958.
An attempt to understand the political causes for North Korean and Chinese prisoners-of-war behavior. Task TICK III report.

1534 No, Kum-Sok and J. Roger Osterholm. A MiG-15 to Freedom: Memoir of the Wartime North Korean Defector Who First Delivered the Secret Fighter Jet to the Americans in 1953. Jefferson, North Carolina: McFarland, 1996.
The author, also known as Kenneth H. Rowe, brought his MiG to an American air base and delivered it to authorities. He says he did not know of the $100,000 reward offered by General Clark.

1535 Page, William F. The Health of Former Prisoners of War: Results from the Medical Examiner Survey of Former POW of World War II and the Korean Conflict. Washington, D. C.: National Academy Press, 1992.
Comparison of the health of returned prisoners looking at the poor health of Korean prisoners against World War II.

1536 Pate, L. C. "Survival Lies in Training" Combat Forces Journal 6 9 (April 1956): 20.
An American sergeant taken captive by the communists talks about how his survival depended on training.

1537 Pelser, Frederick and Marcia E. Pelser. Freedom Bridge. Fairfield, California: Fremar Press, 1984.
A personal narrative of prisoner life and release across "freedom bridge."

1538 Polk, David. Ex-Prisoners of the Korean War. Paducah, Kentucky: Turner Publishing Company, 1993.
This is a yearbook variety account and is of limited value.

1539 POW, The Fight Continues After the Battle. A Report on Prisoners of War by the Secretary of Defense Advisory Committee. Washington, D. C.: Government Printing Office, 1955.
The prisoner question was never settled to anyone's satisfaction, and as it turns out, President Eisenhower was aware that some prisoners were still begin held by the communists. This early accounting makes no such claim.

1540 POW-MIA Fact Book. Washington, D. C.: Department of Defense, 1990.
   Twenty-eight page annual report of basic data and accounts.

1541 POW/MIA's In Indochina and Korea: Hearing Before the Subcommittee on Asian and Pacific Affairs, June 28, 1990. Washington, D. C.: Government Printing Office, 1990.
   An attempt to locate, or prove the lack of, prisoners still in Korea. Information continues to be gathered about Soviet involvement.

1542 Praugh, G. S., Jr. "Justice for all Recap-K's" Combat Forces Journal 6 4 (November 1955): 13-26.
   Maintains that there is no universal reason for POW behavior. Rather there is a need to look at each repatriated prisoner separately in order that justice may be done.

1543 The Prisoner of War Situation in Korea. Washington, D. C.: Government Printing Office, 1952.
   Report of a hearing before a Senate subcommittee on the treatment, and behavior of POWs in Korea.

1544 "Real Story of Returned Prisoners" U. S. News & World Report 34 22 (May 29, 1953): 54-58.
   An analysis of tape recordings made by GIs back from Korea, showed intensive "softening-up" and brainwashing.

1545 "Red Successes with British POW's" America 92 (March 26, 1955): 663.
   Only forty or so of the nearly one thousand British prisoners showed any signs of doubting their nation, and most of these had pro-communist leanings before the war.

1546 "Red Torture Broke Few G.I.'s" U. S. News & World Report 39 9 (August 26, 1955): 38-39.
   Of 7,190 captives, 2,730 died, and only 192 betrayed their country. Article describes new code of conduct for United States fighting soldiers.

1547 Reinhardt, G. C. "Frame-up, Communist Style" Combat Forces Journal 4 3 (October 1953): 35-36.
   Discusses the fate of soldiers in communist hands and how the captors used confession instruments to take advantage of United States prisoners-of-war.

1548 Report of Conference with Repatriated P. O. W. Personnel, Medical Corps, U. S. Army. Washington, D. C.: Department of the Army, 1953.

The army, especially the medical people, were very interested in the condition of returned prisoners.

1549 Return of American Prisoners of War Who Have Not Been Accounted for by the Communists. Washington, D. C.: Government Printing Office, 1957.
Effort to identify and arrange the return of prisoners not identified by the communists.

1550 Roskey, William. Koje Island: the 1952 Korean Hostage Crisis. Arlington, Virginia: Institute of Land Warfare, 1994.
One of the darkest events of the war was the taking of American hostages at Koje prison, and the Army's capitulation to the communist demands.

1551 Sander, H. J. Analysis of the Korean War Prisoner of War Experience. Springfield, Virginia: Monroe Corporation, 1974.
A narrative which tries to describe what the prisoner-of-war experience was really like.

1552 Sanders, James. Soldiers of Misfortune: Washington's Secret Betrayal of American POWs in the Soviet Union. Washington, D. C.: National Press Book, 1992.
The untold story of American POWs who were sent to Russia for interrogation and imprisonment. [Alternate title and publisher: Soldiers of Misfortune: The Cold War Betrayal and Sacrifice of American POWs. New York: Avon Books, 1992.]

1553 Schein, Edgar H. "The Chinese Indoctrination Program of Prisoners of War: A Study of Brainwashing" Psychology 19 (1956): 149-172.
Discusses the methods of indoctrination used by the Chinese. This study focuses on the techniques of upsetting the elements of social organization and the use of reward and punishment to control prisoners.

1554 Schein, Edgar H. A Psychological Follow-up of Former Prisoners of War of the Chinese Communists. Cambridge: Massachusetts Institute of Technology, 1960.
A follow-up study, five years after the war, of two hundred former prisoners, which showed that they were leading normal lives.

1555 Schopfel, U. G. Prisoners of War: A Commander's Dilemma, New Initiatives and Approaches? Newport, Rhode Island: Naval War College, 1986.

Addresses the problem which unit commanders had with the prisoner-of-war issue.

1556 Segal, Julius. "Factors Related to the Collaboration and Resistance Behavior of U. S. Army POW's in Korea" Humrgo Technical Report No. 3. Washington Human Resources Research Office, George Washington University, 1956.

Showed that only thirteen percent of prisoners collaborated with the enemy, and few paid much attention to the constant propaganda value of their "statement" to the Chinese.

1557 Shiratsuki, Thomas T. Notes on the CCF Prisoner of War. no publisher, 1953.

Brief (thirteen page) comments on the political nature of the communist prisoner-of-war, beliefs, and understandings.

1558 Special Report of Prisoner of War Incident, 291805, 1 June 1953. APO: United Nations Command POW Camp, #1, Koje-do, 1953.

Official report on the Koje-do incident. The United States military was clearly out of control at the time.

1559 "Status of Twenty-one Americans who Refused Repatriation" U. S. Department of State Bulletin 33 (July 4, 1955): 20.

Identifies the twenty-one American "turn-coats" as dishonorably discharged civilians who, if they returned, would be held and tried by the Department of Justice.

1560 Sterr, Ronald M. "Koje-do: United Nations Prisoner of War Camp During the Korean Conflict" MST thesis, University of Wisconsin, 1970.

MS: prisoners

1561 Thimayya, Kodendera Subayya. Experiment in Neutrality. New Delhi: Vision Books, 1981.

Diary of POW and the armistice release of General K. S. Thimayya, neutral nations repatriation commissioner.

1562 Thornton, John W. Believed to Be Alive. Middlebury, Utah: Eriksson, 1991.

A prisoner-of-war provides a personal narrative of his years of imprisonment and mistreatment, and how he stayed committed.

1563 Todd, Joe L. Prisoners of War: Interviews with Former Prisoners or War in the Collection of the Oklahoma Historical Society. Oklahoma City, Oklahoma: Oklahoma Historical Society, 1989.

A good collection of prisoner interviews for World War II, Korea, and Vietnam.

1564 Tosi, George. The Parallel Exchange. New York: Carlton Press, 1987.
A very brief narrative which describes the prisoner exchanges.

1565 Treatment of British Prisoners of War in Korea. London: Her Majesty's Stationary Office, 1955.
Brief and less than helpful look at early reports on how British prisoners-of-war were treated.

1566 Tsouras, Peter G. and Timothy R. Lewis. The Transfer of U. S. Korean POWS to the Soviet Union. Washington, D. C.: United States Department of State, 1993.
Increasing evidence suggests that some American prisoners were taken to the Soviet Union for interrogation. This working paper is an early investigation.

1567 U. S. Charges Communists are Holding Fifteen Servicemen "Political Prisoners" in Violation of Korean Armistice. Washington, D. C.: Department of Defense, 1954.
After the war, the charge of holding illegal prisoners was directed toward both sides. This is an official charge to that effect.

1568 U. S. Prisoners of War in the Korean Operation: A Study of Their Treatment and Handling by the North Korean Army and the Chinese Communist Forces. Fort Meade, Maryland: Army Security Center, 1954.
Using interviews from exchanged prisoners, the army compiled a study of the general treatment, comparing North Korean and Chinese captors.

1569 United Nations Command. The Communist War in POW Camps: The Background Incidents Among Communist Prisoners in Korea. no publisher, 1953.
United Nations command tried to understand how the communists were so able to control what happened in the prisoner camps where their people were imprisoned.

1570 United Nations P.O.W.'s in Korea. Peking: Chinese People's Committee for World Peace, 1953.
Commentary of the role of United Nations prisoners-of-war held by the communists, the people's view.

1571 United States. The History of Compound 65. Armed Forces Far East: no publisher, 1954.

Stories of life among prisoners of North Korean camp, particularly one compound.

1572 United States. Prisoners of War in the Korean Hostilities Report (to Accompany H. R. 4121). Washington, D. C.: Government Printing Office, 1959.

Statement about prisoners-of-war which was attached to House Bill 4121.

1573 United States Army. Question of Atrocities Committed by the North Korean and Chinese Communist Forces against United Nations Prisoners of War in Korea. no publisher, 1953.

Compilation of documents and comments to support the American charge of communist atrocities.

1574 United States Congress. Accounting for POW/MIAs from the Korean War and Vietnam War. Washington, D. C.: Government Printing Office, 1997.

Report of congressional hearing held on June 20, 1996.

1575 United States Congress. Korean War Atrocities: Hearing Before the Subcommittee on Korean War Atrocities. Washington, D. C.: Government Printing Office, 1954.

Congressional hearing on "war atrocities" which were conducted by both sides.

1576 United States Congress. Status of POW/MIA Negotiations with North Korea. Washington, D. C.: Government Printing Office, 1997.

Report of congressional hearing held on September 17, 1996.

1577 United States Department of the Army. Comments Concerning a Report by the Red Cross Society of China entitled "Report on the Investigation of Medical Atrocities and Malpractices Committed by U. S. Armed Forces in Korea on Sick and Wounded Chinese People's Volunteers Prisoners of War". Washington, D. C.: Office of the Surgeon General, 1954.

Official reaction to the Chinese Red Cross charges, that of American sanctioned atrocities, against Chinese troops.

1578 United States Department of the Army. Communist Interrogation, Indoctrination, and Exploitation of Prisoners of War. Washington, D. C.: Government Printing Office, 1956.

Pamphlet designed to provide information about the attempted brainwashing of prisoners-of-war. Not very reliable.

1579 Vetter, Harold J. Mutiny on Koje Island. Rutland, Vermont: C. E. Tuttle, 1965.
Effort to understand what happened at the prisoner uprising at Koje-do, which results in an interesting but not too accurate account.

1580 Voelkel, Harold. Behind Barbed Wire in Korea. Grand Rapids, Michigan: Zondervan, 1953.
American missionary who became a chaplain and who ministered to the POWs.

1581 White, William L. The Captives of Korea: An Unofficial White Paper on Treatment of War Prisoners: OUR Treatment of Theirs; Their Treatment of OURS. New York: Charles Scribner's Sons, 1957. Westport, Connecticut: Greenwood Press, 1977.
Used a comparison between United Nations and communist POW techniques to counteract communist charges that the United Nations had mistreated its prisoners to force Chinese and North Korean POWs to repudiate communism and refute repatriation.

1582 Zellers, Larry. In Enemy Hands: A Prisoner in North Korea. Lexington, Kentucky: University of Kentucky Press, 1991.
Recounts his own story and that of civilian missionaries, diplomatic and journalists imprisoned by North Korea and Chinese. He focuses on the interrogations.

Support Functions

Medical

1583 Battle Casualties of the Army. Washington, D. C.: Department of the Army, 1954.
The official accounting of battle casualty statistics.

1584 Best, Robert J. Analysis of Personnel Casualties in the 25th Infantry Division 26-31 July 1950. Chevy Chase, Maryland: Johns Hopkins University, 1952.
Looks at casualties in select units and attempts to identify causes.

1585 Best, Robert J. A Study of Battle Casualties Among Equivalent Opposing Forces, Korea, September, 1950. Chevy Chase, Maryland: Johns Hopkins University, 1953.

An inquiry into the comparative casualties in an effort to identify troop use efficiency.

1586 Biderman, Albert D. Social-Psychological Needs and "Involuntary" Behavior as Illustrated by Compliance in Interrogation. Indianapolis, Indiana: Bobbs-Merrill, 1967.
This article on involuntary behavior among prisoners also appears in Sociometry 232 (June 1960).

1587 Birch, Jack W. and David Konigsburg. Pretesting Procedures for Psychological Warfare: Printed Media: Phase II, Ranking and Other Methods. Chevy Chase, Maryland: Johns Hopkins University, 1953.
An effort to determine what psychological materials will be most useful under a variety of situations.

1588 Bower, Warner F. "Evacuating Wounded from Korea" Army Information Digest 5 12 (December 1950): 47-54.
Discusses the speed with which the medical community overcame the difficulty of casualty care, and established the line from the "front to California."

1589 Casualties Sustained by the British Army in the Korean War, 1950-1953. London: London Stamp Exchange, 1985.
An account of casualties in British forces during the Korean War, with rather extensive information and analysis.

1590 "Casualties: The Toll Rises" Newsweek 37 (February 5, 1951): 26.
Reports that United States casualties had now exceeded, in 1951, the number in seven full American divisions. Fifteen thousand soldiers were being sent to Korea monthly.

1591 Cleaver, Frederick W. US Army Battle Casualties in Korea. Chevy Chase, Maryland: Johns Hopkins University, 1956.
Standard consideration of casualties, causes, and what it tells the reader about the nature of battle.

1592 Cowdrey, Albert E. "'Germ Warfare' and Public Health in the Korean Conflict" Journal of the History of Medicine and Allied Sciences 39 (1984).
Consideration of the germ warfare charges leveled against the United Nations and the general nature of public health in Korea.

1593 Dyer, Murray. Strategic Radio Psywar in FEC. Chevy Chase, Maryland: Johns Hopkins University, 1951.

An inquiry into the use and value of the radio in FEC psychological warfare.

1594 Ewin, JV Haasem. "Fighting For Life in Korea" Asian Defense Journal (December 1989): 92-96.
The medical resources, and the care for wounded in the early days of the Korean War, have much to teach about the nature of United Nations preparedness. The high costs that were paid for not being well prepared cannot be repeated.

1595 Fitzgerald, Helen M. "A History of the United States Navy Nurse Corps From 1934 to the Present" MA thesis, Ohio State University, 1968.
A good history of the Navy nurse in World War II, the Korean War, and the war in Vietnam.

1596 Fontana, Alan and Robert Rosenheck. "Traumatic War Stressors and Psychiatric Symptoms Among World War II, Korea, and Vietnam War Veterans" Psychology and Aging 9 1 (March 1994).
Korean veterans are more likely to suffer stress and suicide than veterans of other wars, because they never received any public thanks and were criticized and presumed to have delivered a poor performance in the Korean War.

1597 George, Alexander L. Psychological Aspects of Tactical Air Operations (Korea). Santa Monica, California: Rand Corporation, 1962.
Inquiry into the psychological aspects of United States Air Force aerial operations.

1598 Groth, John and Mary G. Phillips. "Army Nurses in Korea" What's New 159 (July/August 1951): 11-18.
Observation of nurse medical functions as they were identified in MASH (Mobile Army Surgical Hospital) 8063.

1599 Groth, John and Raymond W. Bliss. "Mobile Army Surgical Hospital 8063" What's New 158 (June 1951): 12-20.
A rather brief but informative look at the effectiveness of the MASH unit in Korea.

1600 Howard, John M. Battle Casualties in Korea: Studies of the Surgical Research Team. four volumes. Washington, D. C.: Walter Reed Army Institute, 1955.
Comments on wounds, injuries, and resuscitation by surgical units.

1601 Hume, Edgar E. "United Nations Medical Service in the Korean Conflict" Military Surgeon 109 (1951): 91-95.

A look at the United Nations service activities, including the multi-national force provisions for medical service. The need, and initial response, felt during the first few months of the war, is reviewed.

1602 Korean Conflict Casualties: 1950-1957: (Includes Only Hostile Casualties). Washington, D. C.: National Archives, 1989.

Register of the dead—combat hostilities—during the expanded Korean War.

1603 Korean War Battle Casualties of the Army. Washington, D. C.: Office of the Adjutant General, 1954.

A listing of official battle casualties in the Army during the Korean War.

1604 Lifton, Robert. "Psychotherapy with Combat Flyers" U. S. Armed Forces Medical Journal 4 4 (April 1953): 525-537.

Identifies three phases of anxiety for combat flyers: reaction to early missions, external stress during missions, and tension related to their final mission.

1605 Manning, Frank E. and Daniel F. Goodacre. Interview with Korean Casualties: A Pilot Study: Final Report. Institute for Research in Human Relations, 1951.

Final report on a series of interviews about Korean War casualties designed to determine reactions to wounds.

1606 Marsh, Walter. "Army Surgical Hospitals at Work in Korea" Army Information Digest 8 (1953): 48-52.

Describes the utilization of Army Surgical Hospitals during the first months of the war when three units were in operation. Medical evacuation was cut considerably by the success of these units.

1607 Morgan, Len. "M*A*S*H Epilogue" Flying 110 (March 1983): 60-63.

Using the popular TV series as background, the author discusses the early role of the mobile medical units, the introduction of the helicopter ambulances, and their success particularly during the early days of the war.

1608 Paul, John R. and William McClure. "Epidemic Hemorrhagic Fever Attack Rates Among United Nations Troops during the Korean War" American Journal of Hygiene 68 (1958): 126-139.

One of the great fears of the Korean War was the irrational beliefs held about the dangers of hemorrhagic fever. This looks at the rate of the disease among troops.

1609 Reister, Frank. Battle Casualties and Medical Statistics: U. S. Army Experience in the Korean War. Washington, D. C.: The Surgeon General, 1973.
    An action-by-action listing of battle casualties as well as supporting medical statistics for the serious inquirer.

1610 Sams, Crawford F. Medic. Carlisle Barracks, Pennsylvania: United States Army Military History Institute, 1986.
    A biography of a brigadier general medic in World War II and Korea. Contains a good deal on tropic medicine.

1611 Sams, Crawford F. Organization of Civilian Medical Service in the Theater of Operations. Washington, D. C.: Walter Reed Army Institute, 1955.
    Discussion of civilian sources and the organization of disaster medicine.

1612 Schwarz, Benjamin C. Casualties, Public Opinion & U. S. Military Intervention: Implications for U. S. Regional Deterrence Strategies. Santa Monica, California: Rand Corporation, 1994.
    An excellent look at the relationship between casualties and their deterrence concepts in Korea, Vietnam, and the Gulf War.

1613 Sheldon, Richard C. and Henry Senft. Preliminary Evaluation of Psywar Leaflets and Broadcasts from IPOR POW Interrogation. Chevy Chase, Maryland: Johns Hopkins University, 1951.
    An evaluation of psychological warfare materials based on prisoner interviews. The materials proved to be less effective than believed.

1614 Snyder, Francis. "Wartime Dentistry" Military Surgeon 112 3 (1953): 182-189.
    Study of field dentistry offered during the Korean War, in this case with the 1st Marine Division.

1615 Taylor, Alex R., Seymour Jablon and Claire M. Kretschmann. Posttraumatic Symptoms in Head Injured Veterans of the Korean Campaign. no publisher, 1971.
    One of the few looks at post-traumatic symptoms for head wounds, presented in a highly technical manner.

1616 Thornton, W. H. "The 24th Division Medical Battalion in Korea" Military Surgeon 113 (1953): 27-31.

Traces the 24th Division Medical Battalion (as an example) during the first two months of the war. Takes into accounts the difficulty of the abrupt move from Japan, setting up a medical service with such limited supplies, and providing medical aid during the long retreat.

1617 Unit History of the 45th Surgical Hospital (8076th AU): Unit Activation to 10 August 1953. archive/manuscript control, 1953.

An expanded regimental history of a significant surgical unit.

1618 United States. Army Deaths: Korean War Conflict. Washington, D. C.: Government Printing Office, 1970.

The official register of the dead from the Korean War.

1619 United States Department of Defense. U.S. Military Personnel Who Died From Hostile Action (Including Captured) in the Korean War, 1950-1957, Arizona. Washington, D. C.: National Archives, 1957.

Listing and narrative describing Americans killed or captured (no return) during the Korean War.

1620 Van Der Water, Marjorie. "The Human Price of Combat" Combat Forces Journal 4 8 (March 1954): 24-25.

Discusses medical research done during the Korean War to determine how much combat stress soldiers can stand. Men usually break after the emergency is over, and need twelve days to recover from the strain of being in combat.

1621 Watts, John C. Surgeon at War. London: Allen, 1955.

Experiences of a front-line British surgeon who saw combat duty in World War II and Korea. Well-written and full of descriptive stories.

1622 Weintraub, Stanley. War in the Wards: Korea's Unknown Battle in a Prisoner-of-War Hospital Camp. Garden City, New York: Doubleday, 1964. San Raphael, California: Presidio Press, 1976.

Communist POWs carried on a highly successful war in the hospital wards of the POW camps. Excellent account.

1623 White, William L. Back Down the Ridge. New York: Harcourt Brace, 1953.

An account of a mobile army surgical hospital; "the story of some typical Korean casualties: how they came by their wounds, how they were gotten down off the ridge to a battalion aid station, and what happened then."

Intelligence

1624 Arnold, Joseph C. "Omens and Oracles" <u>United States Naval Institute Proceedings</u> 106 8 (1980): 47-53.
        An analysis of the mismanagement and misuse of intelligence information which prevented acceptable warnings prior to the Chinese entry into the Korean War.

1625 Cohen, Eliot A. and John Gooch. <u>Military Misfortunes: The Anatomy of Failure in War</u>. New York: Vintage Books, 1991.
        Contains an interesting chapter on the failure of the intelligence community to anticipate the Communist Chinese Force invasion of Korea in the winter of 1950.

1626 "Data for a Pearl Harbor Echo: Did We Muff It in Korea?" <u>Newsweek</u> 36 (July 10, 1950): 26-29.
        Two days of secret hearings by the Senate Appropriations Committee drew admissions from General Lemnitzer, and John H. Ohly of the Mutual Defense Assistance, that America was uninformed, and unprepared for events in Korea.

1627 Headquarters, United States Army Forces, Far East (Advanced), Office of the Assistant Chief of Staff, G-2. "Selected Intelligence Items During Period 16 June-30 June, 1952" <u>Intelligence Digest</u> 26 (2 July 1952): iii, v-vi, 17-19, 44-54.
        Selected (limited) intelligence materials available to the FEC, concerning communist activities.

1628 "Indo-China Next on Kremlin's List?" <u>Newsweek</u> 36 (August 14, 1950): 15-19.
        In battles along the Naktong River line the United States meets the communist who are desperate. Evidence grows that the Chinese are training and equipping Viet Minh troops for an expanded war. The question is, can the war be stopped in Korea?

1629 "Korea: Test of Strength" <u>Combat Forces Journal</u> 1 1 (August 1950): 38-39.
        From the beginning it was apparent that the army of the Republic of South Korea was outmatched and outsmarted. They could not hold Korea. The real test was if the United States could control the North Korean advance long enough for reinforcements and supplies to arrive from America.

1630 Nichols, Donald. The North Korean Intelligence Organization. no publisher, 1956.

Brief (eleven page) report does little to help the reader seriously understand the North Korean intelligence efforts.

1631 Poteat, George. "Strategic Intelligence and National Security: A Case Study of the Korean Crisis (June 25–November 24, 1950)" Ph.D. dissertation, Washington University, 1973.

Suggests that United Nations failures to read intelligence gathered was due to pre-conceived notions about Korea, rather than a lack of understanding or information.

1632 "Too Little, 45 Days Too Late" Collier's 126 (1950): 24-25.

Questions the leadership in Washington who, it contends, had forty-five days notice, delivered by the South Korean Defense Minister, of the impending attack. Washington, therefore, is responsible for so many deaths.

1633 Willoughby, Charles A. Intelligence in War: A Brief History of MacArthur's Intelligence Service, 1941-1951. Tokyo: Dai-Nippon Printing Company, 1959.

Willoughby was criticized for his inability to tell what the Chinese were doing. This yearbook variety account is of no help at all.

Financial and Legal

1634 Alapatt, George K. "The Legal Implications of the Repatriation of War Prisoners in Relation to the Korean Armistice and in View of the Division of Korea" Ph.D. dissertation, St. Louis University, 1958.

The existing rules of international agreement failed to meet the needs in Korea, so the armistice agreement itself made a significant contribution to precedents in neutralist law.

1635 Brandt, Charles H. "An Examination of the Fiscal and Monetary Policies of the United States in a Period of Limited War; Specifically, the Korean War, 1950-1953" MBA thesis, St. John's University, 1967.

MA: fiscal policy

1636 Fisher, Louis. Constitutional Conflict Between Congress and the President. Princeton: Princeton University Press, 1985.

The failure to seek congressional action, and the conflict over presidential power which resulted, was responsible for the 1973 War Powers Act and changed the role of the presidency.

1637 Graebner, N. A. "The President as Commander in Chief: A Study in Power" Journal of Military History 57 1 (January 1993): 111-132.
Discusses the president's legal rights and authority to send America into war, as was done in Korea.

1638 Hoyt, Edwin P. "The United States Reaction to the Korean Attack: A Study of the Principle of the UN Charter as a Factor in American Policy-Making" American Political Science Review 55 1 (January 1961): 45-76.
A legalistic argument which claims the United States used the United Nations charter to get its own way.

1639 Kim, Myong-gi. The Korean War and International Law. Claremont, California: Paige Press, 1991.
Excellent account of the legal problems facing a divided Korea. The Korean War added to the difficulties.

1640 Kirkendall, Richard. Harry S. Truman: The Decision to Intervene. St. Louis, Missouri: Forum Press, 1979.
Discusses the use of executive power and the implications of the lack of a declaration of war.

1641 Lo, Clarence Y. H. "The Truman Administration's Military Budgets During the Korean War" Ph.D. dissertation, University of California, Berkeley, 1978.
Truman was determined not to lose "butter" to buy bombs. But the national debt grew vastly during this period.

1642 Matray, James I. "America's Reluctant Crusade: Truman's Commitment of Combat Troops in the Korean War" Historian 42 (May 1980): 437-455.
Matray's analysis of the decision suggests that neither Truman's decision to commit troops, or his decision to do so without congressional approval, were outside the scope of normal policy. An interesting view of "the other side" of the debate.

1643 Maurer, Maurer. "The Korean Conflict Was a War" Military Affairs 24 7 (Fall 1960): 137-141.
Dealing with the continued United States use of the term "Police Action" the author claims that, despite the lack of congressional action, it was still a war.

1644 Oldham, Donald E. The Finance Section: World War II and Korean War. Oklahoma City, Oklahoma: 45th Infantry Division Museum, 1994.
Considers the role of the finance section in a war situation. Also provides a brief regimental history.

1645 Parker, Edith H. <u>Summary of Finance Corps Activities Relating to the Korean Conflict for the Period 25 June 1950 through September 1951</u>. no publisher, 1951.

Good report of the role of the Finance Corps, but dull reading.

1646 "President's Stand on Korea" <u>Army Information Digest</u> 5 8 (August 1950): 3-11.

Provides and discusses extracts from President Truman's 19 July 1950 message to Congress in which he justifies both his action to involve the United States in the Korean War, and to do so without congressional action.

1647 Verplaetse, Julien G. <u>The Ius in Bello and Military Operatives in Korea, 1950-1953</u> Heidelberg: W. Kohlhammer, 1963.

A discussion of international law and the legal implications of the "unauthorized" Korean War.

Religion, Recreation, and Chaplains

1648 Brooks, Jerrold L. "In Behalf of a Just and Durable Peace: The Attitudes of American Protestantism Toward War and Military-related Affairs Involving the United States, 1945-1953" Ph.D. dissertation, Tulane University, 1977.

Following World War II the Protestant community leaders felt they had a good chance to build a Christian world order. They were frustrated by American foreign policy which they believed would lead to World War III.

1649 Dunn, Joe P. "The Church and the Cold War: Protestants and Conscription, 1940-1955" Ph.D. dissertation, University of Missouri, Columbia, 1973.

Reviews of Protestant reaction to compulsory military service during World War II and Korea.

1650 Graham, Billy. "I Saw Your Sons at War" Minneapolis, Minnesota: Billy Graham Evangelistic Association, 1953.

Account of the evangelist's visit to American soldiers on the battlefield at Korea.

1651 Griepp, Frank R. <u>The Circuit-Riding Combat Chaplain</u>. Palos Verdes, California: F. Griepp, 1988.

The narrative of an Army chaplain during the first year of the war, who served with the 7th Cavalry. Good insights into the role of the chaplain in combat.

1652 Jaeger, Vernon. "Experiences in Korea" <u>Military Chaplain</u> (October 1950): 1-2.

A United States Army chaplain serving on the line makes some observations on what took place during the first few months of the war. He was astonished at the poor preparation and support of the troops thrown into battle.

1653 MacDonald, Margaret F. "A History of the American Red Cross Mobile Recreation Program in Korea, 1953-1956" MA thesis, Oregon School of Health and Physical Education, 1957.

A better than expected account of the Red Cross "donuts and tennis" program in Korea.

1654 Mulvey, Timothy J. <u>These Are Your Sons</u>. New York: McGraw-Hill, 1952.

This Catholic priest lived with the combat troops, followed their stories, and wrote of their lives of combat. Sentimental and overly patriotic.

1655 Osmer, Harold H. <u>U. S. Religious Journalism and the Korean War</u>. Lanham, Maryland: University Press of America, 1980.

A discussion of how various religious presses reacted to the American involvement in Korea. Generally supportive of the nation but not the war.

1656 Osmer, Harold H. "United States Religious Press Response to the Containment Policy During the Period of the Korean War" Ph.D. dissertation, New York University, 1970.

The United States religious press was not as supportive as might be anticipated, as is shown by this study.

1657 Muller, John H. <u>Wearing the Cross in Korea</u>. Redlands, California: J. Muller, 1954.

United States Navy chaplain who served in Korea with the 1st Marines, details his work as chaplain and humanitarian.

1658 Sharp, Robert L. "God Saved My Life in Korea" <u>Saturday Evening Post</u> 223 29 (1951): 26-27, 95-96.

Basically a story of life as a prisoner by an Army private who was captured and credits God with his eventual escape.

1659 Tonne, Arthur. <u>The Story of Chaplain Kapaun: Patriot Priest of the Korean Conflict</u>. Emporia, Kansas: Didde, 1954.

Kapaun, who elected to stay with a group of wounded, was taken prisoner. He died while in captivity.

1660 Weston, Logan E. The Fightin' Preacher. Cheyenne, Wyoming: Vision Press, 1992.

World War II and Korean War Christian leader biography which was first printed in 1940 and then revised to include the Korean War years.

Propaganda and Psychological Warfare

1661 Barnet, John A., Jr. Soviet Propaganda and the Korean War. no publisher, 1957.

Brief (forty-two page) effort to identify Soviet support of the war, and to offset the propaganda effort.

1662 Bradbury, William C., Samuel M. Meyers Albert D. Biderman, editors. Mass Behavior in Battle and Captivity: The Communist Soldier in the Korean War. Chicago: University of Chicago Press, 1968.

After interviewing communist POWs the study tries to explain why two-thirds of the Chinese prisoners refused repatriation.

1663 Brauer, Albert G. Albert G. Brauer Psychological Warfare Propaganda Leaflets Collection. Archive/Manuscript Control, 1951.

A history and analysis of 638 United States Army propaganda leaflets produced by EUSAK.

1664 Chung-kuo jen. . . . Stop U. S. Germ Warfare: Protest, Statements, Appeals and Other Documents Concerning the Use of Bacteriological Weapons Against the People of Korea and China. Peking: Chinese People's Committee for World Peace, 1952.

Documents and appeals concerning the United States and the communist charges of germ warfare.

1665 Clews, John C. Communist Propaganda Techniques. London: Methuen. New York: Praeger, 1964.

Use of biological warfare, and prisoner mistreatment, were used to explain just how good the communist effort was during the Korean War.

1666 Clews, John C. The Communist's New Weapon: Germ Warfare. London: Praeger, 1953.

Sees the communist claim that the United States use of germ weapons, as a weapon in itself, was used to full measure by the communists and produced a lasting stain on the American reputation.

1667 Cooper, Berman. "Radio Broadcasting to Chinese and Korean POW's: A Rhetorical Analysis" Ph.D. dissertation, Stanford University, 1956.

A look at the style and content of radio appeals made from 1952 to 1953 by the United Nations command.

1668 Daugherty, William E. Evaluation and Analysis of Leaflet Program in the Korean Campaign, June-December 1950. Chevy Chase, Maryland: Johns Hopkins University, 1951.
A look at the early efforts to provide effective propaganda leaflets for use against the communists.

1669 Davison, W. Phillips. The Lesser Evil. Santa Monica, California: Rand Corporation, 1951.
United States Air Force Project, 28 March 1951, which deals with the psychological aspects of war.

1670 Endicott, Stephen L. "Germ Warfare and the 'Plausible Denial': The Korean War 1952-1953" Modern China 5 1 (January 1979): 79-104.
The author tends to support charges against the United States, suggesting that they did indeed use germ warfare. No good evidence is given to support this.

1671 Germ Warfare in Korea. New York: Far East Spotlight, 1952.
Deals with the questions of atrocities and biological warfare and attempts to identify causes and blame.

1672 Gittings, John. "Talks, Bombs and the Germs—Another Look at the Korean War" Journal of Contemporary Asia 5 2 (1975): 205-217.
The author rejects the communist claims that the United States was mistreating prisoners, using germ arfare, and bombing which delayed negotiations.

1673 Glad, Betty, editor. Psychological Dimensions of War. Newbury, California: Sage Publications, 1990.
A series of articles collected to provide an analysis of the psychological aspects of the Korean War.

1674 Kahn, Lessing A. and Julius Segal. Psychological Warfare and Other Factors Affecting the Surrender of North Korea and Chinese Forces. Chevy Chase, Maryland: Johns Hopkins University, 1953.
Part of project POWOW designed to determine the success of United Nations activities by interviewing POWs. Interesting but of limited value.

1675 Kendall, Willmoore. <u>An Evaluation of Psywar Influence on Chinese Communist Troops</u>. Chevy Chase, Maryland: Johns Hopkins University, 1953.

An evaluation based on prisoner interviews (project POWOW) shows the effects were not so effective.

1676 Kendall, Willmoore. <u>An Evaluation of Psywar Influence on North Korean Troops</u>. Chevy Chase, Maryland: Johns Hopkins University, 1951.

Project POWOW, based on interviews with prisoners, shows that psywar efforts were proving effective.

1677 Kendall, Willmoore. <u>FEC Psychological Warfare Operations: Theater Staff Organization (as of 1 January 1952)</u>. Chevy Chase, Maryland: Johns Hopkins University, 1952.

Attempts to provide justification for psychological warfare units in theater organization.

1678 Kendall, Willmoore, Lawrence F. O'Donnell and John Ponturo. <u>Eighth Army Psychological Warfare in the Korean War</u>. Chevy Chase, Maryland: Johns Hopkins University, 1952.

Research project to determine the value of psychological warfare waged by the Eighth Army in Korea.

1679 Kim, Kilchoon and E. A. Johnson. <u>Evaluation of Effects of Leaflets on Early North Korean Prisoners of War</u>. Chevy Chase, Maryland: Johns Hopkins University, 1951.

Part of Project POWOW trying to evaluate the effectiveness of surrender leaflets by interviewing North Korean POWs.

1680 Paddock, Alfred H. "Psychological and Unconventional Warfare, 1941-1952: Origins of a 'Special Warfare' Capability for the United States Army" Ph.D. dissertation, Duke University, 1979.

Special, in this case, means psychological. The study follows the creation of the Office of the Chief of the Army.

1681 Pease, Stephen E. <u>Psywar: Psychological Warfare in Korea, 1950-1953</u>. Harrisburg, Pennsylvania: Stackpole, 1992.

An attempt to understand the psychological effort in Korea. Not well done.

1682 Pettee, George S. <u>US Psywar Operations in the Korean War</u>. Fort McNair, Johns Hopkins University, 1951.

Good account of psywar operations in Korea, which considers how they were effective.

1683 Ponturo, John. <u>Psychological Warfare Operations at Lower Echelons in Eighth Army, July 1952-July 1953</u>. Chevy Chase, Maryland: Johns Hopkins University, 1954.

The study shows the operation was more effective at the lower level units.

1684 Redock, Sanford A. "Psychological Operations Used Against North Korean and Chinese Captives During the Korean Conflict, 1950-1953" archive/manuscript control, Fort Bragg, North Carolina, no date.

Manuscript providing an evaluation of the use of psychological operation against prisoners-of-war.

1685 United States Congress. "Investigation of Communist Propaganda" Washington, D. C.: Government Printing Office, 1983.

Report by John E. Nelson on communist techniques of propaganda.

1686 Warner, Denis. <u>The Germ Warfare Hoax: How It Was Fabricated</u>. Seoul: United Nations Korean War Allies Association, 1977.

Another discussion of the germ warfare hoax. Provides little new information.

Nuclear Considerations

1687 Anders, Roger M. "The Atomic Bomb and the Korean War: Gordon Dean and the Issue of Civilian Control" <u>Military Affairs</u> 52 (January 1988): 1-6.

Outlines the argument over control, and the development of policies for civilian control of nuclear power.

1688 Borowski, Harry R. "Air Force Atomic Capabilities from VJ Day to the Berlin Blockade" <u>Journal of Military History</u> 44 3 (October 1980): 105-110.

Air capacity to deliver the atom bomb was seriously restricted by the shortage of pilots and trained air crews.

1689 Botti, Timothy. <u>The Long Wait: The Forging of the Anglo-American Nuclear Alliance, 1945-1956</u>. Westport, Connecticut: Greenwood Press, 1987.

The American side of the nuclear agreement was finally worked out. The British were very afraid the United States would use the bomb in Korean or China without prior consideration.

1690 Bundy, McGeorge. <u>Danger and Survival: Choice About the Bomb in the First Fifty Years</u>. New York: Random House, 1988.

Supports the Rosemary Foot thesis that Eisenhower and Dulles believed threats of nuclear attack would influence the Chinese role. Stalin's death was more responsible, however, for the Chinese decision to go along with the armistice.

1691 Calingaert, Daniel. "Nuclear Weapons and the Korean War" Journal of Strategic Studies 11 2 (June 1988): 177-202.
A vital source of discussion about the nuclear threat and the possibility of nuclear air war in Korea.

1692 Clark, Joseph and William Weinstone. The Atom Bomb and You. New York: New Century Publications, 1951.
Looks at the religious (ethical) aspects to be considered in consideration of the nuclear bomb, and America's use of it as either a threat or policy.

1693 Dinerstein, H. S. War and the Soviet Union: Nuclear Weapons and the Reevaluation in Soviet Military and Political Thinking. Westport, Connecticut: Greenwood Press, 1962.
Excellent look at the role of nuclear weapons in the development of Soviet political and policy decision.

1694 Dingman, Roger. "Atomic Diplomacy During the Korean War" International Security 13 (Winter 1988-1989): 61-89.
Holds that President Eisenhower did not use nuclear pressure at the armistice talks. Truman, on the other hand, had used the threat very effectively.

1695 Foot, Rosemary. "Nuclear Coercion and the Ending of the Korean Conflict" International Security 13 (Winter 1988-1989): 99-112.
The author expresses considerable doubt that the bomb played the significant role that both Eisenhower and Dulles said. The Chinese concessions were small indeed.

1696 Friedman, Edward. "Nuclear Blackmail and the End of the Korean War" Modern China 1 1 (January 1975): 75-91.
Author agrees that the story of atomic blackmail was a fable. He is one of the few to think so.

1697 Herken, Gregg. The Winning Weapon: The Atomic Bomb in the Cold War. New York: Knopf, 1981.
Herken gives the atomic bomb more credit as a potential weapon, than it probably deserved.

1698 Kissinger, Henry A. Nuclear Weapons and Foreign Policy. New York: Harper and Brothers, 1957.

Foreign policy from 1945 on was influenced by the atomic bomb. Just how, and how much is considered in this work.

1699 Rosenberg, David Alan. "American Atomic Bomb Strategy and the Hydrogen Bomb Decision" Journal of American History 66 (June 1979): 63-87.

The hydrogen bomb decision was endorsed by National Security Council 68 (April 1950) and was a political response to the Soviet explosion of the atomic bomb, and the fall of China to the communists.

1700 Ryan, Mark A. Chinese Attitudes Toward Nuclear Weapons: China and the United States During the Korean War. London, England: An East Gate Book, 1989.

The title is somewhat misleading. It is about the willingness to go to war even in the shadow of nuclear weapons. The early phases of the book deal with the Korean War and the misunderstandings (thus probably lack of fear) concerning the power of the bomb.

1701 Sherwin, Martin. A World Destroyed: The Atomic Bomb and the Grand Alliance. New York: Vantage, 1977.

A serious study of Truman's use of the atomic bomb, and how the knowledge of America's willingness to use the bomb influenced the formation of Cold War politics.

1702 Snyder, Jack. Atomic Diplomacy in the Korean War. Washington, D. C.: Pew Charitable Trusts, 1993.

Discusses the role of Great Britain in the use of the bomb threat as a diplomatic tool, as well as the views of Truman and Eisenhower.

1703 Soman, Appu K. "An Unequal Fight?: Nuclear Diplomacy Toward the Non-Nuclear: The United States and China 1950-1958" Ph.D. dissertation, Vanderbilt University, 1995.

Examines the Korean War under the two Taiwan strait crisis, concluding that nuclear diplomacy was the basis for America's dealing with China.

1704 Spaatz, Carl. "Some Answers to Korean Questions" Newsweek 36 (July 31, 1950): 17.

This retired Air Force general answers questions about nuclear war, the F-80, the build-up of the Air Force; all questions raised by American involvement in Korea and the fears it generated.

1705 Spaight, J. M. "Korea and the Atomic Bomb" Journal Royal United Service Institution 95 (November 1950): 566-570.

Much can be learned from the Korean War non-use of the atom bomb. The lack of targets in North Korea made the use of an atomic bomb different than other places.

1706 Trachtenburg, Marc. "A 'Wasting Asset': American Strategy and the Shifting Nuclear Balance, 1949-1954" International Security 13 3 (Winter 1988-1989): 5-49.
     Author considers how Americans failed to take full advantage of the power of atomic warfare consideration.

1707 Wheeler, Michael O. Nuclear Weapons and the Korean War. McLean, Virginia: Center for National Security Negotiations, 1994.
     Author sees the atomic bomb as a threat, as being far more important than do most scholars.

Women in the Military

1708 Alsmeyer, Marie Bennett. The Way of the Waves: Women in the Navy. Conway, Arkansas: Hamba Books, 1981.
     An account of women serving in the United States Navy. The coverage of the Korean War period is unnecessarily brief.

1709 Commandant of the Marine Corps (General Alfred M. Gray). Report on Progress of Women in the Marine Corps. Washington, D. C.: Headquarters, United States Marine Corps, 1988.
     More report than progress—lists in narrative form the expansion of female roles in the Marines.

1710 Curtin, Ann. "Army Women on Active Duty" Army Information Digest 8 6 (1953): 22-30.
     The 11,500 female force was used in all but the six combat military occupational specialties (MOS) during the Korean War.

1711 Douglas, Deborah G. United States Women in Aviation: 1940-1985. Washington, D. C.: Smithsonian Institute Press, 1990.
     Broad-based consideration of women in the aviation sector of the military with good coverage of Korea.

1712 Ebbert, Jean and Marie-Beth Hall. Crossed Currents: Navy Women from WWI to Tailhook. Washington, D. C.: Brassey's, 1993.
     This excellent coverage of women in the Navy begins with a good historical base. The coverage of Korea is limited but informative.

1713 May, Elaine Tyler. Pushing the Limits: American Women, 1940-1961.
New York: Oxford University Press, 1994.
        Holds the view that while women came to the aid of the nation, they
were quick to return to domestic duties, only a very few indicating any desire
to remain in the military.

1714 Mitchell, Brian. Weak Link: The Feminization of the American
Military. Washington, D. C.: Regnery Gateway, Inc., 1989.
        The idea of women in military service, especially in combat, was
opposed by some on the grounds that it weakens the military with "feminist"
attitudes and expectations.

1715 Morden, Bettie J. The Women's Army Corps, 1945-1978. Washington,
D. C.: Center of Military History, 1990.
        Until it was incorporated into the army in 1978, the WACS were a
separate unit. This work centers on the role of the WACS during the Korean
War experience.

1716 Skelly, Anne. "Women Marines—The First 50 Years" Marine Corps
League 49 (Autumn 1993): 38-46.
        A lively account of women in the Marine Corps.

1717 Soderbergh, Peter A. Women Marines in the Korean War Era.
Westport, Connecticut: Praeger, 1994.
        Only real account of women in the Marines which focuses on the
Korean War era. Well-done and a must for the serious student.

1718 Stiehm, Judith H. Army and the Enlisted Woman. Philadelphia,
Pennsylvania: Temple University Press, 1989.
        A general survey of the role of enlisted women in the Army. A good
survey of a less-than-wonderful experience.

1719 Stremlow, Mary V. Coping with Sexism in the Military. New York: The
Rosen Publishing Group, 1989.
        Stremlow, an accomplished historian, deals with the question of
sexism as it affects women and the military.

1720 Stremlow, Mary V. A History of Women Marines, 1946-1977.
Washington, D. C.: U. S. Marines History and Museum Division, 1986.
        Good account of the increasing role of women in the military. Korea
coverage limited.

1721 Willenz, June A. Women Veterans: America's Forgotten Heroines.
New York: Continuum Publishing, 1983.

If ever there has been any forgotten heroines, it is in those who served with the military.

Racism and Integration

1722 Ansel, Raymond B. From Segregation to Desegregation: Blacks in the U. S. Army 1703-1954. Carlisle Barracks, Pennsylvania: United States Army War College, 1990.
    Excellent study of the contribution of blacks in the military up to, and including, the integration push in the early 1950s.

1723 Balmforth, E. E. "Getting Our ROKs Off" Combat Forces Journal 1 7 (February 1951): 22-25.
    Discusses the effect of the integration of thousands of ROK soldiers into the 7th United States Division as replacement. The experiment was not well planned.

1724 Banks, Samuel L. "The Korean Conflict" Negro History Bulletin 36 3 (1973): 131-132.
    Claims black United States soldiers were subject to great amounts of bigotry, receiving bad assignments, and gaining few promotions.

1725 Bowers, William T. Black Soldiers, White Army: The 24th Infantry Regiment. Washington, D. C.: Center for Military History, 1996.
    A study of the much criticized 24th Infantry Regiment. Gives a better picture than most accounts.

1726 Bussey, Charles. Firefight at Yechon. New York: Brassey's, Inc., 1991.
    The author, an officer of the 77th Engineers (Combat), was a member of the black outfit which fought at the battle of Yechon. He is very supportive of the black as a fighting man—though favoring the integration of troops that was taking place—and critical of Appleman's reporting of the inefficiency of black troops.

1727 Clark, Mark W. "Negro Battalions 'Weakened Battle Line'" U. S. News & World Report (May 11, 1956): 54-56.
    This Korean War general held the view that black troops did not do well when they moved as teams and that integration did not work well.

1728 Dalfiume, Richard M. Desegregation of the U. S. Armed Forces: Fighting on Two Fronts, 1939-1953 Columbia, Missouri: University of Missouri Press, 1969.
    The accepted work on the decision to end segregation, via executive order in 1948, including the armed services.

1729 Ducksworth, Selika M. "What Hour of the Night: Black Enlisted Men's Experiences and the Desegregation of the Army During the Korean War, 1950-1" Ph.D. dissertation, Ohio State University, 1994.

Case study of Afro-American enlisted experience, primarily in the 24th Regiment, which claims black enlisted men took leadership in the development of the desegregation policy and implementation.

1730 Gropman, Alan. The Air Force Integrates 1946-1964. Washington, D. C.: Center for Air Force History, 1985.

The percentage of blacks in the Air Force in 1949 was ten percent and racism was still a major problem. This is more of a public relations piece than a true inquiry.

1731 MacGregor, Morris J., Jr. Integration of the Armed Forces, 1940-1965. Washington, D. C.: Center of Military History, United States Army, 1981.

This analysis of integration in the Armed Forces credits the Korean War with speeding up the process, but disagrees on the combat value of integrated units.

1732 Martin, Harold H. "How Do Our Negro Troops Measure Up?" Saturday Evening Post 23 (June 16, 1951): 30-31.

The combat record of the black 24th Infantry Regiment was not all that good. But when integrated into other units black troops served with distinction. Argues that segregation in the military must end.

1733 Morrow, Curtis. What's a Commie Ever Done to Black People? A Korean War Memoir of Fighting in the U. S. Army's Last All Negro Unit. Jefferson, North Carolina: McFarland, 1997.

Primarily a personal narrative of life in a black outfit, but also an excellent look at the treatment of blacks in the Korean War Army.

1734 Nalty, Bernard C. Strength for the Fight: A History of Black Americans in the Military. New York: The Free Press, 1989.

Good accompanying work for MacGregor, deals with blacks in the individual service components.

1735 Shaw, Henry I., Jr. and Ralph W. Donnelly. Blacks in the Marine Corps. Washington, D. C.: History and Museums Division, Headquarters, United States Marine Corps, 1975.

Good study of the role and the success of blacks who served in the Corps.

1736 Skaggs, D. C. "The KATUSA Experiment: The Integration of Korean Nationals into the U.S. Army, 1950-1953" Journal of Military History 38 2 (April 1974): 53-58.

In an effort to supply quick replacements, MacArthur assigned ROK troops to American units, primarily the 7th Division. It was a disaster from almost every point of view.

1737 University Publications of America. Papers of the NAACP, Part Nine, Discrimination in the U. S. Armed Forces, 1918-1955. Frederick, Maryland: University Publications of America, 1989.

Documented view of the facts, and effects, of discrimination of blacks who served in the United States military.

RESPONSE TO THE WAR

Media and the War

1738 Altieri, James J. "The Story Behind Army Feature Films" <u>Army Information Digest</u> 7 (1952): 37-42.
  Army cooperation on the production of Korean War films, of which more than thirty-five feature films were finally made. Uses "The Big Push" as an illustration.

1739 Aronson, James. <u>The Press and the Cold War</u>. Indianapolis, Indiana: Bobbs-Merrill, 1970.
  The press was primarily supportive of Truman's stand against communism. The fear of the "Reds" made good press.

1740 Avery, Robert K. and Timothy L. Larson. "U. S. Military Documentary Films: A Chronological Analysis" paper presented at the annual meeting of the Speech Communication Association in San Antonio, Texas, November 10-13, 1979.
  Chronology of films from World War I through Vietnam. Compares "Why We Fight" to "Why Korea" and finds the first superior because of more visual, music, and narration.

1741 Blair, William D., Jr. "Journey Beyond Fear" <u>Reader's Digest</u> 59 (1951): 1-4.
  Blair, a war correspondent, was present during the September 1950 battle for Seoul. He was wounded. This provides a sensitive account of the fear, pain, and anxiety of combat.

1742 Blazing Combat: Vietnam and Korea! Greencastle, Pennsylvania: Apple Press, 1993.

The reprint of two comic books, dealing with combat in Asia, originally published in 1965.

1743 Broadbooks, Jon K. "Reporting from the Devil's Cauldron: The Wartime Associated Press Dispatches of Don Whitehead" MS thesis, University of Tennessee, Knoxville, 1993.

MS: reporting

1744 Brun, Ellen and Jacques Hersh. "The Korean War: 20 Years Later" Martan Review 25 2 (1973): 44-53.

Retrospective look which blames the war on the interface of imperialist motives and unclear United States policy.

1745 Butler, Lucius A. and Chaesoon T. Youngs. Films for Korean Studies. Honolulu: Center for Korean Studies, 1978.

Identifies more than one hundred and twenty 16mm films on different aspects of the Korean War. The list is heavy with films from the early phases of the war, and includes several repeat films under different titles.

1746 Caspary, William. "Public Reaction to International Events" Ph.D. dissertation, Northwest University, 1968.

Examines how the attitudes of the public change during major international events. However, the author says there was consistent support for action against Red China.

1747 Cheek, Leon B., Jr. "Korea Decisive Battle of the World" Military Review 32 12 (1953): 20-26.

Claims the conflict was one of the decisive victories in world history, when the United Nations was strengthened and communism slowed.

1748 Cho, Chong Hyuk. "The Press Censorship of the United States Eighth Army, Under Douglas MacArthur During the Korean Conflict" MA thesis, University of Akron, 1978.

MA: censorship

1749 Cho, Sung-Kyu. "The Korean War as Portrayed in Korean and American Novels" MA thesis, Miami University, 1966.

MA: literary criticism

1750 CiCola, Louis F. "The Korean War as Seen by the Chicago Tribune, the New York Times, and the Times of London" MA thesis, Kent State University, 1981.

An analysis of how the war was covered by three major newspapers. They reflect not only national policy but local interests.

1751 Cleary, Thomas J., Jr. "Aid and Comfort to the Enemy" Military Review 48 (August 1968): 51-55.

During the first few weeks of the fighting, the United States press corps managed to print every bit of military information they got their hands on, including a great deal about the limitations of troops and supplies, which aided the enemy in fighting the war. Local and jurisdictional commanders quickly put a lid on the press but information still got out.

1752 Cumings, Bruce. War and Television. London: Verso, 1992.

Cumings, a respected historian of the Korean War, uses five chapters to describe the conflicts that exist between official and unofficial documentaries, and to describe the difficulty in filming the story of the Korean War. It is part "apology" for the failure of the British "Korea" film and part analysis of the television coverage of American wars.

1753 Dorn, Frank. "Briefing the Press" Army Information Digest 6 (1951): 36-41.

Describes the procedure by which the Department of Defense disseminated news to the press during the first six months. The news that was released rarely told the American people what was happening, and was especially quiet about the difficulties involved.

1754 Edwards, Paul M. A Guide to Films on the Korean War. Westport, Connecticut: Greenwood Press, 1997.

The only guide specifically prepared for films about the Korean War provides technical information and analysis.

1755 Engles, Gene. "Public Opinion During the Korean Conflict" MEd thesis, Millersville, Pennsylvania: State College, 1974.

MA: public opinion

1756 Erwin, Ray. "Censorship, Communications Worry 200 K-War Correspondence" Education Public 83 (1950): 7, 44.

Erwin discusses the problems of war correspondents during the early weeks of the war. Rules of reporting constantly changed depending on what military jurisdiction was calling the shots. The confusion was not simply policy but reflected a growing anger at what the military considered to be "unwise" reporting. This article's value is that it includes the names of most correspondents on the scene at the time.

1757 Falk, Louis Kaye. "The Korean Conflict in Film: A Thesis" MA thesis, University of New Orleans, 1989.
     MA: film

1758 Fraser, Benson P. "The Broadcast Coverage of the Korean War" MA thesis, Fullerton: California State University, 1981.
     MA: broadcasting

1759 Habgood, Carol Anne. "Hollywood and the Korean Conflict: A Survey of Films about the War, 1950-1953" MA thesis, University of Southern California, 1970.
     Limited, and unaware of some of the films, but useful.

1760 Higgins, Marguerite. "Terrible Days in Korea" Saturday Evening Post 223 (August 19, 1950): 26-27.
     Account of the war's most famous female correspondent who accompanied troops on the Seoul to Taejon retreat. A well-written folksy approach which makes no effort to hide opinions which are, generally, unfavorable.

1761 Higgins, Marguerite. War in Korea: The Report of a Woman Combat Correspondent. Garden City, New York: Doubleday & Company, 1951.
     A highly critical and overly dramatic book by Marguerite Higgins, the first of the women correspondents at the front in Korea. She went ashore as a "member in good standing" of the fifth wave of Marines at Inchon. While critical of the Army troops during the first few months, and the "unnecessary" retreat, she gives the Marines good press.

1762 Hubbert, Joseph G. "American Catholic Editorial Opinion and the Korean War, 1950-1953" MA thesis, Catholic University of America, 1983.
     MA: editorial

1763 Hulse, Ed. "The Forgotten War" Video Review (November 1990): 57-59.
     A review of Korean War movies. Not only were there very few such movies, but they were generally very poor. The author, however, is unaware of several films available.

1764 Johnson, Lisa D. "No Place for a Woman: A Biographical Study of War Correspondent Marguerite Higgins" MA thesis, East Texas State University, 1983.

This thesis describes Higgins as an aggressive correspondent who sent daily dispatches during the early months of the war despite the misgivings of the military commanders.

1765 Kaff, Al. "War Correspondents Revisit Korean Battlefields" Editor & Publisher 123 28 (July 14, 1990): 30.
    An interesting account of early correspondents during the war, including Bill Shinn's story on the Inchon landing before the operation was announced. All in all more that 350 correspondents were accredited to the United Nations command and eighteen were killed.

1766 Kagan, Norman. The War Film. New York: Pyramid Publication, 1974.
    Good early account of military movies, including some on the Korean War.

1767 Kahn, Ely J. The Peculiar War: Impressions of a Reporter in Korea. New York: Random House, 1952.
    Kahn considers the nature of the Korean War, and also gives a lot of attention to the early military leaders, their prejudices and failures, as well as the successes.

1768 Kim, Myung Jun. "Coverage of the Korean War by the New York Times and Asahi Shimbon: Foreign Policy as the Key Constraint on the War Reporting" Ph.D. dissertation, Temple University, 1991.
    Views the Korean War from key American and Japanese newspapers, arriving at the hardly enlightening conclusion that each reflected their country's policy toward Korea.

1769 Lande, Nathaniel. Dispatches from the Front: News Accounts of American Wars, 1776-1991. New York: H. Holt, 1995.
    Brief account of specific war coverage, interesting but of little use.

1770 Lee, Raymond S. H. "Early Korean War Coverage" Journalism Quarterly 55 (1978): 789-792.
    Reviewing four South Korean papers, and three large American papers, the author suggests that American papers were more accurate than Korean ones.

1771 Lee, Seong-Hyon. "Comparative Study of Certain Korean and American Newspapers Early in the Korean War" MA thesis, Kent State University.
    A journalistic study of various newspapers showing the great diversity of coverage and point of view.

1772 Maynard, Richard A. Propaganda on Film: A Nation at War. Rochelle Park, New Jersey: Hayden Book Company, 1975.
A look at film propaganda used by United States producers.

1773 Mee, Charles L. "Are You Telling Them That It Is an Utterly Useless War?" Horizon 18 1 (Winter 1976): 110-111.
The role of the war correspondent in Korea is compared to the reporting of other wars, suggesting American soldiers were not told the truth, either as to what they were doing, or how well they were doing it.

1774 Moeller, Susan D. Shooting War: Photography and the American Combat Experience. New York: Basic Books, 1991.
Part four "The Korean War" deals with the role of, and use of, combat photography during the Korean Conflict. Asserts photojournalists were less restricted than other correspondents. A really excellent book.

1775 Myrick, Howard A. "A Critical Analysis of Thematic Content of United States Army Orientation Films of the Korean War" Ph.D. dissertation, Unviersity of Southern California, 1968.
Analysis of five films designed to sell the Korean War to United States soldiers, which found them very much like the same type of film in World War II.

1776 Rifas, Leonard. "The Forgotten War Comics: The Korean War and American Comic Books" MA thesis, University of Washington, 1991.
MA: war comics

1777 Riley, John W. Jr. and Wilbur Schramm. The Reds Take a City: The Communist Occupation of Seoul. New Brunswick, New Jersey: Rutgers University Press, 1951.
A somewhat dramatic eyewitness account of the North Korean occupancy of the capital on 28 June 1950. While early accounts discuss the failed efforts at defense and the defeat of the city, most of the work, however, is spent dealing with questions of survival in Seoul.

1778 Smith, Howard. "The BBC Television Newsreel and the Korean War" Historical Journal of Film, Radio, and Television 8 (1988): 227-252.
Smith discovered that war coverage on the BBC was more analytical than that offered by American news media.

1779 Suid, Larry H. Guts and Glory: Great American War Movies. Reading, Massachusetts: Addison-Wesley, 1978.
Good discussion of war films, but weak and incomplete coverage of Korean War efforts.

1780 Suid, Larry H. and David Culbert. Films and Propaganda in America: A Documentary History. volume 4. "1945 and After" Westport, Connecticut: Greenwood Press, 1991.
  Discusses film as the means to greatly influence public opinion. Not clear always about relation between cause and effect, but considerable information.

1781 Taylor, Barry M. "Press Reaction to the Issue of the Korean War in the 1952 Election" MA thesis, University of California, Berkeley, 1964.
  MA: press

1782 Toplin, Robert Brent, editor. Hollywood as Mirror: Changing Views of "Outsiders" and "Enemies" in American Movies. Westport, Connecticut: Greenwood Press, 1993.
  Views Hollywood and the film industry as responsible for much of the creation of minority identification and the focus of "enemy," particularly in military films.

1783 Wallis, Hal. "Movie Star You Never Saw: Filming of Cease Fire" 75 Reader's Digest (November 1958): 122-124.
  Describes the use of soldiers as actors in filming the documentary/narrative movie Cease Fire.

1784 White, Marilyn M. "The Korean War and Journalism: An Annotated Bibliography" MS Project, University of Kansas, 1987.
  MS: journalism

1785 Willenz, Eric. German Press Reaction to the Air War in Korea. Santa Monica, California: Rand Corporation, 1951.
  Analysis of Germany's dealing with the United Nations and American activity in Korea. Not all that supportive.

1786 Winnington, Alan. I Saw the Truth in Korea: Facts and Photographs That Will Shock Britain! London: People's Press, 1950.
  Brief fifteen-page book that charges, in comment and photos, that the United States and the United Nations troops were committing war atrocities.

1787 Youn, Keun. "The Korean War: Its Coverage and Editorial Opinions" MA thesis, University of Missouri, Columbia, 1964.
  MA: editorial

Home Front

1788 Caine, Philip D. "The United States in Korea and Vietnam: A Study in Public Opinion" Air University Quarterly Review 20 1 (1968): 49-58.
    By the end of the Korean War only about half of the American people were supportive of the war effort.

1789 Coontz, Stephanie. The Way We Never Were: American Families and the Nostalgic Trap. New York: Basic Books, 1992.
    Interesting account of Americans on the home front, in the Korean War period.

1790 Epstein, Laurence B. "The American Philosophy of War, 1945-1967" Ph.D. dissertation, University of Southern California, 1967.
    At the end of World War II the traditional philosophy of war was radically changed. The disassociation between political policy and military power could no longer be tolerated. The author raises six issues which caused the contemporary attitude. Korea was one of them.

1791 Gietschier, Steven P. "Limited War and the Home Front: Ohio During the Korean War" Ph.D. dissertation, Ohio State University, 1977.
    Holds the view that Ohio's major institutions in politics and economics were affected by the Korean War, but that international implications were more important than domestic.

1792 Hamby, Alonzo L. "Public Opinion: Korea and Vietnam" Wilson Quarterly 2 3 (Summer 1978): 137-141
    Provides a comparison between the American attitude toward Korea and Vietnam, finding that the protests against the Korean War came from the political right, who used and honored the American flag in their protests.

1793 Hennessy, Peter. Never Again: Britain 1945-1951. London: Jonathan Cape, 1992.
    Discusses the fact that the press, British in particular, provided material which brought aid and comfort to the enemy. Considered a law to discourage a "distorted press."

1794 Herzon, Frederick D. and others. "Personality and Public Opinion: The Case of Authoritarianism, Prejudice and Support for the Korean and Vietnam Wars" Polity 11 1 (1978): 92-113.
    Argues that there is a strong case to be made linking those with racial prejudice and an aggressive view of the Korean War.

1795 Hoare, J. H. "British Public Opinion and the Korean War" British Association on Korean Studies paper 2 (1992).
   Brief effort to identify British opinion which reflected both mainline and socialist views of the Korean War.

1796 Mantell, Matthew E. "Opposition to the Korean War: A Study in American Dissent" Ph.D. dissertation, New York University, 1973.
   Considers American opposition to the Korean War finding that it comes from the pacifist movement, the political left who considered the war imperialistic, and the pragmatists who originally supported the war but soon felt it was not a war that could be won.

1797 Mueller, John E. "Trends in Popular Support for the Wars in Korea and Vietnam" American Political Science Review 65 2 (1971): 358-375.
   The Korean War, as well as the Vietnam War, saw the initial support available at the beginning of the war quickly erode.

1798 Mueller, John E. War, Presidents and Public Opinion. New York: John Wiley & Sons, Inc., 1973.
   A highly readable discussion of the popularity of both the Korean War and the Vietnam War. Contains several surveys dealing with period response to the war, and a chapter dealing with retrospective support.

1799 Paik, Seung Gi. "Korean Attitudes toward United States Military During the War, 1950-1953" MA thesis, University of Dayton, Ohio, 1967.
   MA: opinion

1800 Salopek, Marijan. "A Survey of Western Canadian Concerns and Fears During the Korean War, 1950-1953" MA thesis, University of Alberta, 1984. Published Ottawa: National Library of Canada, 1986.
   Views Canadian involvement as it was reflected in the concerned citizens: no clear image.

1801 Sung Sin Women's University Press. The Impact of the Korean War on the People and Society of Korea. Seoul: Sung Sin Women's University Press, 1986.
   Deals with the results of the war, the impact of the armistice, and the limited cease-fire, on the South Koreans. Lot of information but less than clear analysis.

1802 Toner, James H. "American Society and The American Way of War: Korea and Beyond" Parameters 11 1 (1981): 79-90.

The impact of social and cultural views on the Korean War is the theme of this excellent study. For example safety standards in troop training frequently led to greater casualties in combat.

1803 Whitfield, Stephen. "The 1950s: The Era of No Hard Feelings" South Atlantic Quarterly 74 (Summer 1975): 289-307.
        Makes an effort to explain the role of the peace movement which, during the 1950s, tried to control nuclear arms.

1804 Wiltz, John E. "The Korean War and American Society" in Francis H. Heller, editor. The Korean War: A 25-Year Perspective. Lawrence, Kansas: Regents Press of Kansas, 1977.
        Wiltz expresses the view that the war frustrated people at home, but that it was not seen with any great fear.

1805 Wood, Hugh G. "American Reaction to Limited War in Asia: Korea and Vietnam, 1950-1968" Ph.D. dissertation, University of Colorado, 1974.
        Reviewed public opinion through newspapers and reported that United States goals in Korea were unrealistic but it was only in Vietnam that they came to realize the folly of United States Asian policy.

Memorials

1806 Casey, Charles E. In Memory—Lest We Forget: Korean War, 1950-1954: KIA, MIA and Others. Plattsmouth, Nebraska: Potter Offset Print, 1993.
        A register of those killed in action, and those missing in Korea.

1807 Craig, Berry. The Forgotten War . . . Remembered. Paducah, Kentucky: Turner Publishing Co., 1990.
        Published for the Korean War Veterans Association, 1000 copies only. Simple narrative account.

1808 Euwer, Robert M. No Longer Forgotten: The Korean War and Its Memorial. Baltimore, Maryland: Gateway Press, 1995.
        A personal narrative of the memorial.

1809 Highsmith, Carol M. Forgotten no More: The Korean War Veterans. Washington, D. C.: Chelsea Publication, Inc. 1995.
        The story of the Korean War Memorial, from innovation to completion.

1810 Kerin, James R. "The Korean War and American Memory" Ph.D. dissertation, University of Pennsylvania, 1994.

An inquiry from literature, sociology, and psychology into the phenomenon of "forgotten" and the questions of realistic memorialization of the Korean War. Very abstract, yet very interesting.

1811 "Major General George L. Marby, Jr." Veterans Memorial Park Dedication Ceremony: May 28, 1990. Sumter, South Carolina, 1990.
Ceremonial brochure.

1812 Soderbergh, Peter A. "Remembering Korea—Thirty-five Years Later" Congressional Record. (June 25, 1985).
Address given on the 35th anniversary of the Korean War, read into the Congressional Record S8713-8714.

1813 United States. Joint Resolution Approving the Location of the Korean War Memorial. Washington, D. C.: Government Printing Office, 1988.
Record of congressional approval.

1814 United States. Korean War Veterans War Memorial Amendments Act of 1991 Report. Washington, D. C.: Government Printing Office, 1991.
Alterations in memorial project.

1815 United States. Memorial to Honor Members of the Armed Forces Who Served in the Korean Conflict. Washington, D. C.: Government Printing Office, 1985.
Statement of memorial intentions by the Korean War Veterans Association.

1816 United States Joint Resolution to Designate June 25, 1990, as "Korean Remembrance Day" Washington, D. C.: Government Printing Office, Superintendent of Documents, 1990.
Resolution approved.

1817 Vitz, Carl P. P. Homage to Those Who Gave their Lives to Keep Us Free: World War I, World War II, Korea, Vietnam, Desert Storm. Cincinnati: Public Library, 1992.
Register of dead from five American wars.

1818 "We Can't Forget: Memories of WWII, Korea, Vietnam, and Desert Storm, in War Zones and on the Homefront" Evanston, Illinois: Chicago Spectrum Press, 1995.
Memorial narrative from heroes of American wars.

Oral History

1819 Berry, Henry. Hey, Mac, Where Ya Been? New York: St. Martin's Press, 1988.
    An excellent collection of oral history memories of the United States Marines during the Korean War. These personal accounts are both humorous and deadly. The retelling of the soldier's story gives an excellent picture of the war as it was seen by those fighting it. The assault and landing at Inchon is reviewed in five interviews.

1820 Breece, Katharine A. Memories: A Collection of Korean Conflict Oral Histories From Veterans and Others. Arlington, Virginia: Yorktown High School, 1993.
    American history students of Ms. Breece assisted with personal stories of veterans.

1821 Gardam, John. Korea Volunteer: An Oral History from Those Who Were There. Burnstown, Ontario: General Store Publishing House, 1994.
    Canadian Army personal narrative.

1822 Knox, Donald. The Korean War, Pusan to Chosin: An Oral History. volume 1. San Diego: Harcourt, 1985.
    An oral account of the war, the first volume dealing with Pusan to the Yalu. Knox includes several accounts including MacArthur's "flamboyance and penchant for grand gestures."

1823 Stillwell, Paul. United States Naval Institute Oral History Collection: Catalog of Transcripts. Annapolis, Maryland: Naval Institute Press, 1983.
    Provides an excellent guide to oral histories of naval officers; available at Annapolis.

1824 Tomedi, Rudy. No Bugles, No Drums: An Oral History of the Korean War. New York: John Wiley and Sons, 1993.
    An oral history of the Korean War as seen by the average participant.

Novels and Narratives

1825 Abcede, Salvador. Nita: Salvador Abcede's Historical Novel. Philippines, 1985.
    A fiction about World War II, the Korean War, and Negros Island.

1826 Aichinger, Peter. The American Soldier in Fiction, 1860-1963. Ames: Iowa State University Press, 1975.

The author holds the view that the novels of the Korean War represent a greatly demoralized soldier facing limited war and undefined goals.

1827 Alexander, James Edwin. Inchon to Wonsan: From the Deck of a Destroyer in the Korean War. Annapolis, Maryland: United States Naval Institute Press, 1996.
    Fictionalized account of USS John J. Borland, a symbol of destroyer actions, which the author views as the workhorse of the fleet during the days of the early counterattacks.

1828 An, Chong-hyo. Silver Stallion: A Novel of Korea. New York: Soho Press, 1990.
    An account of the nation and the Korean War by this Korean nationalist.

1829 Anders, Curtis. The Price of Courage. New York: Sagamore Press, 1957.
    The experiences of Lieutenant Eric Holloway, an infantry combat officer, who describes life on the front line.

1830 Anderson, Thomas. Your Own Beloved Sons. New York: Bantam Books, 1956.
    A novel about six men on patrol during the Korean War. The usual fare, but more than usual information provided, and the fight sequences are especially well written.

1831 Anderson, William. Banner over Korea. London: Evans Brothers, 1960.
    The personal narrative of a British soldier who performed national service.

1832 Andow, A. Andy. Letters to Big Jim Regarding Narrul Purigo, Cashinum Iman. New York: Vantage Press, 1994.
    Wonderful narrative of this recalled Marine reservist who served in Korea.

1833 Axelsson, Arne. Restrained Response: American Novels of the Cold War and Korea, 1945-1962. New York: Greenwood Press, 1990.
    An analysis of Korean War novels, as few as there are, which deal with the various phases of the war as seen in fiction.

1834 Bailey, Hubert. Black Boy, What Are You Fighting For? New York: Pageant Press, 1966.
    A personal narrative of personal and unit danger.

1835 Balgassi, Haemi. Peacebound Trains. New York: Clarion Books, 1996.
A novel of a family escape from Seoul during the Korean War.

1836 Barbeau, Clayton C. The Ikon: A Novel. San Francisco, California: Ikon Press, 1995.
A serious novel of emotions and commitment.

1837 Barton, Donald E. You Be the Judge. New York: Carlton Press, 1973.
Prisoner-of-war narrative which shows the problems of dealing with poor treatment and torture.

1838 Becker, Stephen. Dog Tags. New York: Random House, 1973.
Frustration is not knowing how to tell who your enemies are.

1839 Beech, Keyes. Tokyo and Points East. Garden City, New York: Doubleday, 1954.
Personal narrative by Chicago News reporter who provides good firsthand reports on MacArthur.

1840 Blair, Clay. Beyond Courage: Escape Tales of Airmen in the Korean War. New York: McKay, 1955.
Accounts of escapes and personal narrations from the Korean War. Forward by General Nathan F. Twining.

1841 Boeck, James H. Flight Home. Santa Ana, California: Pioneer Press, 1972.
Short personal narrative.

1842 Bond, Larry. Red Phoenix. New York: Warner Books, 1989.
A novel about a new war in North Korea which comes close to unleashing World War III.

1843 Bostwick, Ronald. The Iron Ring. New York: Avon, 1963.
A novel of the Korean War.

1844 Bowersox, Rex L. The Wings of Destiny. Chicago: Adams Press, 1994.
A novel of the Air Force in Korea.

1845 Boyne, Walter J. Air Force Eagles. New York: Crown Publications, 1992.
A novel based on Air Force action in Korea.

1846 Brady, James. The Coldest War: A Memoir of Korea. New York: Orion Books, 1990.

A personal account of the war told by a Marine officer who later became a highly respected reporter.

1847 Brodie, Howard. "Hill 233" Collier's 27 11 (1951): 28-29.
Artist sketches of infantry unit attacking an enemy-held unit.

1848 Busch, Frederick. War Babies. New York: New Directions, 1989.
A novel of tension as two young adults deal with the behavior of their fathers' roles in a Korean POW camp.

1849 Byrnes, David Thomas. Corporal C. J. Batchelor's Collaboration With the Communists. Annapolis, Maryland: United States Naval Academy, term paper on microfiche.
A remembrance dealing with POWs and the nature of collaboration with the enemy.

1850 Campbell, John T. Raid on Truman: A Novel. Novata, California: Lyford Books, 1991.
A novel of frustration, danger, and commitment.

1851 Campigno, Anthony. A Marine Division in Nightmare Alley. New York: Comet Press Books, 1958.
A personal narrative of life as a Marine.

1852 Chamberlain, William. Combat Stories of World War II and Korea. New York: The John Day Company, 1962.
A collection of short stories about combat in Korea.

1853 Chamberlain, William. More Combat Stories of World War II and Korea. New York: The John Day Company, 1964.
A collection of combat action stories, some of which take place during the Korean War.

1854 Chamberlin, Al. Circle of Courage. New York: Vantage Press, 1991.
A combat related novel of the day-by-day courage of the ordinary solider.

1855 Chung, Donald K. Remembrances of the Forgotten War: A Korean-American War Veteran's Journey for Freedom. Pacifica, California: Pacific Press, 1995.
Personal narrative of war, imprisonment, and the search for freedom.

1856 Chung, Donald K. The Three Day Promise: A Korean Soldier's Promise. Tallahassee, Florida: Father and Son Publishing, Inc., 1989.
   The story of an ROK soldier who became a doctor and returned home after many years. His war experiences are well told.

1857 Cleveland, Les. Dark Laughter: War in Song and Popular Culture. Westport, Connecticut: Praeger, 1994.
   An excellent collection of stories, poetry, and songs which deal with the dark humor of war.

1858 Collenette, E. J. Korean Raid: An R. N. Frigate in Action, London: Brown, Watson Ltd., 1958.
   A novel of naval operations in Korea.

1859 Condon, Richard. The Manchurian Candidate. New York: Jove Books, 1959.
   A popular novel of brainwashing and assassination which was made into a first class movie.

1860 Connolly, John B. Underway: Tour of a Tin Can Soldier. Baton Rouge, Louisiana: Connolly, 1990.
   A personal narrative of a destroyer crew member.

1861 Coon, Gene L. Meanwhile Back at The Front. New York: Crown, 1961.
   Narrative of the 1st Marine Division's Public Information Section in Korea.

1862 Cox, Keller and Raymond L. Frazier. Buck: A Novel of a Tennessee Boy in Korea. Clarksville, Tennessee: Chogie Publishers, 1982.
   A rather ordinary novel of adjustment to war.

1863 Crane, Robert. Born of Battle. New York: Pyramid Books, 1962.
   A novel.

1864 Crawford, C. S. The Four Deuces: A Korean War Story. Novato, California: Presidio Press, 1989.
   Memoirs of a member of the lst Marines during the final days of the Korean War.

1865 Crawford, William. Give Me Tomorrow. New York: Morrow, 1962.
   Deals with the physical and psychological stress of combat on a young Marine, as he complains that United States citizens do not care about the war.

1866 Crawford, William. Gresham's War. Greenwich, Connecticut: Fawcett, 1968.
>American's hostility toward South Korean citizens.

1867 Crosbie, Philip. Three Winters Cold. Dublin: Brown and Nolan, 1955.
>Fiction of prisoners and prisons based on Korean experiences.

1868 Davis, Franklin. The Naked and the Lost. New York: Lion, 1954.
>A poor effort in trying to do a Korean The Naked and the Dead.

1869 Deane, Philip. Captive in Korea. London: H. H. House, 1953.
>A fictionalized account of life as a prisoner which in America was titled I Was a Captive in Korea.

1870 Deane, Philip. I Should Have Died. Ontario: Longman, 1976.
>Canadian published personal narrative of the life as a prisoner during the Korean War.

1871 Deerfield, Eddie. The Psy-Warrior. Salt Lake City, Utah: Northwest Publishers, 1994.
>United States reservists are found in harm's way in a North Korean trap.

1872 Dibble, Birney. Taking of Hill 1052. Salt Lake City, Utah: Northwest Publishers, 1958.
>Highly fictionalized account of a physician's war.

1873 Dickinson, Theodore and David McNichol. Korea Illustrated. Rutland, Vermont: Tuttle, 1952.
>Combat illustrations by two Marine Corps artists.

1874 Dillon, Lester R. Battle Scarred: The Autobiography of Lester Reed Dillon, Sr., The Fighting Man. New York: Vantage Press, 1977.
>A personal narrative of World War II and the Korean War.

1875 Drummond, William. Oh Well, St. Michael. New York: Vantage, 1987.
>A fictionalized autobiography.

1876 Early, Charles. The Tigers Are Hungry. New York: Modern Literary Editions Publishing, Co., 1967.
>Fictionalized account of prisoners and prisons.

1877 Edwards, Paul M. The Hermit Kingdom: Poems of the Korean War. Dubuque, Iowa: Kendall/Hunt Publishing Company, 1995.

An interesting collection of poems about the Korean War. One of the few collections of poetry available about the Korean period.

1878 Etter, Orval and Raleigh Pickard. The Adventures of a Nonregistrant Doctor. Berkeley, California: Fellowship of Reconciliation, 1951.
      The story of a physician from California who registered as a conscientious objector during the war.

1879 Eunson, Robert. MiG Alley. New York: Ace Books, 1959.
      A novel of air war; heroism in the face of military restrictions.

1880 Fairless, Benjamin Franklin. How Not to Kill a Flea. New York: United States Steel Corporation, 1951.
      A short twelve-page address to the Alumni Society, November 12, 1951, about business and industry in the Korean War.

1881 Fast, Howard. Korean Lullaby. Sydney: Current Book Distributors, 1950.
      A small collection of Korean War poems from the early war, and available on microfilm.

1882 Faucher, Elizabeth, Jim Thomas and John Thomas. The Rescue: A Novel. New York: Scholastic, 1987.
      Fiction based on the motion picture by Touchstone Pictures about a prisoner-of-war.

1883 Felton, Monica. That's Why I Went. London: Lawrence & Wishant, 1953.
      Describes the travels to Asia of a British delegation of women, from 1945 on, where one lady found evidence that South Korea and the United States planned the attack on Korea.

1884 Flinn, Robert Francis. Letters. West Point: United States Military Academy, 1951.
      Letters from classmate of William De Graf who was killed in the Korean War.

1885 Flood, Charles Bracelen. More Lives Than One. Boston: Houghton Mifflin, 1967.
      Fictionalized story of three doctors in the Korean War who are captured and performed well.

1886 Flynn, Robert. Living with the Hyenas: Short Stories. Ft. Worth, Texas: Texas Christian University Press, 1995.

A series of short stories dealing with life in combat, including Korea.

1887 Forrest, Williams. <u>Stigma for Valor</u>. Greenwich, Connecticut: Fawette Books, 1958.
   A fictionalized account of a British POW in Korea.

1888 Frank, Pat. <u>Hold Back the Night</u>. New York: Lippincott, 1952.
   One of the best Korean War novels (later made into a less spectacular motion picture) about a United States Marine involved in the withdrawal from the Chosin Reservoir to Hungnam.

1889 Frank, Pat. <u>The Long Way Round</u>. Philadelphia: Lippincott. 1953.
   Autobiographical and personal narrative of a correspondent who finally arrives in Korea.

1890 Frankel, Ernest. <u>Band of Brothers</u>. New York: Macmillan, 1958.
   A fictionalized account about Marine Bill Patrick and his company withdrawal from Chosin via Hungnam. Shows bitterness against unaware civilians at home.

1891 Franklin, Edward Herbert. <u>It's Cold in Pongo-ni</u>. New York: Vanguard Press, 1965.
   Novel of an eight-man Marine patrol on a night raid. A good read. The author contends that the results of the war was "zero."

1892 Fuinderburk, Robert. <u>Heart and Soul</u>. Minneapolis: Bethany House, 1995.
   A novel with more heart than action.

1893 Gaither, Charles E. <u>Memoirs of a U. S. Marine Sergeant of World War II, Korea, and Vietnam</u>. Pittsburgh, Pennsylvania: Dorrance Publishing Company, 1992.
   An interesting remembrance of this marine sergeant's military career.

1894 Gardella, Lawrence. <u>China Maze</u>. New York: Worldwide, 1987.
   Biography first published in 1981 as <u>Sing a Song to Jenny Next</u>. It is the story of a group of United States Marines (including the author) dropped behind enemy lines to destroy a nuclear research facility. Of questionable authenticity.

1895 Glasgow, William M. <u>Platoon Leader in Korea</u>. no publisher, 1992.
   A personal narrative.

1886 Gogan, John P. The Hard Way: A Novel. J. Gogan, 1995.
        A highly fictionalized story of a Marine Rifle Company in Korea
1951.

1897 Goldman, William. Soldier in the Rain. New York: Bantam, 1966.
        Fictionalized account of military life, primarily in the inter-war army,
and during the early period of Korea. Made into a motion picture in 1963.

1898 Goldsmith, David H. "The Restaurant" MA thesis, Bowling Green State
University, 1961.
        MA: drama

1899 Goodrich, John G. How Lucky Can You Get?: A Korean Odyssey. no
city: Goodrich, 1995.
        Personal narrative of member of Company C, 1st Battalion, 5th
Regiment Marine Corps.

1900 Gore, Gene L. The Outer Edge of Glory. Salt Lake City, Utah:
Northwest Publishing, 1995.
        Fictionalized life of a World War II and Korean War soldier.

1901 Green, Lewis W. Spirit Bells: A Novel of the Korean War. Fairview,
North Carolina: Indian Rock Publishers, 1995.
        An emotive novel.

1902 Griffin, Bobby. The Search. Tampa, Florida: Grace Publishing
Company, 1974.
        A fictionalized account and personal narrative of Christianity and
witness-bearing in war.

1903 Hackworth, David. About Face: the Odyssey of an American Warrior.
New York: Simon & Schuster, 1989.
        Biography of the man on which Kurtz (Apocalypse Now) was
focused. Most decorated soldier who was destroyed by the war.

1904 Hackworth, David H. and Julie Sherman. Brave Men. New York:
Pocket Books, 1993.
        Condensed version of About Face, a biographical work and personal
narrative about Korea and Vietnam and the United States Army.

1905 Hadley, M. S. Korea? I've Had It! The Candid-Camera Biography of
A Korean Quote Hero Unquote. Rutland, Vermont: C. E. Tuttle, 1954.
        Humor, caricatures, and general nonsense from the Korean War
period.

1906 Harris, Alfred Martin. The Tall Man. New York: Pocket Books, 1958. New York: Farrar, 1960.

Account of a tall Australian who led two civilians on a dangerous and fatal mission.

1907 Henry, Edward F. PFC Crazy Hank. New York: Carlton Press, 1992.

A lively and down-to-earth account of a United States Army grunt who landed at Inchon and worked his way north.

1908 Herbert, Anthony. Herbert—The Making of a Soldier. New York: Hippocrene Books, 1982.

A personal narrative of Herbert's role in the military. An outstanding soldier, this work it more about the Korean War than his other book. Fair reading.

1909 Herbert, Anthony with James T. Wooten. Soldier. New York: Holt, Rinehart, and Winston, 1973.

Autobiography of Master Sergeant (later Lieutenant Colonel) Anthony Herbert who was identified as the nation's "outstanding soldier" of the Korean War and was court-marshalled and relieved as a Regimental Commander during the Vietnam War.

1910 Herbert, Anthony and Robert L. Niemann. Conquest to Nowhere. Herminie, Pennsylvania: Keystone Publishing Company, 1955.

Somewhat dramatic personal narrative of the authors.

1911 Hess, Dean E. Battle Hymn. New York: McGraw-Hill Book Company, Inc., 1956.

Story of the clergyman pilot who flew three hundred missions in World War II and Korea. Later made into a movie.

1912 Hickey, James Richard. Chrysanthemum in the Snow: A Novel of the Korean War. New York: Crown, 1990.

One of the best novels of the war, which is clearly a memorial to those who forgot the war. Supports "the communists own the night" thesis.

1913 Hinojosa, Roland. The Useless Servants. Houston, Texas: Arte Publico Press, 1993.

A fictionalized account of the Mexican-American participation in the Korean War.

1914 Hirsch, Phil. Great Combat Stories of the Korean War. New York: Pyramid Books, 1968.

Selection of short narratives.

1915 Holinger, William. The Fence Walker. Albany, New York: State University of New York Press, 1985, 1995.
   An excellent novel of guard duty along the DMZ, walking the long dividing fence.

1916 Hollands, Douglas J. Able Company. New York: Houghton, 1956.
   Novel of a British platoon commander along the broad front of the Commonwealth Division.

1917 Hollands, Douglas J. The Dead, the Dying, and the Damned. London: Cassell, 1956.
   A novel of the Rockinghamshire Regiment which asks what the purpose of war is other than to further military careers.

1918 Holliday, Kate. Troopship. New York: Doubleday, 1952.
   A reporter's account of a Korean-bound troopship and the soldiers on it, heading for Korea.

1919 Hooker, John. Standing Orders. New York: Fontana, 1986.
   Narrative of a New Zealand soldier.

1920 Hooker, Richard (pseudonym). MASH. New York: Morrow, 1968.
   One of the most loved stories of the Korean War which gave a humorous account of the medical unit 4077.

1921 Horwitz, Dorothy. We Will Not Be Strangers. Urbana: University of Illinois Press, 1997.
   Letters between a MASH surgeon, Mel, and his wife during the days of the Korean War.

1922 Hunt, Bruce F. Am I My Brother's Keeper? Wildwood, New Jersey: Leslie A. Dunn, 1950.
   A novel based on the religious aspects of politics, government, and war.

1923 Hutchinson, Dave. Remembrances: Metis Veterans. Regina: Gabriel Dumont Institute, 1994.
   Canadian's World War II and Korean War personal narratives.

1924 Irwin, Lester R. Korean War. Youngstown, Ohio: Youngstown State University Press, 1989.
   A very short (twenty-one page) collection of personal memories in transcript form. Part of an oral history program.

1925 Jacques, Maurice J. and Bruce H. Norton <u>Sergeant Major, U. S. Marines</u>. New York: Ivy Books, 1995.
Biography about experiences in Vietnam and Korea.

1926 Jones, Francis S. <u>No Rice for Rebels: A Story of the Korean War</u>. London: Bodley Head, 1956.
A personal narrative of prison life during the Korean War.

1927 Jones, Ken. <u>I Was There</u>. New York: Lion Books, 1953.
Journalist first-person narrative which assumes a knowledge of life in combat.

1928 Joo-Young, Kim. <u>The Sound of Thunder</u>. Seoul, Korea: Si-sa-yong-o-sa, Inc. 1990.
A novel set in the bedlam of the Korean War, it is an example of what has become known as "division-literature" a genre of novels concerning the division of Korea and the response to the atrocities of war.

1929 Kelleher, Brian. <u>The Gathering Storm</u>. New York: Signet/Nal, 1989.
A novel of combat and decision-making in Korea.

1930 Kestner, Franklin D. R. <u>To the Last Man! Kolbes' Mongrels of the Chosin Reservoir</u>. Tucson, Arizona: Westernlore Press, 1991.
A personal narrative of the war.

1931 Killingbeck, Arthur. R. <u>U. S. Army Privates, Sergeants, Fire and Smoke</u>. New York: Vantage, 1991.
Privately printed fiction of military life which is long on glory and short on information.

1932 Kim, Chu-yong. Chondung Sori, translator. <u>The Sound of Thunder</u>. Seoul: Si-Sa-young-o-sa, 1990.
A novel.

1933 Kim, Hyong-Cha. <u>The Tunnel of Destiny</u>. Seaul [sic]: Christian Literature Society of Korean, 1971.
Personal narrative, a translation of <u>Unmyong ui</u>.

1934 Kim, Seyong. "This Is Our War" MA thesis, Wichita State University, 1955.
MA: a play in three acts with music.

1935 Kingsland, Gerald. <u>In Quest of Glory: Korean War Memories</u>. London: New England Library, 1989.

Personal narrative about service in Korea with the British.

1936 Krause, Walter C. The Sergeant's Colonel. Pompano Beach, Florida: Exposition Press, 1985.
A personal narrative with an unusual twist.

1937 Kriendler, I. Robert and Malcolm K. Beyer. Diary: Korea, Summer 1953. no publisher, 1953.
A short personal narrative of a summer in combat and occupation.

1938 Kroll, Clare M. Jump into Hell. Folsom, California: Miskar Publishing Company, 1986.
A novel relating the personal experiences of the author.

1939 Larby, Ron. Signals to the Right, Armoured Corps to the Left. Royal Leamington Spa: Korvet, 1993.
A personal narrative of this soldier's national service with Great Britain Royal Signals.

1940 Large, Lofty. One Man's War in Korea. Wellingborough: Kimber, 1988.
A personal narrative with a highly individual point of view.

1941 Lasly, Walt. Turn the Tigers Loose. New York: Ballantine Books, 1956.
Fictionalized story of Colonel Tom Loving and his B-26 Night Intruders on raids into Korea.

1942 Leatherneck's Book of Gyrene Gyngles and Cartoons. no city: Leatherneck Association, 1951.
Book of Marine Corps humor.

1943 Lemon, James Anthony. The Robin Must be Fed. New York: Comet Press Books, 1954.
Korean veteran rediscovers himself in small town.

1944 Lewis, Jack P. Chosen Tales of Chosin. North Hollywood, California: Challenge Books, 1964.
A series of personal narratives from Marines who took part in the Chosin retreat.

1945 Lindland, Frances K. Memoirs of the Morning Calm. New York: Times Journal Publishers, 1992.
A novel of service in Korea.

1946 Llewellyn, Stephen Peter. The Score at Tea Time. London: P. Davies. 1957.
> Highly romanticized novel.

1947 Lloyd, Adrien. Inchon Diary. Wayne, Pennsylvania: Dell/Banbury Books, Inc., 1983.
> A worse than usual novel of a woman correspondent covering the early phases of the Korean War.

1948 Lu, Chu-kuo and Andrew M. Condron. The Battle of Sangkumryung. Peking: Foreign Language Press, 1961.
> Communist inspired fiction.

1949 Lucas, Jim Griffing. Report from Korea. New York: New York World Telegram, 1950, 1959.
> A thirty-page account of several well-known Scripps-Howards war correspondents in Korea.

1950 Lydens, Peter F. Opus USMCR: The Experiences of a Young Marine During the Korean War. Charleston, West Virginia: P. Lydens, 1991
> Biography of a member of Company D, 8th Infantry Battalion.

1951 Lynch, Michael. An American Soldier. Boston: Little, Brown, 1969.
> Novel which focuses on the inadequacies of South Korean troops.

1952 MacDonnell, James E. Wings Off the Sea. London: Constable, 1953. Melbourne: Transworld Publishers, 1955.
> Canadian novel about Australian aircraft operation off a carrier in the Korean War.

1953 Macho, Dean C. The Day I Went Regular. Maxwell Air Force Base, Alabama: Air War College University, 1970.
> A personal narrative of the Air Force.

1954 Maddron, Ernie. Love, Shame and Honor. Virginia Beach, Virginia: Cornerstone Books, 1993.
> Fictionalized life of grandfather and farm life of a soldier in Korean War.

1955 Maher, William L. A Shepherd in Combat Boots: Chaplain Emil Kapaun of the 1st Cavalry Division. Shippensburg, Pennsylvania: Burd Street Press, 1997.
> Another treatment of this chaplain who became a prisoner-of-war and died in captivity.

1956 Manne, Robert. <u>Agent of Influence: The Life and Times of Wilfred Burchett</u>. Toronto, Canada: Mackenzie Institute, 1989.
    Biography of journalist and war correspondent

1957 Maton, Sonny. <u>A Leaf Falls but Once</u>. New York: Carlton Press Corporation, 1994.
    Romanticized fiction of the Korean War.

1958 Matthias, Howard. <u>The Korean War: Reflections of a Young Combat Platoon Leader</u>. Tallahassee, Florida: Father & Son Publishers, 1993.
    A personal reflection of a young combat leader in war.

1959 Mauldin, William H. <u>Bill Mauldin in Korea</u>. New York: Norton, 1952.
    This World War II artist/correspondent provides a well-written and illustrated story of his experiences in Korea.

1960 McAleer, John J. and Billy D. Dickson. <u>Unit Pride</u>. New York: Bantam, 1982.
    A poorer-than-usual story of two Americans in combat, full of sex, booze, and arduous mountain fighting in Korea.

1961 McCaffery, Patrick J. <u>The Knolls of Korea</u>. New York: Comet Press Books, 1959.
    Reflections of a young Marine lieutenant who was given command of a combat platoon until wounded and returned to the United States. An excellent account.

1962 McCaull, Julian. <u>The Hinge</u>. New York: Alcyone Publication, 1984.
    A fictionalized account of minesweepers and destroyers, <u>Aware</u>, <u>Award</u>, and <u>Merritt</u> at work on mines at Wonsan.

1963 McCloskey, Paul N. and Helen Hooper McCloskey. <u>The Taking of Hill 610: And Other Essays on Friendship</u>. Woodside, California: Eaglet Books, 1992.
    Narratives of men of the 5th Marines, 1st Battalion, C Company.

1964 McKenna, Lindsay. <u>Dawn of Valor</u>. New York: Silhouette, 1991.
    One of the few war romances, located during the Korean War.

1965 McLeod, Alistair. <u>Banzai Attack Korea 1951</u>. Bangnor Regis: New Horizon, 1981.
    A fictionalized account of the Argyll and Sutherland Highlanders, 1st Battalion.

1966 Meader, Stephen W. Sabre Pilot. New York: Harcourt, Brace and Company, 1956, 1957.
        Juvenile novel of pilots in the air war.

1967 Michener, James A. The Bridges at Toko-Ri. New York: Ballantine Books, 1953.
        An exciting flag-waving story of destiny, jet planes, Korean air war, and life aboard a carrier.

1968 Michener, James A. Sayonara. New York: Random House, 1954. multiple others.
        A story of love, sex, war, and humor in Asia during the Korean War. Not one of Michener's best.

1969 Millar, Ward M. Valley of the Shadow. New York: D. McKay Co., 1955.
        Personal narrative of life in the prisons by a United States Air Force pilot who was captured and then managed to escape.

1970 Molloy, Tom. The Vandal. Ambler, Pennsylvania: Cumpac Readers Group, 1990.
        A novel with confused intentions.

1971 Montyn, Jan. A Lamb to the Slaughter. New York: Viking, 1985.
        Translation of a Dutch narration.

1972 Moore, Robin. Oh! Inchon. no city: One Way Productions, 1981.
        Used by One Way Productions for the filming of Inchon. Less than objective.

1973 Moreno, Ruben, Rudy Lucero and Annie M. Lopez. E-Company Marines Remembered. Tucson, Arizona: R. L. Moreno, 1994.
        Narratives of Hispanic Americans in the 13th Infantry Battalion.

1974 Moscatelli, Arthur. The Korean War As I Saw It. Chisholm, Minnesota: Iron Range Research Center, 1989.
        Personal narrative and biography.

1975 Moses, Lloyd R. and Gerald W. Wolff "The Korean War Journal of Lloyd R. Moses" South Dakota Historical Collections 40 (1981).
        A personal narrative.

1976 Nichols, Donald. How Many Times Can I Die? Autobiography of Donald Nichols. Brookville, Florida: D. Nichols, 1981.

Account of spies and action based on the author's experience.

1977 North, John. Men Fighting: Battle Stories. London: Faber and Faber, 1958.
     Personal narrative of World War II and Korea.

1978 Oden, Kenneth. Yeah, Brave Coward. Rutland, Vermont: Charles Tuttle, Co., 1960.
     Novel of soldiers who do their job simply and bravely in Korea. Humorous and well-written.

1979 O'Kane, Henry. O'Kane's Korea: A Soldier's Tale of Three Years of Combat and Captivity in Korea, 1950-53. Kenilworth: H. O'Kane, 1988.
     A lively account of interrogation as a prisoner-of-war.

1980 Ottoboni, Fred. Korea Between the War: A Soldier's Story. Sparks, Nevada: Vincente Books, 1997.
     A personal narrative that covers the occupation, invasion, and involvement.

1981 Out of Line: A Collection of Cartoons From the Pacific Stars and Stripes. Tokyo: Pacific Stars and Stripes, 1952, 1954.
     Printed in Stars and Stripes: humor from the Korean Conflict.

1982 Pa, Chin. Living Amongst Heroes. Peking: Foreign Language Press, 1956.
     Chinese personal narrative of the Korean War.

1983 Paananen, Eloise. Dawn Mission: A Flight Nurse in Korea. New York: John Day Company, 1962.
     Juvenile fiction which romanticizes the role of the military nurse.

1984 Paschall, Rod. Witness to War: Korea. New York: Berkley Publishing Group, 1995.
     Collection of narratives.

1985 Pasley, Virginia. 22 Stayed. London: W. H. Allen, 1955.
     Biographies of prisoners who did not desire repatriation and stayed with their captors in North Korea. American book was titled 21 Stayed because one prisoner was a British soldier.

1986 Pate, Lloyd W. Reactionary! New York: Harper, 1956.
     A shorter version appeared in the New York Herald Tribune called "Soldiers on the Hook." It is a personal narrative of life in the prison camps.

1987 Peacock, Robert S. <u>Kim-chi, Asahi, and Rum: A Platoon Commander Remembers Korea, 1952-1953</u>. Toronto: Lugus, 1994.
> The leadership narrative of a Canadian officer in combat duty.

1988 Peters, Ralph. <u>The Perfect Soldier</u>. New York: Pocket Books, 1995.
> Fictionalized account of a soldier's life in a Soviet prison.

1989 Peterson, Bernard W. <u>Short Straw: Memories of Korea</u>. Scottsdale, Arizona: Chuckwalla Publishing, 1996.
> Marine Corps biography of fighter pilots and aerial operations.

1990 Pettigrew, Thomas H. <u>The Kunu-ri (Kumori) Incident</u>. New York: Vantage Press, 1963.
> Personal narrative based on a historical event.

1991 Philpot, Van B. <u>Battalion Medics: A Novel of the Korean War</u>. New York: Exposition Press, 1955.
> Fictionalized story of a United States medic serving in Korea.

1992 Plemmons, Dallas. <u>Hell in the Land of the Morning Calm</u>. Vabeca, Virginia: McDonough Group, 1987.
> A biography and personal narrative of time spent in Korea.

1993 Pollard, Freeman. <u>Seeds of Turmoil: A Novel about American PWs Brainwashed in Korea</u>. New York: Exposition Press, 1959.
> Fiction about American prisoners-of-war.

1994 Pollini, Francis. <u>Night</u>. Boston: Houghton Mifflin, 1960.
> This is a story of the confrontation between a United States Army sergeant, a prisoner-of-war, and his Chinese "education" officer. His resistance is weakened by the presence of "progressives."

1995 Polster, Edward C. <u>The Bloody Hills of Korea: A Boy's Initiation to War</u>. Dallas, Texas: L. S. Simmons, 1954.
> Personal narrative of growing up quickly in Korea.

1996 Porcelli, Joe. <u>The Photograph</u>. Charleston, South Carolina: Wyrick & Company, 1995.
> Fictionalized account of Korean War orphans.

1997 Potok, Chaim. <u>I Am the Clay</u>. New York: Knopf, 1992.
> An excellent tale of suffering and redemption of refugees caught in the cross-fire of the Korean War.

1998 Price, Oliver M. Kim-Walk-in-My-Shoes. New York: Howard-McCann, 1968.
    A novel of a Korean boy, befriended by an American doctor, during the Korean War.

1999 Racing Towards Victory: Stories from the Korean Front. Peking: Foreign Language Press, 1954.
    Communist stories of life fighting the imperialists.

2000 Redstreake, William N. The Wine of Life. New York: Vantage Press, 1968.
    A novel of Korea.

2001 Reinburg, J. Hunter. Aerial Combat Escapades: A Pilot's Logbook: The True Combat Aerial Adventures of an American Fighter Pilot. Grand Canyon, Arizona: GCBA Publishers, 1988.
    Personal narrative of Marine Fighter Squadron (VMF) 121 during World War II and the Korean War.

2002 Rhee, Jhongman. My Memoirs of the Leathernecks. Pohang: United States Army Memorial, 1970.
    Personal narratives of members of a United States Marine Corps Wing.

2003 Rishell, Lyle. With a Black Platoon in Combat: A Year in Korea. College Station, Texas: Texas A & M University Press, 1993.
    A personal narrative, very effective.

2004 Roskey, William A. Muffled Shots: A Year on the DMZ. Simpsonville, Maryland: Eighund Publishing, 1986.
    A story of the demilitarized war zone.

2005 Ross, Glen. The Last Campaign. New York: Harper, 1962.
    Fictional account of a young army corporal who was stationed in Japan in 1950 playing a musical instrument in the division band. When the war broke out he and his friends were sent off to Korea in that first group whose primary role was to make an appearance. The idea was still held that just having Americans there would stem the tide. Describes the horrors and suffering they experienced.

2006 Ruggero, Ed. 38 North Yankee. New York: Pocket Books, 1990.
    A highly speculative novel about the outbreak of hostilities and the completion of the unfinished war in Korea.

2007 Russ, Martin. The Last Parallel: A Marine's War Journal. New York: Rinehart and Company, 1957.
 Journal of a twenty-one year old Marine who goes through training and service in Korea with the 1st Division.

2008 Salter, James. The Hunters. New York: Bantam Books, 1958. Washington, D. C.: Counterpoint, 1997.
 A fictionalized account of aerial operations in the Korean War which follows an Air Guard unit in the sky near the Yalu River, and the difficulties of an over-anxious commander.

2009 Sauter, Jack. Sailors in the Sky: Memoir of a Navy Aircrewman in the Korean War. Jefferson, North Carolina: McFarland, 1995.
 Biography of aerial and navy aircrewman.

2010 Sayers, Dick. No Victory, No Sting. Pittsboro, North Carolina: Town House Press, 1992.
 A good novel of the "trench war" and hill fighting of the last days in Korea.

2011 Sellers, Con. Brothers in Battle. New York: Pocket Books, 1989.
 Stresses the communist infiltration movement, and the value of South Korean troops.

2012 Sheldon, Walt. Troubling of a Star. Philadelphia: Lippincott, 1953.
 Pilot is troubled by the napalm he has been dropping.

2013 Sidney, George. For the Love of Dying. New York: Morrow, 1969.
 The story of a Marine officer who is activated and survives the horrors of war by telling himself, "somebody has to do it."

2014 Skomra, F. P. Behind the Bamboo Curtain. New York: Greenwich, 1957.
 A fairly interesting but highly overstated novel dealing with United States airmen fighting the air war in Korea.

2015 Slaughter, Frank G. Sword and Scalpel. New York: Doubleday and Co., 1957.
 A novel depicting the experiences of Paul Scott, an American surgeon in the Korean War, taken prisoner and then released. Accused of collaboration.

2016 Snowden, Ron A. Pak's Palace. Los Angeles: California: Spartan Books, 1959.

Fiction based on Major William E. Meyers, psychiatrist, interviews with one thousand POWs and how they responded to pressure.

2017 Snyder, Don J. A Soldier's Disgrace. Dublin, New Hampshire: Yankee Books, 1987.
Proclaims the truth of Ronald Alley who died while trying to clear his name.

2018 Sprioff, Boris. Korea: Frozen Hell on Earth. New York: Vantage Press, 1995.
A personal narrative based on an old formula.

2019 Stephens, Rudolph W. Old Ugly Hill: A G.I.'s Fourteen Months in the Korean Trenches, 1952-1953. New York: McFarland and Co., 1955.
Well-written account of Stephens' tour in Korea, and his fight on "Old Baldy."

2020 Stevens, Clifford J. Wild Dogs of Chongdo. Huntington, Indiana: Our Sunday Visitor, 1979.
A novel about a Korean child who escaped from the ravages of war with the aid of wild dogs.

2021 Storrs, James L. The Expendable Innocents: A Novel of Truth and Comedy. New York: Vantage Press, 1992
Rather good story about Marine Corps history.

2022 Styron, William. The Long March. New York: Random, 1968.
Short novel which looks at training for the Korean War, in the eyes of a traditional colonel and rebellious captain, who objects to recall.

2023 Sullivan, John A. Toy Soldier: Memoirs of a Combat Platoon Leader in Korea. New York: McFarland and Co., 1951.
Short, well-written account of the author who faces the twin problems of war at its most difficult, and his own lack of confidence as a platoon leader.

2024 Swanson, Earl R. Service in the U. S. Army Reserve, 1939-1952. Urbana, Illinois: Earl R. Swanson, 1996.
Personal narrative and brief biography of service in World War II and Korea.

2025 Taylor, George. Infantry Colonel. Upton-upon-Severn: Self Publishing Association, 1990.

The World War II and Korean War campaigns of this field officer of the British army.

2026 Thomas, Melvin. <u>Boondocker Ballet</u>. Pittsburgh: Dorrance Publishing Company, 1996.
    Marine Corps personal narrative of World War II and the Korean War.

2027 Thompson James. <u>Camp 5: 1004 Days of North Korean Prison</u>. Laguna Beach, California: Voyager Press, 1981. <u>True Colors: One Thousand and Four Days as a Prisoner-of-War</u>. Port Washington, New York: Ashley Books, 1989.
    The story of Sergeant Major James Thompson, a black, who was held as a prisoner even after the first exchanges. His story relates to both his status as a prisoner and the plight of a black man.

2028 Thompson, Reginald. <u>An Echo of Trumpets</u>. London: G. Allen & Unwin, 1964.
    Autobiography of the author's experiences in combat during World War II and the Korean War.

2029 Thorin, Duane. <u>A Ride to Panmunjom</u>. Chicago: H. Regnery Company, 1956.
    Poorly-constructed fiction of a Swedish helicopter pilot who is eventually taken prisoner.

2030 Tibbets, Albert. <u>Courage in Korea: Stories of the Korean War</u>. Boston: Little, Brown & Co., 1962.
    Collected stories of events and action in the Korean War.

2031 Trooper. <u>Korean Raider</u>. Ranfurly, New Zealand: Hawkspur Productions, 1994.
    A fictionalized account also titled <u>Hawkspur</u>.

2032 Truchinski, L. E. <u>I Cheated Death: A True Story</u>. Wisconsin Rapids, Wisconsin: L. E. Truchinski, 1984.
    Story of the Korean War.

2033 Turner, Richard E. <u>Big Friend, Little Friend: Memoirs of a World War II Fighter Pilot</u>. Garden City, New York: Doubleday, 1969. Mesa, Arizona: Champlin Fighter Museum Press, 1983. <u>Mustang Pilot</u>. London, Kimber, 1970. London: New English Library, 1975.
    354th Fighter Group aerial operations in World War II and Korea.

2034 Turnstall, Julian. I Fought in Korea. London: Lawrence & Wishant, 1953.
        The personal narrative of a British soldier, strong on hardships and atrocities.

2035 Valot, Wilbur. Korean War. Youngstown, Ohio: Youngstown State University, 1989.
        A twenty-one page transcript of an oral history interview on personal experiences.

2036 Verdi, John M. First Hundred: A Memoir of the Korean War, 1952-1953. Northport, Alabama: J. Verdi, 1989.
        A personal narrative of a year in Korea.

2037 Voorhees, Melvin B. Korean Tales. New York: Simon, 1952.
        Collection of personal essays by the man who was the chief censor of the United States Eighth Army.

2038 Voorhees, Melvin B. Show Me a Hero. New York: Simon, 1954.
        This is the story of three men; a general officer, chaplain, and journalist who suffer during the long peace negotiations.

2039 Walker, Wilbert L. Stalemate at Panmunjom: A Novel. Baltimore: Heritage Press, 1980.
        A novel about the armistice talks.

2040 Walker, Wilbert L. We Are Men: Memoirs of World War II and the Korean War. Chicago: Heritage Press, 1972.
        The personal story of two American blacks who served as combat soldiers in World War II and Korea.

2041 White, Link S. Chesi's Story: One Boy's Long Journey from War to Peace. Tallahassee, Florida: Father and Son Publishing, Inc., 1995.
        This is the story of a preteen Korean boy and his survival of the destruction of home and family. He was adopted by Americans and became a company mascot.

2042 Whitehouse, Arthur. Combat in the Sky. New York: Duell, Sloan and Pearce, 1961.
        Air combat story from World War II and Korea.

2043 Whitehouse, Arthur G. J. Fighters in the Sky: Adventure Tales of Fighter Pilots in Three Wars. New York: Universal Publishers, 1965.
        Short stories of air combat, some in Korea.

2044 Wilkinson, Allen B. <u>Up Front Korea</u>. New York: Vantage Press, 1967.
     The narrative of a young 2nd Infantry Division soldier told with fictional characters in an exaggerated battle.

2045 Williamson, John I. <u>Dearest Buckie: A Marine's Korean War Memoir</u>. Austin, Texas: R. J. Speights, 1993.
     Correspondence and personal narrative of author's time in Korea.

2046 Wilson, Arthur W. <u>Korean Vignettes: Faces of War</u>. Thayer, Missouri: Artwook Publications, 1996.
     A fine collection of short vignettes of men who served in Korea. It gives a wide look at the many services performed, and something of the "feel."

2047 Wilson, Jim. <u>Retreat, Hell! We're Just Attacking in Another Direction</u>. New York: William Morrow and Company, Inc., 1988.
     A classic account of the Marine retreat from Chosin, but he does begin with a highly informative account of the landing of the Marines at Inchon.

2048 Winder, Charles R. <u>Escape and Evasion</u>. New York: Carlton Press, 1992.
     A "true story" biography of escape.

2049 Wolfe, Gene. <u>Letters Home</u>. Weston, Ontario, Canada: U. M. Press, 1991.
     Correspondence and personal narrative of Korea.

2050 Yang, Shuo. <u>A Thousand Miles of Lovely Land</u>. Peking, Foreign Language Press, 1957, 1979.
     A Chinese novel of war in Korea.

2051 Young, Neil F. <u>The Cornfield Commando</u>. New York: Vantage Press 1990.
     Personal narrative of a soldier in Korea and Vietnam.

2052 Zdanavage, Tony and Esther Zdanavage. <u>Korea, 25 June 1950-27 July 1953: The War America Forgot to Remember</u>. Berwick, Pennsylvania: Zdanavage, 1991.
     The author's biography and personal narrative about the Korean War.

Picture Histories

2053 Brodie, Howard. War Drawings: World War II, Korea. Palo Alto, California: National Press, 1962.
     Drawings by a famous combat artist who records the Marines in Korea.

2054 Cabot, Hugh. Korea. Tokyo: World News and Publishing Company, 1954.
     Picture history of the Korean War.

2055 Campbell, John M. and Donna Campbell. B-17 Flying Fortress Nose Art Gallery. Osceola, Wisconsin: Motorbooks International, 1993.
     Colorful and interesting account of the nose paintings on B-17s in Korea.

2056 Campbell, John M. and Donna Campbell. Talisman: A Collection of Nose Art. West Chester, Pennsylvania: Schiffer Military History, 1992.
     Colorful account of nose art on aircraft in Korea.

2057 Campbell, John M. and Donna Campbell. War Paint: Fighter Nose Art for World War II and Korea. Shrewsbury: Airlift, 1990. Osceola, Wisconsin: Motorbooks International, 1990.
     Nose art from the Korean War.

2058 Cassino, Jay A., editor. Pictorial History of the Korean War. New York: Wise, 1951.
     Covers the early United Nations forces during the beginning stages of the conflict. This edition was identified as the memorial edition for the Veterans of Foreign Wars.

2059 Chang, Albert. This Way to War: A Pictorial Monograph. Honolulu: Tongg Publishing Company, 1952.
     About the United States 24th Division, 5th Regiment Combat Team.

2060 Doll, Thomas E. USN/USMC Over Korea. Carrollton, Texas: Squadron/Signal Publications, 1988.
     Essentially a picture book of planes involved in the United States Navy and Marine Corps flyers in Korea.

2061 Duncan, David. "The First Five Days" Life 29 2 (1950): 20-27.
     Duncan, a photographer for Life, was one of the first photo-journalists in Korea. His words and photos narrate events from the evacuation of American citizens to the first visit from MacArthur.

2062 Duncan, David. This Is War! A Photo-Narrative of the Korean War. New York: Harper, 1951. New York: Little, Brown, 1990.

Duncan, a world class photo-journalist covers the United States Marines fighting in Korea. A short text and uncaptioned photography tells a graphic story. While it covers the whole war there is plenty of coverage of the defense of Pusan Perimeter.

2063 Dvorchak, Robert J. Battle for Korea: The Associated Press History of the Korean Conflict. Conshohocken, Pennsylvania: Combined Books, 1993.

A photographic history.

2064 "Free Koreans Meet the Test of Battle" Army Information Digest 5 (1950): 25-31.

A pictorial account of the contribution made by the South Koreans during the early months of the fighting, and the toll taken upon the civilians as the army rushed into retreat.

2065 Giangreco, Dennis M. War in Korea, 1950-1953: A Pictorial History. Novato, California: Presidio Press, 1990.

Pictorial history of the Korean War with several previously unpublished photographs, many very descriptive, as well as an excellent set of captions.

2066 Gurney, Gene. A Pictorial History of the United States Army. New York: Crown, 1966.

Chapter on Korea provides about one hundred fifty pictures, some not generally seen.

2067 Jones, Charles and Eugene Jones. The Face of War. New York: Prentice-Hall, Inc., 1951.

A photo essay of the 1st Marine Division at war. The essays are very informative, but the pictures themselves present an excellent story as well.

2068 The M-1 Does My Talking!: The U. S. M1 Garand Rifle. Sandston, Virginia: Robert Bruce Photography, 1952.

The history and development of the M1 Rifle is told in pictures in this eighty-page book.

2069 Miller, John, Jr., Owen J. Carroll and Margaret E. Tackley. Korea 1951-1953. Washington, D. C.: Office of the Chief of Military History, Department of the Army, 1956, 1989, 1997.

Uses official photos to show the United States Army in action the last two years of the war. Particularly good coverage on the hill war.

2070 Mitchell, Kenneth F. and Eugene Newhall. <u>47th Viking Infantry Division: Pictorial Review</u>. Atlanta: Love, 1951.
    Picture history.

2071 Moody, Jerry. <u>67th Tactical Reconnaissance Wing With the United Nations Forces, Korea</u>. United States: 67th Tactical Reconnaissance Wing, 1952.
    A pictorial work of war photography.

2072 Packwood, Norval E. Jr. <u>Leatherhead in Korea</u>. Quantico, Virginia: Marine Corps Gazette, 1952.
    A cartoon look at the 1st Marine Division from reorganization and staffing by reserves through the fight at Inchon and Seoul. This is a strong editorial piece which gives quick insight into the political climate of the time.

2073 <u>Pictorial Korea 1951-1953</u>. Seoul: International Publicity League of Korea, 1952.
    Illustrated history of the Korean War.

2074 Stadtmauer, Saul A., editor. <u>24th Forward: The Pictorial History of the Victory Division in Korea</u>. Tokyo: Koyosha, 1953.
    Good account as well as fine pictures of the 24th Division in Korea.

2075 United Nations. <u>United Action in Korea</u>. New York: United Nations, Department of Public Information, 1951.
    Brief (twenty-one page) pictorial work.

2076 Veterans of Foreign Wars. <u>Pictorial History of the Korean War</u>. no city: Veterans' Historical Book Service, 1951, 1954.
    In this very complete collection, the various photographs are used to explain the numerous aspects of the United Nations Command.

ANALYSIS

General Analysis

2077 "Analysis of Issues by Korean Commission" United Nations Bulletin 9 (October 1, 1950): 301-304.
United Nations Commission lists the North Korean invasion as "an act of aggression initiated without warning and without provocation."

2078 Barclay, C. N. "Lessons of the Korean Campaign" Brassey's Annual (1954): 122-133.
From the British point of view much was learned about joint operations, but this article questions the use of the tank and the vast administrative baggage imposed on the Commonwealth Division.

2079 Barham, Pat and Frank Cunningham. Operation Nightmare: The Story of America's Betrayal in Korea and the United Nations. Los Angeles: Sequoia University Press, 1953.
Generally an exposé of the United Nations failures and a strong support of General Douglas MacArthur "our great living general and American, a victim of governmental blundering and treason. . . "

2080 Benben, John S. "Education of Prisoners of War on Koje Island, Korea" Educational Record (April 1953): 157-175.
Discusses the value of the education program set up by the United Nations for the communist prisoners at Koje prison compound.

2081 Bennett, Bruce W. <u>Two Alternative Views of War in Korea: The North and South Korea Revolutions in Military Affairs</u>. Santa Monica, California: Rand Corporation, 1995.
    A computer simulation account of other options.

2082 Best, Robert J. <u>The Structure of a Battle: Analysis of a UN-NK Action North of Taegu, Korea, September 1950</u>. Chevy Chase, Maryland: Johns Hopkins University, 1954.
    Analysis of technical, unit casualties, statistics, and troop movements.

2083 Bhagat, B. S. "Military Lessons of the Korean War" <u>Journal Royal United Service Institution</u> (January-April 1952): 5-21. [Reprinted in <u>Military Review</u> 32 9 (December 1952).]
    This article discusses military lessons learned during each phase of the war. It acknowledged the fact intelligence was very poor; and stressed the value of inter-service cooperation.

2084 Bradley, Omar N. "The Path Ahead" <u>Army Information Digest</u> 5 10 (1950): 24-26.
    The Chairman of the Joint Chiefs of Staff addresses both the question of why America is involved and why there will be a delay in getting support troops to Korea.

2085 Bradley, Omar N. "US Military Policy: 1950" <u>Reader's Digest</u> 57 (October 1950): 143-154.
    The Chairman of the Joint Chiefs of Staff identifies the shift in American policy from the simple concept of containment to contesting communism. Stresses the need to protect Western Europe.

2086 Brooks, Robert O. <u>Russian Airpower in the Korean War: The Impact of Tactical Intervention and Strategic Threat on United States Objectives</u>. Maxwell Air Force Base, Alabama: Air University, 1964.
    Analysis piece trying to evaluate Soviet air power in Korea and what it says about Soviet threat to the United States.

2087 Cagle, Malcolm W. "Inchon: The Analysis of a Gamble" <u>United States Naval Institute Proceedings</u> 80 1 (1954): 47-51.
    A critical look at MacArthur's decision to invade at Inchon. A well-constructed view.

2088 Carpenter, William M. "The Korean War: A Strategic Perspective Thirty Years Later" <u>Comparative Strategy</u> 2 4 (1980): 335-353.

An American image of weakness and indecision probably led to the "start" of the Korean War. Now thirty years later it is leading America to the same position again.

2089 Carter, Gregory A. Some Historical Notes on Air Interdiction in Korea. Santa Monica, California: Rand Corporation, 1966.

A Rand Corporation study prepared for the Vietnam era provides an analysis.

2090 Chen, Jian. "China's Changing Aims During the Korean War, 1950-1951" The Journal of American East Asian Relations 1 (Spring 1992): 8-41.

Holds the view that China's decision to move into the Soviet camp was influenced by failure of American policy.

2091 Christensen, Thomas. "Threats, Assurances, and the Last Chance for Peace: The Lessons of Mao's Korean War Telegrams" International Security 17 (Summer 1992): 122-154.

Excellent piece which uses primary material to argue Mao's decision to enter the war was based on the United States decision to cross the 38th Parallel.

2092 Cottrell, Alvin J. and James E. Dougherty. "The Lessons of Korea: War and the Power of Man" Orbis 2 (Spring 1958): 39-64.

An interesting account of the impact of limited war, and the failure of the United States to see the Korean Conflict in light of its strategic background. The United States never fully understood the relationship between military success and political movement in Korea.

2093 Cronin, Mary M. "An Analysis of Wartime Agenda: The Korean War Reporting of Marguerite Higgins" Boston, Massachusetts: Emerson College, 1990.

Talk presented to the Association for Education in Journalism at the 1990 convention in Minnesota which discusses the character of Higgins' reporting.

2094 Crowe, Clarance. An Analysis of the Inchon-Seoul Campaign. Maxwell Air Force Base, Alabama: Air University, 1983.

This is an evaluation of the military effort, and achievement, from the point of view of command. It is the product of students at the command classes of the Air Command and Staff College. It is located at the University library. The work is not classified, but unavailable to the scholar, unless they receive special permission from the staff at the college.

2095 Crushman, John H. <u>Command and Control of Theater Forces: The Korean Command and Other Cases</u>. Cambridge, Massachusetts: Center for Information Policy Research, 1986.

Serious indepth study of command, which finds that in many cases the command area was too large to match responsibility.

2096 Cumings, Bruce. "'Revising Postrevisionism,' or the Poverty of Theory in Diplomatic History" <u>Diplomatic History</u> 17 4 (Fall 1993): 539-571.

A long scholarly article, an attack on post-revisionism, suggesting others failed to see, or read much primary evidence. Very significant article.

2097 Deagle, Edwin A., Jr. "The Agony of Restraint: Korea, 1951-1953" Ph.D. dissertation, Harvard University, 1970.

Looks at military decision limited by restraints imposed by a limited war mentality.

2098 "The Defeat of the American Eighth Army in Korea, November-December, 1950" in Eliot A. Cohen and John Gooch. <u>Military Misfortunes: The Anatomy of Failure in War</u>. New York: The Free Press, 1990.

While actually addressing the military failure at Chosin, it takes a look at the "aggregate failure" which began at Inchon and which in turn frightened the Chinese into action.

2099 DeWeerd, Harvey A. "Lessons of the Korean War" <u>Yale Review</u> 40 (Summer 1951): 592-603.

At the time of its writing, the author saw the Korean war as undeclared, limited, of minor importance, and in general a confusing event which had already taught some important lessons. These lessons seem to be valid though he wrote before the war was over.

2100 DeWeerd, Harvey A. "Strategic Surprise in the Korean War" <u>Orbis</u> 6 3 (Fall 1963): 435-452.

While this article is directed to the Korean War in general it does deal with the "mishandling of strategic intelligence" and tries to explain why the United States was so unprepared. What is not discussed, and should be in such a work, is the American failure to keep its own activities secret. The surprise is that the United States managed to keep any secrets at all. The Inchon landing was well known long before it was executed.

2101 Drummond, S. "Korea and Vietnam: Some Speculations about the Possible Influence of the Korean War on American Policy in Vietnam" <u>Army Quarterly Defense Journal</u> 97 1 (1968): 65-71.

Concludes a misreading of the mission, and success, in Korea led to some tragic mistakes in Vietnam.

2102 Egbert, Robert L. Fighter I: An Analysis of Combat Fighters and Non-Fighters. Washington, D. C.: George Washington University, 1957.
     A short piece on how soldiers performed when on duty in combat. A serious look at a major problem in armies.

2103 Elowitz, Larry. "Korea and Vietnam: Limited War and the American Political System" Orbis 18 2 (1974): 510-534.
     Discusses the changing nature of public support as public and congressional backing slowly slipped away.

2104 Finletter, Thomas K. "The Meaning of Korea" Army Information Digest 6 9 (September 1951): 3-8.
     The Secretary of the Air Force maintained the position that the American involvement in the war came because of the need to support the aims and ideals of the United Nations. He writes that Korea is the point at which the United States and the United Nations had to take a stand; that the fight is about creating a powerful defense which can be the beginning of the efforts toward disarmament.

2105 Fishel, Wesley R. and Alfred H. Hausrath. Language Problems of the US Army During Hostilities in Korea. Chevy Chase, Maryland: Johns Hopkins University, 1958.
     Discussion of the effect of twenty-one nations operating in a single command.

2106 Fondacaro, Steve. A Strategic Analysis of U. S. Special Operations During the Korean Conflict, 1950-1953. Fort Leavenworth, Kansas: United States Army Command and General Staff College, 1988.
     Account of the secret service and intelligence operations.

2107 Foot, Rosemary. "Historiography: Making Known the Unknown War: Policy Analysis of the Korean Conflict in the Last Decade" Diplomatic History 15 3 (Summer 1991): 411-431.
     An excellent account of the ex post facto histories of the Korean War but particularly interesting in terms of the "meaning" of the first phase of the war. This fine historian has provided a good 1990s look at the Korean War and the bibliographic interpretations of it.

2108 Foot, Rosemary. The Wrong War: American Policy and the Dimensions of the Korean Conflict, 1950-1953. Ithaca, New York: Cornell University Press, 1985.
     Foot addresses the concept of limited war and American involvement in a book which seems to document Omar Bradley's view "the wrong war, at the wrong place, and with the wrong enemy." American

efforts, from the beginning, were designed to keep China out of the war. See chapter three.

2109 Gacek, Christopher M. "Contending Approaches to the Use of Force: The 'Never Again' and 'Limited War' School in American Foreign Policy" Ph.D. dissertation, Stanford University, 1989.
A comparison of the decision, first in Korea and then Vietnam, to use military force.

2110 Gayle, John S. "Korea, Honor with War" Military Review 30 10 (1951): 55-62.
Criticizes Truman's cut in defense areas following the 7th Division withdrawal in 1949. This left the United States unprepared for the coming war.

2111 Goodrich, Leland M. Korea: A Study in U. S. Policy in the United Nations. New York: Council on Foreign Relations, 1956.
Careful handling of the Korean question in the United Nations from V-J Day to the armistice in Korea. Particularly interesting in regards to United Nations versus American political interests.

2112 Ha, Yong Sun, editor. New Approaches to the Study of Korean War: Beyond Traditionalism and Revisionism. Seoul: NaNam, 1990.
A neo-revisionist suggestion about how to reinterpret the Korean War.

2113 Hadaway, Christopher K. "The Vietnam and Korean Wars: A Comparison of Elite and Non-elite Reaction" MA thesis, Memphis State University, 1975.
MA: comparisons

2114 Haggerty, William M. "American Misperceptions and the Korean War" BS thesis, Massachusetts Institute of Technology, 1971.
BS: misconceptions

2115 Hakon, Ostholm. "The First Year of the Korean War: The Road Toward Armistice" Ph.D. dissertation, Kent State University, 1982.
Holds that the Korean War was the most catastrophic of the international conflicts. The event created a situation no one wanted. Chapter four deals with the effect of this view on the fighting of the war, and discusses the dangers seen by the military leadership involved in the war.

2116 Hanguk, Hongbo H. "The Truth Behind the Korean War: A Review" Seoul: Public Relations Association of Korea, 1973.

A review of world news reports and editorials, giving the "real truth" behind them.

2117 Heller, Francis H. The Korean War: A 25 Year Perspective. Lawrence, Kansas: The Regents Press of Kansas, 1977.

This twenty-five-year look at the Korean War contains some very interesting information, but the most significant is the early discussion of the war by a panel of participants. One of the topics is Inchon, during which General Matthew B. Ridgway made some insightful comments.

2118 Holland, Thomas D. Problems and Observations Related to the Korean Forensic Identification of Human Remains Repatriated to the United States by North Korea. Santa Monica, California: Rand Corporation, 1993.

Difficulties in identifying the missing-in-action and prisoner human remains: no one may ever know!

2119 Hoyt, Edwin P. "The United States Reaction to the Korean Attack: A Study of the Principles of the United Nations Charter as a Factor in American Policy-Making" American Journal of International Law 55 1 (January 1961): 45-76.

Hoyt defends the right of the president, as representing a voting member of the United Nations, to involve the United States in the Korean Conflict, including the use of troops.

2120 Hudson, G. W. "The Privileged Sanctuary" Twentieth Century 149 887 (1951): 4-10.

Highly critical of United Nations policy which allowed the communists to hide in the sanctuary of Red China while attacking United States and British forces. Sees Korea as a political defeat for America.

2121 Hughes, Paul D. Battle in the Rear: Lessons from Korea. Fort Leavenworth, Kansas: United States Army Command and General Staff College, 1988.

An analysis of guerrillas and the counterinsurgency effort in Korea. Not all that effective in the overall success of the Korean War.

2122 Ickes, Harold L. "War in Korea" New Republic (July 10, 1950): 17.

Written shortly after war broke out Ickes charges that American hysteria is directly related to years of over-reaction created by McCarthyism.

2123 Jervis, Robert. "The Impact of the Korean War on the Cold War" Journal of Conflict Resolution 24 (December 1980): 563-592.

A rather basic look at the effective influence of the Korean War on Cold War activities and policy making.

2124 Judd, Walter H. How and Why Did We Get into War in Korea: Remarks During Debate on Extension of Mutual Defense Assistance Act of 1949. Washington, D. C.: Government Printing Office, 1950.
   Strongly opinionated view against President Truman and views the war entry as a token anti-communist sympathizer.

2125 KMAG, Public Information Office. The United States Advisory Group to the Republic of Korea, 1945-1955. Tokyo: Diate, no date.
   Primarily an administrative history of the advisory group responsible for the organization of the South Korean armed forces, following KMAG from it conception and taking it through the early fighting (where its success proved doubtful) and on to the post-war role The history is constrained and it tends to make too strong a case for the benevolent nature of the advisors.

2126 Kim, Chull Baum. "An Inquiry into the Origins of the Korean War: A Critique of the Revisionist View" East Asia Review 6 3 (Summer 1994): 3.
   A new look at an old argument. Rephrase of author's "Abandonment or Safeguard" article.

2127 Kim, Hak-Joon. "Trends in Korean War Studies: A Review of the Literature" in Kim Chull Baum and James Matray, editors. Korea and the Cold War. Claremont, California: Regina Books, 1993.
   Kim argues that the Korean War was the direct outgrowth of the 1948 American withdrawal.

2128 Kim, Kyoung-Soo. "The Genesis of Non-Alignment: A Study of India's Foreign Policy with Specific Reference to the Korean War (1950-53)" Ph.D. dissertation, State University of New York at Albany, 1983.
   India had used the non-aligned status as a diplomatic policy for years. India's role in Korea is a good example of how it gave this nation considerable power in international events even though it has a small military.

2129 Kim, Nam G. From Enemies to Allies: The Impact of the Korean War on U. S.—Japan Relations. San Francisco: International Scholastic Studies, 1997.
   The war in Korea had the effect of bringing the Japanese-American war to an end.

2130 Kim, Sam Kyu. History of the Korean War: Reevaluation of Modern History. Tokyo: Korean Hyoronsha, 1967.
   Provides a leftist analysis of the cause and meaning of the Korean War.

2131 Kim, Soon Nam. "The Conduct of The Korean War, 1950-1953: With Emphasis on the Civilian Control over the Military in the United States" Ph.D. dissertation, University of Aberdeen, 1987.

In a very interesting study of civilian control in general the author addressed the role of General Douglas MacArthur. The author deals with the Inchon decision and presents the case that the decision to land troops at Inchon was an example of how MacArthur was able to take preeminence over civilian authority both by the power of his argument and power of this position.

2132 Korea and the Cold War: Division, Destruction, and Disarmament. Claremont, California: Regina Books, 1993.

Articles by numerous authors provide an analysis of the Korean War and the diplomacy of the war. Well done.

2133 Khong, Yuen Foong. Analogies at War: Korea, Munich, Dien Bien Phu, and the Vietnam Decisions of 1965. Princeton, New Jersey: Princeton University Press, 1992.

Another attempt to place the Korean War within the larger context of the Cold War, all of which led to American involvement in Vietnam. The author's position is that what the United States thought they had learned in Korea explains why the Johnson administration felt it necessary to be involved in Vietnam.

2134 King, O. H. P. Tail of the Paper Tiger. Caldwell, Idaho: The Caxton Printers, Ltd., 1961.

A highly critical account of the war by participant, Associated Press reporter O. H. P. King, who describes Korea as a war that "was never meant to be won."

2135 Knight, Charlotte. "Korea: A Twenty-Fifth Anniversary" Air Force 58 (1975): 59-63.

Based on an August 1950 field report during which the author tries to describe and evaluate the air operations during the first few months of war. The article is supportive of the American air effort but not of the effect.

2136 Kriebel, P. Wesley. "Unfinished Business—Intervention Under the U. N. Umbrella: America's Participation in the Korean War, 1950-1953" in Robin D. Higham, editor. Intervention or Abstention: The Dilemma of American Foreign Policy. Lexington: University Press of Kentucky, 1975.

In this article the author attempts to identify the attitude of the communist states about American policy, and the ultimate decision to intervene in the Korean War.

2137 Lee, Chae-Jin, editor. <u>The Korean War: 40 Year Perspective</u>. Claremont McKenna College: Keck Center for International and Strategic Studies, 1991.

    This is the first of the Center's monographs dealing with the Korean War. This perspective looks at the war from both political and military points of view, nearly half-a-century after the armistice was signed.

2138 Lee, Daewoo. "The Consequences of War: Economic Impact of Regional Total War" Ph.D. dissertation, Claremont Graduate School, 1995.

    Uses the "simple-trend-fitting-methodology" to evaluate the costs of regional total wars, including the price of the Korean Conflict.

2139 Lee, Suk Jung. <u>Ending the Last Cold War: Korean Arms Control and Security in Northeast Asia</u>. Brookfield, Vermont: Dartmouth Publishers, 1997.

    An important look at the analysis of how the Korean War affected and continues to affect the Asian policy.

2140 Leopold, Richard W. "The Korean War: The Historian's Task" in Francis H. Heller, editor. <u>The Korean War: A 25 Year Perspective</u>. Lawrence: The Regents Press of Kansas, 1977.

    A dated but very good statement which addresses the lack of historical perspective concerning the Korean War. While Leopold makes a good case, the production of some fine Korean War history would seem to lessen the impact of his remarks. His general perspective, as well as his footnotes, are very helpful.

2141 Lindley, Ernest. "Counters to the Kremlin's Designs" <u>Newsweek</u> 36 (July 31, 1950): 20-21.

    This author maintains that if the Korean attack was intended as a diversionary action preluding to a Russian attack on Western Europe, it was not well done. And the prompt action by the United States prevented the Russians from being successful.

2142 Lofgren, Charles A. "How New is Limited War?" <u>Military Review</u> 47 7 (1967): 16-23.

    Says that Korea does not qualify for what is usually meant by "limited war," however, Vietnam does.

2143 Lowe, Herbert S. "United Nations Action in Korea—A Test Case in the Development of International Security" MA thesis, Tulane University of Louisiana, 1952.

    MA: security

2144 Lowe, Peter. "The Significance of the Korean War in Anglo-American Relations" in Michael Dockrill and John W. Young, editors. British Foreign Policy, 1945-1956. London: Macmillan, 1989.

Tries to analyze the value of British opinion in the formation of American diplomacy.

2145 Maghroori, Gholam R. "The First World War and the Korean Conflict: An Application of the War Threshold Theory" MA thesis, California State Unviersity, San Jose, 1973.

MA: threshold theory

2146 Making Known the Korean War: Policy Analysis of the Korean Conflict in the Last Decade. unknown publisher, date.

An overview of historiographic trends in considering the Korean War policies and analysis during the 1980s. Listed in several bibliographies, and listed at the Command and Staff College Library.

2147 Marshall, S. L. A. "Our Mistakes in Korea" Atlantic 192 3 (1953): 46-49.

Truman was unwilling to make a commitment to manpower needed to win in Korea.

2148 Marshall, Thurgood. Report on Korea: The Shameful Story of the Courts Martial of Negro GIs. New York: National Association for the Advancement of Colored People, 1951.

This case of the mistreatment of black soldiers is used in an analysis of how blacks were dealt with.

2149 Mayers, David A. Cracking the Monolith: U.S. Policy Against the Sino-Soviet Alliance, 1949-1955. Baton Rouge: Louisiana State University Press, 1986.

A wide look at the long-range diplomatic plan to divide the unity of the communist block. Of interest here only in its interpretations of the landing and victory at Inchon. The assumption of victory, and the opportunity to cross the 38th Parallel, is seen in the light of America's "classical diplomacy," i.e. to somehow drive a wedge between China and Russia.

2150 Ministry of Information. The Origins and Truth of the Korean War: An Analysis of False Perspective by Revisionists. Seoul: no publisher, 1990.

This anti-revisionist history supports the view that the communists were to blame for the war.

2151 Muccio, John J. "Korea and the Explosion of a Communist Delusion" Department of State Bulletin 26 (June 16, 1952): 939-942.
    Discusses the victories won in the Korean War, meaning first, the prevention of a communist state with the division of North and South Korea and United Nations elections; and second, the victory following Inchon.

2152 Nagai, Yonosuke. "The Korean War: An Interpretative Essay" The Japanese Journal of American Studies 1 (1981): 151-174.
    The author contends the war in Korea provided the United States the opportunity to "draw a line in the sand" and proclaim their policy of containment.

2153 Norman, Lloyd. "Washington's War" Army (June 1960): 38-49.
    Claims that the United States was ill-prepared for any war, especially the one in Korea. Not only was the attack made possible because of poor intelligence by United States fact finding bodies, but the early phase of the war was nearly a disaster because of a limited understanding of the enemy, and poor supplies. Demands that the lesson of unpreparedness be learned once and for all.

2154 Oliver, Robert T. Syngman Rhee and American Involvement in Korea, 1942-1952: A Personal Narrative. Seoul: Panmun, 1978.
    This personal friend of Rhee assures the reader that Syngman Rhee was not responsible for causing this war.

2155 Olsen, Edward A. "The Diplomatic Dimension of the Korean Confrontation" Monterey, California: Monterey Institute of International Studies, 1991.
    A conference paper delivered in March of 1991 which tries to explain the diplomatic failure.

2156 Park, Ki-June. "A Systems Analysis of the Korean Conflict" MS thesis, Central Missouri State University, 1977.
    MS: analysis

2157 Park, Sun-yup. Reflections on the Korean War: The Army and I. Seoul: Hanul, 1991.
    Reinterpretation of the role of the military.

2158 Pickett, W. F. "Why We Fight" United States Naval Institute Proceedings 80 7 (1954): 751-753.
    A Marine colonel says Americans fought for what is decent and correct. It was at home that the war was lost.

2159 Poats, Rutherford. Decision in Korea. New York: The McBride Company, 1954.

This American war correspondent's point is that the war was not fought to win, but rather to show Russia the American determination to support any country against communist aggression. It is basically a negative attitude toward leadership.

2160 Price, Joseph E. "The Wages of Unpreparedness: The United States Army in the Korean War, July 1950" MA thesis, East Texas State, 1982.

A well-researched and presented study of why the Army made such a poor showing, placing most of the blame on Army leadership.

2161 Ra, Hong-Yk. The Unfinished War: Korea and the Great Power Politics 1950-1990. Seoul: Jenyewon, 1994.

Analysis of why the war must remain unfinished in order to keep the diplomatic arrangements in order.

2162 Rayburn, Robert. Fight the Good Fight: Lessons from the Korean War. Pasadena, California: Couant, 1956.

Describes the ways in which war can strengthen religious beliefs among servicemen in Korea.

2163 Reed, John C. An Analysis of Chinese Communist Aggression in Korea in 1950 and the Possibility of Recurrence in Vietnam. Maxwell Air Force Base, Alabama: Air War College, 1968.

MA: communist aggression

2164 Reynolds, Robert B., Jr. "Perception and Misperception in the Korean War: The Failure of Rollback" Honors thesis, College of William and Mary, 1992.

Thesis: perceptions

2165 Rubin, Rebecca. "Army, Navy and Air Force Assessments of the Korean Conflict, 1953-58: A Case Study of the Role of Ideology in Military Strategy" AB thesis, Harvard University, 1987.

AB: strategy

2166 Rush, Eugene J. Military Strategic Lessons Learned from the Korean Conflict as They Related to Limited Warfare. Carlisle Barracks, Pennsylvania: United States Army War College, 1974.

Discusses the effect of the Korean War on United States military planners and leadership.

2167 Schopick, Philip J. "The Effects of the Korean War on China: Should the Peoples' Republic of China Have Involved Itself in the Korean War" BA project, Antioch College, 1973.
BA: China

2168 Shapper, John G. "An Analysis of the Origins of the Korean Conflict" thesis, Glassboro State College, 1970.
Thesis: origins

2169 Simpson, David G. "Korea: Learning Ground for the Modern United States Air Force" BGS thesis, Texas Tech University, 1994.
BGS: tactical aviation

2170 Smith, Charles R., John R. Brinkerhoff and Trevor N. Dupuy, Historical Analysis of Reserve Component Tank Battalion Equipment Problem in the Korean War Mobilization: Final Report. Fairfax, Virginia, Historical Evaluation and Research Organization, 1985.
Excellent analysis of armor mobilization, its use and organization.

2171 Spaatz, Carl. "Why We Face a Tough Fight in Korea" Newsweek 36 (July 10, 1950): 23.
Decries the failure of ground forces to take advantage of the major bombing runs. The lack of adequate ground response means that the North Koreans could save most of their supplies, and move quickly. The advantage of American airpower is diminished by whether the North Korean troops are able to save their supplies.

2172 Srivastava, M. P. The Korean Conflict: Search for Unification. New Delhi: Prentice-Hall of India, 1982.
An analysis of the war and its effect in several unification proposals offered.

2173 Stilwell, Richard. "A Victory Not to Be Forgotten" The American Legion (June 1990): 30, 49-50.
Stilwell holds that the Korean War was pivotal in postwar history and politics and thus beneficial to the United States and Allies. Appears to be overly patriotic.

2174 Stueck, William W. "Cold War Revisionism and the Origins of the Korean Conflict: The Kolko Thesis. Pacific Historical Review 42 (November 1973): 537-575.
Very important look at Joyce and Gabriel Kolko's thesis that the United States is responsible and the Soviets were only responding to American aggression.

2175 Tarpley, John F. "Korea: 25 Years Later" United States Naval Institute Proceedings 104 8 (1978): 50-57.
Despite its problems the armistice has provided twenty-five years of stability in Asia.

2176 Tays, George. "The Price of the Korean War" thesis, Seoul, 1951.
Thesis: Korean War

2177 Thomas, James A. "Limited War: The Theory and the Practice" Military Review 53 2 (1973): 75-82.
The demoralized effect of loss in Korea and Vietnam was exaggerated because the Army had every right to have expected victory.

2178 "Threats at Formosa Take Ominous Turn" Newsweek 36 (July 31, 1950): 11-13.
The War in Korea is counterbalanced by concern over the Chinese threat to Formosa. The gloomy picture suggests that it might be spring of 1951 before an offensive can be launched against North Korea.

2179 Toner, James H. "Candide as Constable: the American Way of War and Peace in Korea, 1950-1953" Ph.D. dissertation, University of Notre Dame, 1976.
A discussion of American foreign relations from 1945 to 1953 at it related to affairs in Korea.

2180 United States. Comments and Recommendations of the 1st Marine Division on the Chosin Reservoir Operation, Condensed and Classified Washington, D. C.: Historical Division, United States Marine Corps, 1951.
Resource considers the behavior of Marines at the retreat from the Chosin Reservoir.

2181 United States. An Evaluation of the Influence of Marine Corps Forces on the Course of the Korean War; 4 August 1950-15 December 1950. 2 volumes. Quantico, Virginia: Marine Corps School, 1952.
Very important look at how the Marines were used in the war in Korea and their influence.

2182 Walsh, Thomas L. "The Korean Dilemma: the Decision to Cross the 38th Parallel, July 1-October, 1950" MA thesis, University of Texas at Austin, 1981.
MA: crossing the 38th Parallel

2183 "We Weren't Permitted to Win in Korea" U. S. News & World Report 37 (September 3, 1954): 81-84.

General Stratmeyer testifies before the Senate Armed Services Committee telling them that General "MacArthur's hands were tied" when it came to both political and military concerns. Very supportive of MacArthur but little new.

2184 Weathersby, Kathryn, commentary and translation. "New Findings on the Korean War" Cold War International History Project Bulletin 3 (Fall 1993): 1, 14-18.
      Excellent insights into new materials becoming available.

2185 Wells, Samuel F., Jr. "The Lessons of the War" The Wilson Quarterly 2 (Summer 1978): 119-127.
      The Korean War altered the defense mentality and provided a new willingness to resist communist aggression.

2186 Williams, William J., editor. A Revolutionary War: Korea and the Transformation of the Postwar World. Chicago: Imprint Publications. 1993.
      A major work on the interpretation of the Korean War which contains several excellent articles on significant issues.

2187 Winn, Gregory F. T. "Arms, Attitudes, and Decisions: The Probability of Conflict in Northeast Asia with Particular Emphasis on the Korean Peninsula" thesis, University of Southern California, 1979.
      MA: North Korea emphasis

2188 Wint, Guy. What Happened in Korea: A Study in Collective Security. London: Batchworth, 1954.
      Primarily a study in the motivations of participants with little on the war issue.

2189 Worden, William "We Won Back Korea—And We're Stuck With It" Saturday Evening Post 223 21 (1950): 31, 153.
      Claimed the war was over in November of 1950, and how the United States was now responsible for twenty million "miserable people."

Historiography

2190 Cook, Glenn S. "Korea: No Longer the Forgotten War" Journal of Military History 56 (July 1992): 489-492.
      Claims that by 1972 the Korean War had drawn enough scholarly interest that it is no longer "forgotten."

2191 Cotton, James and Ian Neary. The Korean War in History. Atlantic Highlands, New Jersey: Humanities Press International, Inc., 1989.

A look at the way history as a discipline has recorded the Korean War.

2192 Halliday, Jon. "What Happened in Korea? Rethinking Korean History 1945-1953" Bulletin of Concerned Asian Scholars 5 3 (1973).
New look is in order—old view.

2193 Kang, Taek-koo. "The Korean War in History: A Historiographical Approach" MA thesis, Eastern Washington University, 1986.
MA: historiography

2194 Kaplan, Lawrence S. "American Historians and the Atlantic Alliance" in Walter LaFeber, NATO and the Korean War: A Context. Kent, Ohio: Kent State University Press, 1991.
Papers at a symposium in Brussels, May 1989.

2195 MacDonald, Callum. "Rediscovering History—New Light on the Unknown War; Korea" Bulletin of Concerned Asian Scholars 244 (October 1992): 62-70.
A review of John Merrill Peninsular Origins, Bruce Cumings Roaring of the Cataract and Rosemary Foot Substitute for Victory, all of which require the reader to reconsider the early history of the war. Excellent view of causes.

2196 May, Ernest R. "Lessons" of the Past: The Use and Misuse of History in American Foreign Policy. New York: Oxford University Press, 1973.
Wonderful presentation. If only diplomats would read it.

2197 Park, Hong-Kyu. "Korean War Revisited—Survey of Historical Writings" World Affairs 137 4 (Spring 1975).
After a quick survey of more than fifty works Park offers some areas where additional work remains to be done.

2198 Singleton, Kathy A. "A Survey of the Historiography of the Korean War" MA thesis, University of Arkansas, Fayetteville, 1985.
MA: historiography

2199 Swartout, Robert, Jr. "American Historians and the Outbreak of the Korean War: An Historiographical Essay" 1 Asian Quarterly (1979): 65-77.
Discounts theory that Russia and/or South Korea began the war and suggests it was, as originally held, the North Koreans who were responsible.

2200 Unger, Irwin. "The 'New Left' and American History: Some Recent Trends in United States Historiography" American Historical Review 72 (July 1967): 1237-1263.
    Excellent review of early historical writings.

2201 War Memorial Service—Korea, Korean War Research Conference Committee. The Historical Reillumination of the Korean War. Seoul: War Memorial Service—Korea, 1990.
    Comment about South Korea memorializing the war effort.

2202 Warner, Geoffrey. "The Korean War" International Affairs 56 1 (1980): 98-107.
    Good work by a British historian who analyzes the many explanation of who caused the war.

2203 Watt, D. C. "The Historians Task and Responsibilities" in Yonosuke Nagai and Akira Iriye, editors. The Origins of the Cold War in Asia. Tokyo: University of Tokyo Press, 1977; New York: Columbia University Press, 1977.
    Papers presented in Japan—November 1975.

2204 West, Philip. "Interpreting the Korean War" The American Historical Review 94 (February 1989): 80-96.
    This is a combined review of six major Korean War books which Philip West identified suggesting—taking a phrase from Arthur Schlesinger Jr.—that the war has moved from the "heroic stage to the academic stage." He views the revisionist writings of the war premature, as the real sources of information, North Korean and Chinese sources, are still very limited.

2205 Wubben, H. H. "American Prisoners of War in Korea: A Second Look at the 'Something New in History' Theme" American Quarterly 22 1 (1970): 3-19.
    A new look at the literature which challenges the accepted view that United States prisoners-of-war were easily controlled and brainwashed.

AUTHOR INDEX

Listings are keyed to entry numbers unless indicated as page number.

SUBJECT INDEX

Listings are keyed to entry numbers unless indicated as page number.

About the Compiler

PAUL M. EDWARDS is Director of the Center for the Study of the Korean War in Independence, Missouri. He is the author of several works on the Korean War, including *A Guide to the Films on the Korean War* (Greenwood, 1997).

ISBN 0-313-30317-7

90000>

EAN

9 780313 303173

HARDCOVER BAR CODE